"I was delightfully stunned when reading rare to find a book that seamlessly integrates the latest findings of neuroscience with practical tools for overcoming ingrained toxic lifestyle habits that sap joy and happiness. With its blend of compelling anecdotes, fascinating science, and easy-to-implement practices, *Rewire Your Brain 2.0* will inspire you to change your life in ways you never before dared or even dreamed possible. Dr. John Arden has generously gifted us with a brain-and-life-changing book designed to enhance, heal, and recover our innate sense of wholeness—for body, mind, and spirit. How wonderful!"

—Donald Altman, author of *The Mindfulness Toolbox*,
Simply Mindful, and *Clearing Emotional Clutter*

"There is so much in this book. As I read it, I thought that if I only read one book – this would be it! Dr John Arden's *Rewire Your Brain* draws together the latest research from neuroscience, psychology, biology and genetics to demonstrate how our minds, bodies, and lifestyles interact. Packed with practical ideas, this book details actions we can readily integrate with everyday activity, providing compelling evidence for simultaneously optimizing social, emotional, and physical well-being. Dr Arden eloquently explains and illustrates ways of rewiring our brains and strengthening the mental systems that lead us to long, happy, and healthy lives."

—Jean Annan, PhD, author of *7 Dimensions.*
Children's Emotional Well-being, Auckland, New Zealand

"This book is wonderfully entertaining and inspiring from the first pages. Neurons and even new neurons, intertwining, find new connections in the process of reading this book. Many, weaving into others, as they expand your horizons of new thinking. These new neural connections build powerful ways out of bad habits and attitudes that have blocked your life and recreate yourself. You will find this book thoroughly satisfying, accessible, and rewarding."

—Svitlana Grygorieva, PhD, associate professor,
State University Odessa, Ukraine

"A timely update for those of us invested in keeping our brains and minds healthy. Dr. Arden doesn't offer brain "hacks" or "hot tips," but down-to-earth, thoughtful and encouraging advice grounded in neuroscience."

—Sarah McKay, PhD, author of *The Women's Brain Book*, Sydney, Australia

"Dr. John Arden has that rare ability to take complex biological and psychological science and translate it into easily understood concepts for mental health professionals and the general public alike. Not only does he have this translational gift, but he combines it with a creativity and keen insight that takes him to the cutting edge of what we know about healthy minds and healthy bodies. *Rewire Your Brain* is a powerful synergy of years of accumulated knowledge boiled down to key concepts that are fascinating, intuitive, and practical for you to live a better life. This second edition is a must for anyone who wants to know what key areas are important for overall health, why, and what to do about it, from one of our leading professionals in mental health.

—Matthew Dahlitz, Editor-in-Chief, *The Science of Psychotherapy*, co-author of *The Practitioner's Guide to The Science of Psychotherapy.*

"In Rewire Your Brain 2.0, Dr. John Arden delivers a masterpiece that's sure to appeal to both professional and general readers alike. This book combines a fascinating overview of applied neuroscience with tangible steps we can all take to improve our brain and in turn improve our lives in a lasting way. By explaining how and why principles like mindfulness, social connection, and exercise work the way they do, Arden empowers all of us to foster well-being one practical step at a time. A must-have book!"

—Jonah Paquette, PsyD, author of *Happily Even After, Awestruck,* and *The Happiness Toolbox*

"Everything, you, as a professional, need to know about how to nurture your most important tool—your brain – for achieving sustainable performance and long-term health, is awaiting you in Dr. Arden's remarkably well-written book, *Rewire Your Brain 2.0*. So, what are you waiting for?"

—Sefan Falk, executive coach and author of *Intrinsic Motivation: Learn to Love Your Work and Succeed As Never Before.*

"As a clinical neuroscientist, I have always been fascinated by John Arden's ability to bring the issues of Applied Neuroscience to the ordinary public. The new edition (2.0) of his book *Rewire Your Brain* allows any person to apply, in his or her real life and real world, the biological basis of a positive behavior and welfare, both for brain and mind. Stimulating and beautifully written, the *Rewire Your Brain* 2.0, contributes to develop an innovative approach to mental health."

—*Tullio Scrimali*, MD, PhD, professor of clinical psychology, University of Catania, Catania, Italy, founder and director of ALETEIA, European Scholl of Cognitive Therapy, Enna, Italy

"Dr. Arden explains, in a clear, entertaining, and well-supported way, how gene expression can be activated, how we can stimulate neurogenesis, and develop better mental and emotional states following a series of behavioral guidelines that become healthy habits. This book is the equivalent of Whitman's *Song to Myself*, from the perspective of neuropsychology, a song to freedom to which human beings can aspire. It will add more life to your years.

—Juan Francisco Ramírez Martínez
CENTRO MEXICANO DE PROGRAMACIÓN
NEUROLINGÜÍSTICA

"In this engaging book, Dr. Arden teaches us neuroscience with clear, easy to understand and easy to remember explanations and examples. Interwoven throughout the narrative, he offers practical strategies for preserving and boosting, not only brain health, but also total well-being and happiness. *Rewire Your Brain 2.0* is a must read!"

—Liana Lianov, MD, MPH, president,
Global Positive Health Institute

Rewire Your Brain 2.0

Rewire Your Brain 2.0

Five Healthy Factors to a Better Life

John B. Arden, PhD, ABPP

JB JOSSEY-BASS™

A Wiley Brand

Jossey-Bass
A Wiley Imprint
111 River St, Hoboken, NJ 07030
www.josseybass.com

Jossey-Bass books and products are available through most bookstores. To contact Jossey-Bass directly, call our Customer Care Department within the U.S. at 800-956-7739, outside the U.S. at +1 317 572 3986, or fax +1 317 572 4002.

Wiley also publishes its books in a variety of electronic formats and by print-on-demand. Some material included with standard print versions of this book may not be included in e-books or in print-on-demand. If this book refers to media such as a CD or DVD that is not included in the version you purchased, you may download this material at http://booksupport.wiley.com. For more information about Wiley products, visit www.wiley.com.

Library of Congress Cataloging-in-Publication Data is Available:

ISBN 9781119895947 (Paperback)
ISBN 9781119895954 (ePDF)
ISBN 9781119895961 (ePub)

COVER DESIGN: PAUL MCCARTHY
COVER ART: © GETTY IMAGES | TIMANDTIM

SKY10042285_020223

This book is dedicated to all those people who have incorrectly assumed that they are beyond help, that their mental health problems can be addressed only medically, and to those who support them.

Contents

Preface to the Second Edition

Since the first publication of this book there have been exciting advances in fields of research that were once assumed irrelevant to the brain and mental health in general. Not only has research in the fields of psychology and neuroscience combined to offer new practical insights about how to improve your brain and mental health, but also the fields of metabolism, epigenetics, and immunology have revolutionized our understanding. This book brings together the practical insights from all these fields and explains how you can apply them to your life.

This book is a nontechnical companion to my book *Mind-Brain-Gene*. Whereas that book addresses how the developments in neuroscience, epigenetics, and immunology can be applied to therapy, *Rewire Your Brain 2.0* is meant to be a down-to-earth book for the general public that describes how to change your brain based on well-researched principles that work. If you want more neuroscientific detail, I have added boxes with that information separate from the general narrative. Overall, this book will guide you through the process of rewiring your brain so that you can change how you think and feel for the better.

Each chapter explains key insights from new developments in all these sciences and describes how to apply them to specific areas of your life to help you thrive. I have tried to keep the technical terminology to a minimum, but there are some terms and concepts that are worth remembering.

In Chapter 1, you'll learn about the major discoveries that explain how to rewire your brain. You'll learn how habits are formed, how to increase good habits, and how to stop bad ones. Your brain is always developing new connections between brain cells, called *neurons*, and shedding the old ones that are not being used. You'll learn how to make new connections that promote good habits and shut off those that support bad habits. These brain changes have been described as "Cells that fire together wire together" and "Cells that fire out of sync lose their link."

You'll learn to use the acronym FEED to help you remember the steps to rewire your brain. The mnemonic stands for Focus, Effort, Effortlessness, and Determination. By practicing these steps, you can *feed* and make the rewiring changes described in the rest of the book.

You cannot rewire your brain without producing and utilizing energy efficiently. To understand how this works, in Chapter 2 you will learn about your metabolism and the indispensable energy factories in each of your cells. You will learn that your DNA is not your destiny. Your genes are, of course, critical, but the emerging science of epigenetics has shown that genes can be turned on and off with self-care and positive behavior change. You will also learn about how your immune system, and especially chronic inflammation, has a profound negative effect on your brain. The exciting field of psychoneuroimmunology (which stands for the links between your mind, brain, and immune system) will be explained, and there will be suggestions for achieving mental health.

We all feel a little anxious or down in the dumps at times. You'll learn how to reframe these feelings to feel more positive. In Chapter 3, you'll learn about a part of your brain called the *amygdala* that can detect threat and is sometimes turned on when there is actually just the miss-perception of threat. Since your amygdala can trigger these kinds of false alarms, you will learn how to keep it in check with another part of your brain called the *prefrontal cortex*. You'll also learn about the balance between your sympathetic and the parasympathetic nervous systems: which one becomes excited when need be, and which one helps you to calm down afterward. Also, I'll explain an evidence-based practice called *exposure*, which turns off a false alarm so you may approach life courageously and with vitality.

In Chapter 4, you'll learn how withdrawing from the world can worsen sadness and depression. The underactivation of the left prefrontal cortex (PFC) and overactivation of the right PFC are associated with depression. In contrast, activation of the left PFC, which is associated with taking action, contributes to the alleviation of depression and the promotion of positive feelings. I will explain how the techniques of *behavioral activation* and *cognitive restructuring* can shift your brain activity to your left PFC. You'll learn how chronic inflammation is strongly linked with depression and problems with thinking clearly. Also, I'll explain how full spectrum light affects your biochemistry and your mood. You'll learn how to stay positive and enjoy life with an optimistic attitude.

The next five chapters will describe the lifestyle practices that have received the most consistent research toward brain health. They are encoded in the mnemonic SEEDS, which stands for Social, Exercise, Education, Diet, and Sleep. You'll also learn how these healthy habits enhance your brain's longevity and how to maximize a vibrant life free of self-imposed limitations. The SEEDS factors form the foundation and prerequisite for brain health.

In Chapter 5 specifically, you'll learn how people who maintain positive social relationships live longer and feel more satisfied with their lives and about the brain networks that thrive on social support. I'll describe how these networks help to build healthy relationships and the empathy critical for your mental health.

In Chapter 6, you'll learn that exercise plays an indispensable role in how your brain rewires and creates new neurons. Exercise is one of the most powerful ways to jump-start the neurochemistry of neuroplasticity, and one of the best antidepressants and anti-anxiety techniques that you have immediately available to you. This essential behavior can stimulate neurogenesis, which is a process that can actually grow new neurons in your brain.

In Chapter 7, you'll see how education harnesses your memory skills by wiring together as you learn. Various memory techniques have been used for the last 2000 years, and you can refashion them to enhance your memory capacity. You'll learn mnemonic devices to make your memory skills work optimally, and how education builds what we call *cognitive reserve*, to build added connections between neurons that act like a reserve.

In Chapter 8, you'll learn how a healthy diet ensures that your brain creates the right fuel for your energy factories. Your diet also provides the biochemistry for making your brain cells communicate with one another so that you can be calm, energized, and focused. In addition to consuming the right amino acids, vitamins, and minerals through your diet, you'll need the correct essential fatty acids to ensure that your cell membranes are supple and flexible enough to enable neuroplasticity.

In Chapter 9, you'll learn how sleep plays a central role in brain maintenance. You spend one-third of your life asleep, and the quality of your sleep determines your health and longevity. You will learn how to achieve a healthy sleep cycle and what the stages of sleep do for your brain. There are stages that help to encode memory, boost your immune system, and wash your brain clean of toxins.

In the next part of the book, specifically in Chapter 10, you'll learn what factors increase your resilience and, despite obstacles, allow you to approach life with a can-do attitude. Research in the field of positive psychology illuminates the role of optimism and healthy ambition and offers antidotes to the narcissistic and material focus that is endemic in contemporary society. In addition, the practice of compassion and nonattachment helps to alleviate needless tension and suffering. Since there are always bumps on the road of life, resiliency and openness allow you to rewire your brain to be flexible and accepting of the rich complexity of life.

You'll also learn about the calming yet vitalizing role of nonjudgmental attention, your prefrontal cortex, and an accepting attitude.
The subtle power of parasympathetic meditation can increase your
tolerance of stress and your sense of peace. You'll learn how to
increase your ability to be mindfully present and to maintain a sense
of connectivity with others and the world around you to thrive.

Part 1

Healthy Brain and Body

1

Your Adaptive Brain

A revolution is occurring in many sciences such as neuroscience, epigenetics, immunology, and psychology to reveal how you can rewire your brain. Since the first edition of this book, new insights have illuminated how your mind, brain, genome, metabolism, and immune system need to be in sync for your well-being. This book brings all this new knowledge together in a down-to-earth manner and explains how to apply it to your daily life and how to get better control of your thoughts and emotions.

It was once incorrectly assumed that the brain you were born with was hardwired to function in predetermined ways dictated by your genes. Your brain is not hardwired. Rather, it is soft-wired by experience and how well you take care of it. Neuroscientific research has revealed that the brain is quite plastic. If you think you are stuck with a brain that tortures you with anxiety and depression, you are not. The brain you were born with is modified by your experiences throughout your life and is changing all the time. Neither is your behavior or your emotions rigidly determined by your genes. Genes lay out potential vulnerabilities, but they do not dictate your thoughts, your feelings, or your behavior. You can even turn genes on or off by your self-care behaviors.

It was also erroneously believed that all the brain cells you had at birth would be the only ones you would ever possess. The possibility of developing new neurons was thought to be ridiculous. In fact, when I was first studying neuropsychology, my professor said, "You have as many neurons as you will ever have the day you were born; then you lose 10,000 a day!" Yet it turns out that you can grow new neurons in specific areas of your brain under certain conditions. This phenomenon is called *neurogenesis*.

These discoveries shed light on how you can maximize your potential and minimize your vulnerabilities. This book describes how to apply the findings from these fields to rewire your brain so that you can feel calm and positive. By learning these skills, you can improve your ability to focus, face challenges, reach your goals, and yes, even be happy.

You can learn to feel less tense, less anxious, and less easily stressed. There are parts of your brain that, when not tamed, tend to overreact and add to needless tension, anxiety, and stress. This book will describe how to get those parts rewired and work for you, not against you. The bottom line is this: how you train yourself to think, feel, and take care of yourself on a regular basis will rewire your brain and allow you to be calm, positive, and focused.

This process of rewiring your brain is not merely a taming of parts that are overactivated but also activating the parts that are not. For example, there are parts of your brain that thrive on taking action, and when you do take action you are more likely to enjoy positive feelings. On the other hand, when you sit back passively and wait for positive feelings to emerge, parts of your brain become overactive to promote anxiety and depression.

Thanks to new discoveries, we now know much more about how the brain works and how you can rewire the parts of it that are out of balance with the others. Think of this book as a manual for a brain tune-up. You will learn to tune up the areas that have become either underactivated or overactivated when you feel down in the dumps, lose your optimism, and look only at the dark side. I will describe how to activate the parts of your brain that must be balanced so you feel positive about your life and see the glass as (at least) half full. You'll learn to calm down in the face of stress and boost your mood when you're down. You'll also learn to improve your memory, have better relationships, and get a good night's sleep, all of which rewire your brain and thus enable you to be calmer and feel more positive.

Nurtured Nature

To rewire your brain, the first thing you need to understand is that your brain changes as you adapt to the world around you. Most importantly, you can change how you feel and think. We have moved far away from the old debate about nature versus nurture, and we now know that you are able to "nurture your nature." Since your brain is not hardwired and is instead soft-wired, your experience and behavior play major roles in modifying your nature. In other words, you change your brain by what you do (Figure 1.1).

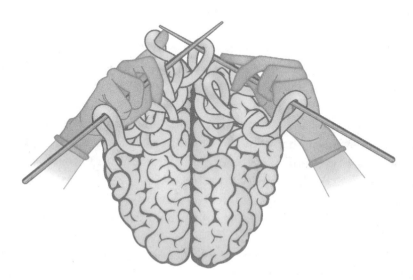

Figure 1.1   The brain weaving itself

Your brain weighs just three and a half pounds, yet it's one of the most advanced organs on the planet. According to the last good count, it has 86 billion brain cells, called *neurons*, and a trillion *glial cells*. All these cells are social, meaning that they need to be activated to stay alive. What you do, how you think, and how you take care of yourself changes your brain, just as muscles change when you exercise them.

Your brain cells communicate with one another all the time. Most of this communication takes place in the gaps between your neurons, called *synapses* (Figure 1.2). Since they are not hardwired but instead are soft-wired, new synapses are made when you learn a new skill. This is called synaptic plasticity or *neuroplasticity*, which you can remember as a rewiring of your brain. Because the synapses between your neurons are modifiable, you can acquire new skills and talents, such as how to speak a new language, play the piano, or read.

When you repeatedly do something, like ride a bicycle, you use the synaptic connections that support that skill, and in turn you strengthen those connections. When you let the skill lie dormant, you weaken those connections. It's similar to atrophy and the way your muscles weaken if you stop exercising. In this very real sense, your brain is a use-it-or-lose-it organ.

The mantra "Cells that fire together wire together" aptly describes the way your neurons make new synaptic connections so that you can learn new skills. The more you do something in a particular way, such as how to speak a new language, ride a bicycle, or play a piano, the more the neurons fire together and wire together to make it happen again with more ease. Repetition and practice strengthen those synaptic connections. The more the neurons fire together, the more likely it is that they will fire together in the future. A saying that describes the opposite effect is "Neurons that fire apart wire apart." Or you could say that neurons that are out of sync lose their link, which is the neural explanation for why you forget things. This can happen when you forget to feel anxious or depressed in a certain situation that previously made you anxious or depressed. I use the

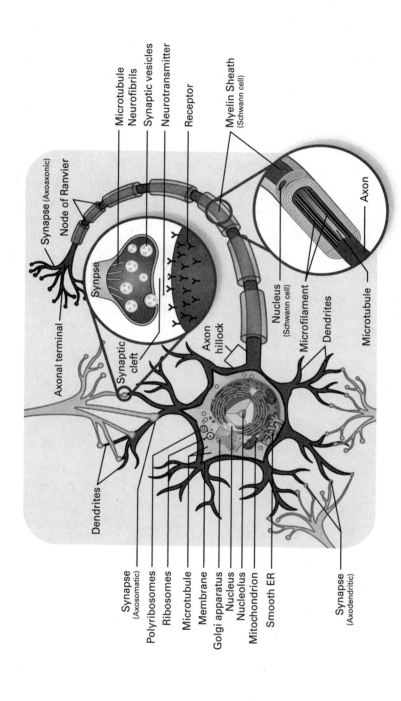

Figure 1.2 Synapses and neurons

words *made you* very lightly because situations do not make you feel this way. They are bad habits that you can break. More about this in Chapters 3 and 4.

The more you do something, the more likely it is that you will do it again in the future. That's why baseball players go to batting practice, golfers go to driving ranges, and piano players practice for hours on end. The same goes for thinking. The more you think about your Aunt Alice, the more she will pop into your mind again and again. That's what studying for exams is all about. Repetition rewires your brain and grooms habits. When preparing for a final exam, you can earn a higher score by studying early and often.

Neuroplasticity makes learning how to be positive possible and how to deal with stress effectively. In fact, if your brain is really hardwired and you were depressed, you would be stuck for life. But this is not true. You are not doomed to suffer. Learning something new *is* rewiring the brain. By making new connections between thoughts and feelings, you make new synapses between the neurons that encode those ideas and images.

LTP vs. LTD

Another way to describe the way neuroplasticity works is by the *long-term potentiation* (LTP) that occurs when the excitation between cells is prolonged and it tends to increase the potential for them to fire together again more easily. This sensitizes and strengthens the connections between the cells to make them more likely to fire together in the future. Thus, LTP promotes long-lasting affinity between neurons by reconfiguring their electrochemical relationship. On the sending side of the synapse, the stores of the excitatory neurotransmitter glutamate become stronger, while the receptor side of the synapse reconfigures to receive more of it. The voltage on the receptor side becomes stronger in its resting state, which attracts more glutamate. If the firing between these neurons continues, the genes within the neurons turn on to construct more building blocks for the synapse, which strengthens its activity.

Just as the brain needs the LTP mechanisms that strengthen the connections between neurons so that you can improve your memory and learn new skills, it also needs mechanisms that will help it to forget. A process known as *long-term depression* (LTD) helps you break bad habits. (Note: LTD has nothing to do with the emotional state called depression.) LTD helps you weaken the connections between the neurons that support an old bad habit—like anxious feelings and depressive thinking. This is what is meant by the saying "Cells that fire out of sync lose their link."

When neurons fire together often, they begin to fire together at a quicker rate. They do not require as much energy as before when you were first learning the skill. This leads to increased efficiency because there is more precision in the number of neurons that are recruited to do that skill. For example, when you learn to ride a bicycle, you use muscles and neurons that have not yet been linked. As you begin to link them when learning to ride, at first you try to avoid wobbling and falling over. Then, once you learn to ride with ease, less effort is required, and your ride becomes much smoother and faster. The neurons required to fire with their partners have teamed up and wired together.

As you become more talented at a specific skill, a greater amount of space in your brain is devoted to making that skill possible. For example, Alvaro Pascual-Leone of Harvard Medical School used measured regional cerebral blood flow with positron emission tomography (PET) to measure specific areas of the cortex. He studied people who are blind who read braille and found that the neuronal networks associated with their reading fingers were larger than the networks for their other fingers and for the fingers of readers who can see. In other words, the sensitivity of their reading fingers involved more connections, which used more space. This means that practice enhances neuroplasticity that creates extra space devoted to that skill in your brain.

In another example of how the brain rewires, musicians who play string instruments such as the violin were examined to see if their brains had reorganized to accommodate more space. There tends to be little difference between the musicians and the non-musicians in how much space was made available for the fingers of the right hand. However, the area of the brain devoted to the fingers of the left hand showed a dramatic difference because they must be nimble and dexterous to make all the fingering movements. The brain space devoted to the fingers involved in fingering was significantly greater in these musicians than in non-musicians. This difference was greatest if the musician had started playing the instrument before the age of 12. In other words, although this use-dependent neuroplasticity occurs during adulthood, it is more dramatic the earlier and the longer that the person plays the instrument.

To understand how neuroplasticity works, consider that the age at which you learn a language affects whether you speak with an accent. If you learn a new language while in your 20s, it's highly probable that you will speak that new language with an accent from your first language. If you learn a new language before age 9, however, you probably won't have an accent tinged by your first language. When you learn a new language as an adult, the neurons that have always connected to make specific sounds tend to continue to fire together even when you try to make different but related sounds. For example, if your first language is German and now you are learning English, you may have trouble with the sounds found at the beginning of the words wish and this, because with sounds don't exist in German. You may therefore pronounce them instead as v and z, which are similar sounds that occur in German. People who speak Japanese often have trouble with the English r and l sounds.

The more you speak to people who don't share your accent, the greater the chance that your accent will fade. For example, both my parents grew up in the Boston area, and a few years after I was born my family moved to California. My parents gradually lost most of their Bostonian accents as they spoke with people who had moved west from all over the country and with people who had grown up in California.

Not only does your behavior rewire your brain; just thinking about or imagining behaviors also can change your brain structure if you repeat those thoughts enough. For example, researchers have shown that simply imagining a session of piano practice contributes to neuroplasticity in the area of the brain associated with the finger movements of playing the piano. Essentially, mental practice contributes to the rewiring of the brain. Of course, mental practice is what studying for an exam is all about. But imagining piano lessons without the figure movements is not as effective as with the finger movements. You get the point: Mental practice establishes new connections and strengthens them.

The bottom line is that repeating a particular behavior strengthens the synaptic connections that make that behavior possible, and not repeating it weakens the connections. To break a habit, your task is to not strengthen it by repeating it. Eventually it will fade. The less you repeat anxious and depressive thoughts and behaviors, the less they will automatically plague you in the future. Chapters 3 and 4 offer methods to specifically eliminate anxiety and depression. The point here is that cells that fire out of sync lose their link.

Neurogenesis

One of the important players in both neuroplasticity and neurogenesis is a growth substance called *brain-derived neurotrophic factor* (BDNF). It belongs to a family of proteins that enhance your brain cells, called *neurotrophic factors*. BDNF helps build, grow, and maintain the infrastructure of brain cell connections. Since I described it in the first edition of this book, it continues to be one of the hottest areas of research in neuroscience, and thousands of articles have been written about its amazing growth functions. I call it organic fertilizer because when it's applied to neurons, it causes them to grow. A vivid illustration of BDNF's super-fertilizing effect occurs when researchers sprinkled BDNF onto neurons in a Petri dish. Those neurons sprouted new branches just like they do in your brain during learning and development.

> BDNF does its magic in a variety of ways. In general, BDNF prevents cells from dying and enhances their growth and vitality. It works within your brain to activate the genes that increase the production of proteins, serotonin, and even more BDNF. It binds to the receptors at the synapse, triggering a flow of ions that increases the voltage, which in turn strengthens the connectivity between the neurons. BDNF is activated indirectly by glutamate and increases the production of internal antioxidants and protective proteins, which stimulates LTP and BDNF. Learning increases BDNF levels. When researchers deprived the brains of BDNF, the brains also lost their capacity for LTP—in other words, learning.

Several factors slow BDNF:

- Chronic inflammation
- Chronic stress
- Recurrent depression
- Marijuana
- Obesity
- Sugar

Several factors promote BDNF:

- Exercise
- Fasting
- Fewer calories consumed (calorie restriction)
- Food content (Omega 3)
- Sunshine and vitamin D

As you can see from this list, exercise and diet play major roles in the possibility of neurogenesis. In addition to maximizing the potential of neurogenesis, both these factors minimize depression, stress, and obesity. Exercise and diet therefore are two of the critical SEEDS factors explained in Chapters 6 and 8. We will explore the neurotrophic factors in Chapter 2.

Your Brain's Brain

To rewire your brain, you need to harness the power of your brain's brain. It is called the *prefrontal cortex* (PFC) because it is in front of our frontal lobes (Figure 1.3). It makes up about 12% of your brain. In comparison, the PFC of a cat occupies about 3.5% of its brain. The PFC is the most recent addition to human evolutionary development and the last part of the brain to mature in humans. Its development is not complete until the middle of the third decade of life. It provides many of your most complex cognitive, behavioral, and emotional control capacities. Your PFC enables you to focus on, develop, and act on a moral system. It allows you to set aside your immediate impulses and reflect on your long-term goals as well as

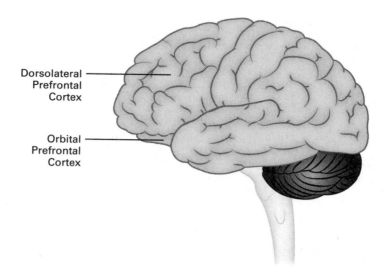

Figure 1.3   Prefrontal cortex and its parts

the needs of others. If your PFC is damaged, you are more likely to engage in antisocial and impulsive behaviors or not engage in any purposeful and constructive behavior at all.

One of the most recent evolutionary advances of our PFC is the *dorsolateral prefrontal cortex* (dlPFC). Yes, this is a mouthful of a term. *Dorsal* means "fin" or "top," and *lateral* means "side." So think of it as the top and to the side part of your PFC. Your dlPFC is very involved in higher-order thinking, attention, and working memory, the latter so named because it processes what you are working on in mind at any one time. You can usually hold information you're working on in mind for 20–30 seconds. In addition to the fact that your dlPFC is the last part of your brain to fully mature, it is also the earliest to falter during the senior years of life. When it does falter, it is the reason behind the phenomenon of walking purposely into a room and then forgetting what you intended to do there. The dlPFC is involved with complex problem-solving, and it maintains rich connections with your hippocampus, which helps you to remember things for later. I am constantly "losing" my reading glasses because of it! I will expand on the key role of the hippocampus for memory and education in Chapter 7.

Another significant part of your PFC is called the *orbital frontal cortex* (OFC), so named because it lies just behind the orbs of your eyes. It maintains a closer relationship with the parts of the brain that control threat detection generated by your amygdala. We will get into the role it plays with your amygdala in the detection of threat and anxiety in Chapter 3.

Your OFC developed earlier in your life than your dlPFC and is closely associated with socially adept parts of your brain. Highly influenced by bonding, your OFC thrives on close relationships as described in Chapter 5. If those relationships are trusting and supportive, your OFC becomes more capable of regulating your emotions. In contrast to your dlPFC, your OFC does not falter much in old age.

Just to put the OFC in perspective, serious damage to it can result in becoming erratic and explosive. Take the famous case of Phineas Gage, who back in 1848 severely damaged his OFC, which destroyed his ability to control his emotions. While working on a railroad crew, a steel rod shot through his OFC but left everything else in his brain intact. Gage retained his cognitive abilities but lost much of his ability to inhibit impulses. He had previously been a supervisor who was widely respected for his emotional reserve, but after the accident he became erratic, rude, and unstable. His skull is on display at Harvard Medical School.

The take-home point in this chapter is that your brain is amazingly adaptable and changes as you learn new skills. You are in more control of your brain than you think. It is time to exercise that control.

FEED Your Brain

Now that you have a better idea of how your brain can change, let's apply a method of rewiring your brain that involves four steps:

- **F:** Focus
- **E:** Effort
- **E:** Effortlessness
- **D:** Determination

To help you remember these steps, use the acronym FEED, as in feeding your brain. Now let's examine each step in detail.

Focus

Focus on the situation, the new behavior, or information that you want to repeat or remember. *Focus* and attention activate your dlPFC, which alerts other parts of the brain to get engaged. Think of this step as the wakeup call. It is a "This is important!" function. You can't rewire your brain without alerting the rest of your brain to open the gate for new information. Focus plays an important role in neuroplasticity. Focus gets the ball rolling.

Since your PFC is your brain's brain, it helps to direct the resources to what is important. This contrasts with when you are on automatic pilot, such as when you are driving on a highway and talking to your friend in the passenger seat, your attention is directed to the conversation. The conversation is what you will remember, not the trees and the houses along the road. On the other hand, if you talk about what you both notice on the highway, your attention has shifted, and you may remember the physical details of the journey.

Yet, simply focusing attention doesn't ensure that your brain has been rewired. You focus briefly on a hundred thousand experiences every day, and your brain can't possibly remember all the things you experienced. Think of how many times you paid attention to all the driving challenges such as the intense traffic. Do you remember the traffic lights when you arrive home? No, because they were not important beyond those moments when you had to bring the car to a stop. Focus allows you to pay attention to what's happening here and now, and this starts the process of neuroplasticity.

Effort

If you talk about these details of the journey later, you'll strengthen those memories. If you don't discuss those details later—that is, you don't direct your attention to them after your initial focus—chances are those memories will fade. Trying to repeat what you want to remember strengthens the new synaptic connections. Maybe you want to remember a particular area along the road that was your habit of traveling so often you did it on autopilot.

Without knowledge of how the brain works, psychologists Robert Yerkes and John Dodson made it clear over a century ago that learning required effort beyond a person's comfort level. They pointed out that if you are too relaxed or extremely anxious, there is little learning possible. The sweet spot is in the middle of what is referred to as the inverse U (Figure 1.4). It is preferable to be moderately out of your comfort zone to learn and change your brain.

Your brain uses a lot of energy when you are trying to learn something new. By observing brain scans, neuroscientists have amassed considerable information about what parts of the brain light up in the scan due to glucose metabolism when someone is thinking or feeling something new. When you're making an effort to do

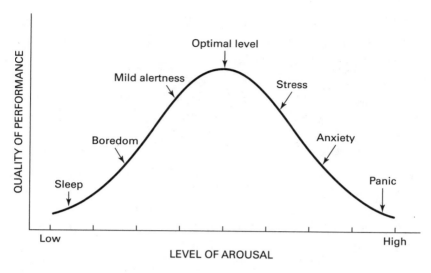

Figure 1.4   Inverse U

something new, the area of your brain associated with that task shows up in the scan as using more energy than other areas.

Effortlessness

After you have made an effort to learn the new behavior, way of thinking, or feeling, it will take less energy to keep it going as your new habit. Like learning a new tennis swing or how to say hello in a new language, in the beginning it takes focus, effort, and more energy in your brain. But after you make the swing or say hello in Spanish enough times, it becomes wired so that it becomes increasingly effortless. This means that to rewire your brain you'll have to stay with the new behavior long enough to make it become automatic—effortless. The bottom line is that after a period of time the new skill will come easier. Your brain won't have to work as hard once you reach this level.

Your brain follows natural laws, and the concept of effortlessness is consistent with the Law of the Conservation of Energy. This means that the things that happen are usually things that happen easily to minimize the energy necessary to make it happen. All water flows downhill, not uphill. The deeper the creek, the more water flows in it.

The same is true for your brain: the more you use certain brain cells together, the more likely you will use them together in the future. It becomes easier and easier. As brain scans illustrate, when you become more proficient in a particular skill, the brain region associated with that skill labors less. This illustrates the fundamental principle of efficiency: what comes easily will be repeated because it's easy.

Determination

Once you have developed a new skill—the tennis swing or saying hello in Spanish with the right accent—it will become easier to do each time. But what if you stop doing it? If you haven't played tennis in 10 years, you won't swing as well immediately. If you go to Spain 10 years after taking a class in Spanish, you won't be as fluent as when you were in the class (unless, of course, you have practiced in the meantime). You must continue to do the activity often to effortlessly retain the ability. You'll certainly play tennis better than if you never played before, and your Spanish will come back more quickly than if you had never learned it before. However, by being determined to stay in practice doing these things, your brain will remain wired to perform them effortlessly.

The final step to FEED your brain involves maintaining determination to stay in practice. You must be determined to engage in the activity again and again. Being determined to continue engaging in that new habit will not be tiring and painful. If you practice the other three steps in feeding your brain, by the time you get to this one, it remains easy. That's because effortlessness precedes it. Determination simply means that you must stay in practice, and you'll complete the feeding process to rewire your brain.

Now that you know the four basic steps or principles, we'll look at how you can apply them in your daily life. In Chapter 3, we'll discuss dealing with anxious feelings, needless worries, or just plain fear, and in Chapter 4 we'll address how you can avoid feeling down in the dumps. Chapters 5 to 8 describe the five healthy brain factors to practice daily. The following story illustrates how important it is to make a commitment to stay with all the steps of the FEED formula in rewiring your brain.

Marlee FEEDS Her Brain

Marlee asked for an appointment, saying that she was "fed up with being moody." She complained that she tended to be irritable and easily stressed.

"I want to be positive like everyone else," she said, shaking her head woefully. "I heard that you know how to rewire people's brains. Please rewire mine."

"It's not me but you that rewires your brain. Are you willing to do the work?" I asked.

"Why can't you do whatever it is that you do?" she insisted.

"They told me that you do hypnosis."

It is true that I was trained in hypnosis, but she needed more to establish a new way of dealing with her emotions.

"I'm tired of trying all these gimmicks that are supposed to work but never do."

"When you try something new, how long do you stay with it?" I probed.

"Long enough to know that it doesn't work," she stated matter-of-factly.

I gently prodded her for a clear answer of how long.

"Until it gets uncomfortable," she said, as if that confirmed her strong effort.

I explained the inverse U learning curve: how a moderate degree of discomfort is critical to rewire the brain. She had to try to stay with the new behavior until it became effortless to actually learn it. "You must practice doing it until it becomes a new habit," I told her. "That means that you must do what you don't feel like doing and continue doing it until it becomes easy to do again."

"Isn't forcing myself to do something against my nature?" she asked incredulously.

"Actually, it's very natural," I answered. "That's how you learn new skills. When you study for a test, you go over material repeatedly until it's easy to remember it, right?"

"No. I just crammed the night before and it worked just fine," Marlee informed me. "I passed the courses. That's all I cared about."

"Do you remember the subject matter now?" I asked.

She shook her head no.

I invited her to pick a habit that she wanted to break.

"My family says I'm irritable," she admitted.

"Do you agree?" I wanted to know.

"When I snap at them, it seems like they deserve it at the time," she noted. "But later it seems that I was shooting my mouth off and they didn't really deserve it."

"Do you really want to change or is it your family wants you to?" I asked. "Your motivation is critical. A passive effort just won't work. With effort, the activation of your brain's brain can direct all the resources to make the change."

"I'm sick of myself like this," she said solemnly. "I'm ready to do something."

"Let's start at the point when you feel the impulse to say something. That's when you need to interrupt your impulse."

I asked Marlee to stop and *focus* her attention on the moment before she reacted impulsively. People who have anger outburst problems react immediately through the fast track to the amygdala and lash out with more fight than flight. We will examine this tendency in greater detail in Chapter 3. In fact, a time-out step like this is used in anger management classes. Yet here, her task had to go further and focus on being an observer who is detached from the immediacy of the emotional reaction. Instead of the fight part of the fight or flight she needs to focus time to put the brakes on her automatic emotional reactions. Marlee's PFC had to develop better adaptive strategies to draw attention to what she was angry about rather than to simply express her anger.

Next, Marlee needed to make an *effort* to interrupt her usual impulsive lashing out. She had to act in a way that was different from her usual irritable way she spoke first and lamented later. Instead, she needed to learn to think first and speak later. She especially needed to make this effort when she didn't feel like it.

Marlee needed to repeat this effort enough times so that she eventually found it *effortless* to do so. She worked with focus and effort until it was effortless, feeding her brain for several weeks; then she came back in and said, "Well, I don't have to work as hard on that anymore—I'm getting the hang of it. So, I can take a break, right?"

I told her that she needed to continue working on these skills. She needs *determination* to wire in the new habit. Rather than take a break, she had to continue to regularly work out to stay in shape. It is only by staying determined that she will be able to rewire her brain to keep the new habit.

Test Yourself

Throughout the rest of the book, we will explore a variety of ways of rewiring your brain. Here is a quick preview quiz that will get to the heart of what's holding you back from rewiring your brain.

1. To rewire your brain, it's important to do what?
   a. Stay within your comfort zone
   b. Do what comes naturally to you
   c. Challenge yourself to change your behavior and then stay with it
   d. Wait until you feel motivated to change
2. What does the acronym FEED stand for?
   a. Feel good, Exhale, Excite, and Dictate
   b. Focus, Effort, Effortlessness, and Determination
   c. Fail, Engage, Encourage, and Describe
   d. Freedom, Effortlessness, Entertainment, and Doing little
3. If you're troubled by anxiety, it's best to do which of the following?
   a. Avoid what makes you anxious until you calm down
   b. Take some medication to numb yourself
   c. Expose yourself gradually to what makes you anxious
   d. Ask your family to shield you from stress

4. If you're down in the dumps, it's best to do which of the following?
   a. Hide out from family and friends until you feel up to seeing them
   b. Dig deep and reflect into why you feel depressed
   c. Get out of the house, exercise, and engage in activities
   d. Self-medicate with alcohol and/or sweets to soothe your feelings
5. When you're trying to improve your memory, it's best to do which of the following?
   a. Relax your mind so that you will have enough energy to remember
   b. Multitask
   c. Rely on your friends to remember things for you
   d. Focus your attention, form associations, and review your memories
6. What should you do to improve your diet so that you can more easily rewire your brain?
   a. Eat large amounts of fried foods, sugar, and processed foods
   b. Eat three balanced meals per day and hydrate with water throughout the day
   c. Eat one good hearty meal and consume plenty of caffeine for energy
   d. Eat only when you feel hunger pains
7. In old age, what is the best way to boost cognitive reserve and delay or prevent dementia?
   a. Minimize your mental strain by staying with a routine
   b. Vary your activities, learn new things, and stay socially connected
   c. Rest and stay away from any kind of demands
   d. Have a cocktail in the evening and ruminate about the past

8. Five habits that form the foundation for a healthy brain can be remembered as planting SEEDS. What does this acronym stand for?
    a. Safety, Escape, Exit, Distance, and Soothingness
    b. Sensation, Entertainment, Ecstasy, Distraction, and Slipping away
    c. Stifle, End, Execute, Don't, and Stonewall
    d. Social, Exercise, Education, Diet, Sleep hygiene
9. To build a resilient brain, you should do which of the following?
    a. Cultivate optimism, inoculate yourself with manageable stress, and challenge yourself
    b. Make pessimism your default mode so that you will never be surprised
    c. Avoid stress at all costs
    d. Save your energy for times of need
10. A mindful brain does which of the following?
    a. Shuts down, checks out, and is otherwise mindless
    b. Is in the here and now, savoring every moment and sensation
    c. Looks for constant distraction from the stress and strain of the moment
    d. Is holier than thou

I will explain in detail what you need to know to answer these questions in the remaining chapters of this book.

2

Energizing Your Brain

You need energy to rewire your brain. And because your energy is not immaculately conceived, you must learn to make it efficiently. This chapter explains how energy is indispensable to life and the functioning of your brain. Since your brain depends on energy to function, I will describe how you can ensure that you make enough of it to keep your brain healthy and your mind sharp.

Without energy you can't turn on and off your genes. That's right, your genes are not always on. In fact, your DNA does not rigidly determine your destiny. The emerging science of epigenetics has shown that your self-care plays a major role in determining which genes are turned on or off. We will also explore how energy, gene expression, and your immune system combine their effects in your brain functioning. When your energy is in short supply or misused your immune system can work against your brain. These malfunctions happen when you don't take care of yourself and can trigger chronic inflammation that results in depressive moods and brain fog.

The differences between people based on their lifestyles could not be more dramatic than between two brothers who shared the same DNA. Sam and Tyler are identical twins, but they diverge dramatically in their lifestyles. Sam describes himself as a home-body. He rarely ventures out into the community other than to go to the supermarket to buy steaks and burgers to barbecue. He enjoys sitting in his den where he watches sports most days and evenings. During the winter it was football, spring basketball, and summer baseball. He even watches games that he recorded.

Tyler is anything but a homebody. Instead of watching sports all day, he is an active member of various community groups. He, too, enjoys sports. But instead of being a passive spectator, he is an active participant in various city leagues, baseball, and tennis. At age 48, he looks 10 years younger, in contrast to his twin brother, who looks 10 years older. Tyler is also 40 pounds lighter than Sam and describes his condition as quite fit. Sam describes himself as looking like he lived the good life. Yet Sam is plagued by high blood pressure and type 2 diabetes.

Tyler is always taking classes in subjects ranging from geology to art at the community college. For his part, Sam says that he is retired. When Tyler asks him what he means by retired, Sam replies by saying, "It means that I can watch the grass grow."

In their ongoing playful and often whimsical and teasing ban-ter Tyler once asked, "Do you mow that grass?" Sam laughed and answered, "I told you I was retired!"

Once Tyler made a deal with the teenager next door to Sam not to mow his lawn that week as scheduled. The teenager agreed to come to Sam's with his mower and accept money for not mowing. Sam became irate. Tyler said, "Not to worry. I will do the job," as a tease. After he finished mowing the lawn, he paid the teenager in front of Sam. The teenager and Sam exchanged a glance with a shoulder shrug and then shook their heads that Tyler needed psychologi-cal help. Playing along, Tyler laughed, then thanked Sam "for the opportunity for some exercise. The gym was closed." Sam's wife was watching the entire scene and turned to Tyler with her eyes rolled. She knew quite well that Tyler's teasing joke was on her husband.

"Where's all this crazy energy coming from?" Sam asked his brother.

"What happened to yours? You aren't the same brother I grew up with."

Though these brothers started out with the same DNA, they became dramatically different in attitudes, activity levels, and overall health. The obvious difference was their lifestyle. Tyler plants and cultivates the five healthy factors encoded in the mnemonic SEEDS (which stand for Social, Exercise, Education, Diet, and Sleep) on a daily basis. Sam seemed resigned to the belief that his energy was retired and rarely engaged in any of the SEEDS factors.

Mitos—Your Energy Generators

Where did Tyler's energy come from? Is it prana or chi? Is it some kind of spiritual energy that we can never totally understand? When producing and harnessing the energy to rewire your brain, we don't need to get lost in those philosophical debates. The answer is right in front of us. Your brain is a biological organ, and it runs on biological energy. So, if you hope to rewire your brain, you should understand how to make and keep energy working efficiently in your brain.

The first thing to appreciate is where and how energy is made. Like all your cells, brain cells contain energy factories called *mitochondria*. Cells contain from 1000 to 2500 mitochondria. To make them simple to remember we will call them *mitos* because they are mighty! See Figure 2.1 for an image of a cell and its mitos. They produce your energy, called adenosine triphosphate, better known as *ATP*. To make ATP simple, think of it as All The Power. ATP plays an indispensable role in determining whether you live or die. Consider that the poison called cyanide will kill you because it immediately kills your mitos. Without your mitos—no ATP, and you die.

Mito health and their product, ATP, determine whether you can read this sentence, rewire your brain, and maintain mental health. While Tyler generates a lot of it, Sam is retiring his mitos.

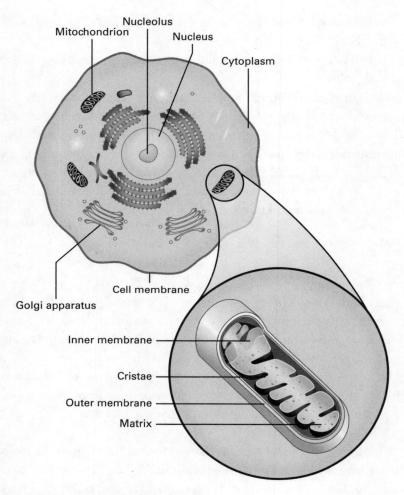

Figure 2.1   A cell and mitochondria

Every day your mitos make two hundred trillion trillion ATP molecules. Another way to grasp the volume and importance of your
mitos is to consider that you produce and recycle your body weight
in ATP. The greater your energy needs and the greater the demand
on your mitos. This also means that there are adverse consequences
when ATP is in short supply. One of the first places you feel loss of
ATP is in your brain.

Though it weighs a mere three and a half pounds, your brain is among the highest energy consumers in your body. So it is no coincidence that your brain cells contain among the greatest number of mitos. There are approximately 10 million billion mitos in your brain. To put this astounding number in perspective, consider that your brain uses 20% of your body's energy, and your synapses use 80% of that energy. This means that much of that energy is devoted to fueling synapses for neuroplasticity. In other words, without enough energy you can't rewire your brain.

Mobile Mitos

Neuroplasticity is facilitated by mobile mitos. They travel on miniature tracks, called *microtubules*, which are like small tubes within your neurons. This mobility allows your mitos to get energy delivered to where the rewiring action is, at your synapses. In other words, mobile mitos provide the energy to rewire your brain.

You may wonder why you have so little energy, cannot think clearly, or cannot maintain a positive mood. If you are already in poor health, you may be accelerating the death of your mitos within your brain cells. You need to maintain your health to give your mitos a chance to help your brain have the capacity to think clearly and produce positive moods.

Just as it is senseless to drive a car without fuel, it's even more senseless to hop in the driver's seat without enough brain energy to drive carefully. Like the engine for your car that needs the right fuel for combustion, to generate energy your mitos must take in the right balance of raw materials to produce ATP. For your car it is refined gasoline, and for your mitos it is oxygen from breathing and glucose, which is derived from the food you eat. Those raw materials travels through your bloodstream to all your cells, at which point the hormone insulin helps get the glucose into your cells so that your mitos can begin to generate ATP. Without this energy your brain cells black out.

Not only do you need the right balance of raw materials for your mitos to produce ATP, but you need to use up the ATP to keep your mitos healthy. Unlike your car that you leave in your garage for a month before driving it again, your brain cannot take a break for one month. Your body needs to use the energy to make more. This is a use-it-or-lose-it must. You must use the energy that you make so that you can make more of it. In other words, exercise is also critical for the health of your mitos. These two self-care factors of exercise and diet will be explained in more detail in Chapters 6 and 8.

Unhealthy mitos don't just produce less energy. They cause ill health. Consider that if you eat mostly junk food and fail to exercise, your mitos will generate excess *free radicals*, which damage your cells. Like a nuclear meltdown that leaks out radiation and destroys the power plant, free radical damage can kill your mitos from which they leak. In other words, eating junk food and failing to exercise blow out your mitos and destroy the cells they inhabit. This damage to your mitos and cells means you lose energy, feel lethargic, can't think clearly, and may even become depressed. This is one of the reasons that Sam looked 10 years older than Tyler and had much less energy and motivation.

Leaky Mitos—Free Radical Toxicity

One way to understand how energy is produced is to think of mitos as following the principles of a hydroelectric dam. As water fills a reservoir within the dam, pressure builds up so that the water is forced out through a channel to drive turbines to create electricity. Just like dams, mitos use pressure so that energy is released from electrons within the pump. The reactions from the released electrons are used to pump protons through the membranes of mitos to generate biochemical reactions culminating with the final product, the synthesis of ATP.

Just as a dam runs the risk of potential leaks, so too can mitos leak. For mitos the main source of leakage is referred to as *reactive oxygen species* (ROS), a type of free radical. Free radicals develop when unmatched electrons leak from your mitos and then steal available electrons from the lipids in cell membranes. Damage to your cells from excessive free radical leakage occurs when you overeat (especially junk food) and fail to exercise. See Figure 2.2 for the difference between a healthy mitochondrial and an unhealthy mitochondrial.

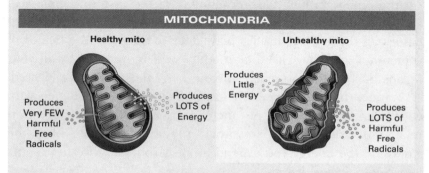

Figure 2.2   A healthy mitochondria and unhealthy mitochondria

Normally, mitos have a shelf life of a few days to a few weeks. Your mitos need to recycle to keep the healthy ones working well and get rid of those that are unhealthy. Their two principal recycling methods are *mitophagy* (killing off old and damaged mitos), and *biogenesis* (the birth of new mitos). These recycling methods work to ensure that underperforming mitos (that are no longer mighty) are killed off. This critical recycling function is facilitated by exercise. When the old and damaged ones are removed, there is room left for the healthy mitos to thrive and new ones to be born. However, this recycling process does not work efficiently if you are suffering from chronic health conditions, in which case low-functioning mitos spew out free radicals and as a result speed up the damage to your brain cells.

This recycling loop can also break down when you, like Sam, don't exercise and eat too much of the wrong foods, such as those with excess calories, simple carbohydrates, and bad fats. This is because overeating increases the half-life of weak mitos so that they remain pooled together. These weak and inefficient mitos are even harder to kill off by mitophagy because you are not exercising. Consequently, the weak mitos produce less ATP and more free radicals than healthy mitos.

Metabolism

All the energy production, recycling, and the resulting biological activity to keep you alive is referred to as your *metabolism*. It encompasses all the work that your body does to maintain the health of your mitos and the ATP they produce which are used by all your organs. Depending on where in your body those cells are located, ATP fuels that organ's metabolism and its interdependence with your other organs. Since your metabolism and the energy are interrelated, one doesn't happen without the other. The total of all the work and the energy you expend to keep yourself alive represents your body's *metabolic rate*.

Impaired brain metabolism leads to many types of dementia such as Alzheimer's and Parkinson's diseases. Metabolic disorders lead to many precursor symptoms of dementia such as cognitive and memory difficulties called mild cognitive impairment (MCI). MCI is on the rise because the Western lifestyle of an unhealthy diet, little to no exercise, and being overweight is quite destructive to the metabolism of the brain.

If you, like Sam, are one of the millions of people caught in the pandemic of overeating, obesity, and lack of exercise, expect that your brain metabolism will suffer. Though your brain cells require considerable ATP for their energy needs, fat cells do not and they tax your metabolism. If you gain extra fat cells, especially if your body mass index (BMI) exceeds 30, your energy production will decrease and so will the number of healthy mitos in your brain cells. Worst yet, excessive weight contributes to metabolic disorders, chronic inflammation, and even brain shrinkage. This means that as your fat cells increase, your brain cells can decrease. The brain areas most vulnerable to damage and shrinking are your PFC and hippocampus. This damage results in problems making decisions and remembering information necessary to make those decisions.

Metabolic syndrome is a growing societal timebomb on our health care system. Don't be part of it. Metabolic syndrome has been estimated to burden around 20–25% of adults in the world, and the numbers are increasing. The most common symptoms metabolic syndrome include:

- High blood pressure
- High levels of LDL cholesterol
- A large waistline

This constellation of destructive health conditions leads to type 2 diabetes, which leads to type 3 diabetes, also called Alzheimer's disease. The question you must ask yourself is: Do you think that you can rewire your brain with all these corrosive things occurring in your brain without changing your lifestyle to prevent them? The answer is that regaining your health is a prerequisite to rewiring your brain.

Consider that your brain is one of the highest energy consumers in the body. If your blood sugar rises too high, it is not only toxic for brain cells but also impairs the ability of your pancreas to produce insulin to deal with the flood of glucose. The effects of metabolic syndrome blunt the receptivity of insulin receptors on cells, which results in type 2 diabetes. No longer will your metabolic system be able to deal with the excess sugar. As cells corrode, you have little energy, making it difficult to think clearly and maintain a positive mood.

The bottom line is that you must maintain metabolic health for the sake of your brain or it will suffer. You need plentiful healthy mitos in each cell not only in your brain but also throughout your body. The energy produced by them is indispensable for the capacity to think clearly and enjoy positive moods. For healthy mitos you must engage in all the SEEDS factors daily, as detailed in Chapters 5–9.

Genomic Plasticity

Until recently many people mistakenly believed that their DNA was their destiny. All too often, I have heard patients say that their depression or anxiety was the result of bad genes. Some said, "There is no use in trying to change because bad genes made my bad brain." Some even thought that their personality was programed by their genes. This kind of simplistic thinking has been called *genetic astrology* by geneticists. Don't buy into this self-defeating silliness. It is antiscience, and believing in it will undermine your motivation to make the lifestyle changes necessary for your brain health.

To understand why you aren't doomed by your genes, we need to first dispel a few myths. There is no simple one-to-one correspondence between your genes and mind. Genes, by themselves, do nothing like that. So, what is a gene, anyway? It is a misnomer to say that there is a gene for this type of thinking or a gene for that type of emotion. To understand the role that your genes play in your life you need first to understand that a gene is a section of your DNA that contains the recipe for a protein. To be more precise, a gene codes for an amino acid which then combines with other amino acids to make a protein. So, genes do not make personalities, prevent you from being happy, or love the color purple. If genes did such things, Tyler and Sam would share personality characteristics. Again, genes simply contain the recipe to make proteins.

Chromosomes, DNA, and Genes

When researchers discovered the entire DNA–protein complex under a microscope, it appeared purplish-brown, so they named it a *chromosome*, from the Greek *khroma* meaning "color." You have 23 chromosomes in each cell. The stuff of chromosomes includes DNA and genes. Your DNA is composed of four nucleotides: adenine, thymine, cytosine, and guanine. These are all arranged in an order that is uniquely you. They are commonly referred to by letters that are abbreviated from the nucleotides as A, T, C, and G. The identification of a particular gene is three letters long, located within your DNA. They can be adjacent or more often separated by many spaces and organized in triplets. To make a protein, the triplet sequence of nucleotides that represents a gene must be copied by DNA's cousin molecule, RNA. Genetic information is sent via messenger RNA to the protein factories in your cells called ribosomes.

From the beginning of your life until death, your body grows new cells to replace old ones. In doing so, cells divide and copy your entire genome, which includes all your chromosomes with your DNA and genes. The two strands of the double helix separate and serve as a template for the creation of another strand to match it. The new double-stranded DNA has exactly the same base sequence as its parent molecule. Each of your cells contains all the three billion base pairs of DNA—half inherited from your father, half from your mother—which combine to produce your unique sequence, referred to as your genome.

We know a lot about our DNA thanks to the Human Genome Project. It was a decades-long international effort involving 32 institutions and 442 scientists at a cost of $288 million. Prior to this project we erroneously believed that humans possessed 100,000 genes. It was surprising to discover that we have only between 20,000 and 25,000 genes. To put this humbling discovery in perspective, a round-worm has roughly 20,000 genes and a grape has 30,434. Since we are much more complicated creatures than worms or grapes, why don't we have more genes? Surely, if individual genes make particular traits and since humans have more traits than worms and grapes, wouldn't we have more genes? What is the answer to this puzzle?

Part of the answer to these questions came from the project's most surprising discovery: that only 2% of human DNA can be described as genes. The remaining 98% was initially called junk

DNA because no one knew what what it did. More recently we discovered that it was wrong to refer to this 98% of our DNA as junk. It is now referred to as noncoding DNA because it does not code for protein and therefore cannot be described as genes.

If only 2% of your DNA can be described as genes, then the question we must ask is what does the noncoding remaining 98% DNA do? One significant clue is that we have far more of noncoding DNA than any other living creature. We now know that the expression of your genes is far more variable and flexible than other living creatures because your noncoding DNA plays a role in how your genes are used in response to the context of your experience and behavior. And it turns out that the noncoding DNA does all sorts of things, including helping turn on and off genes. This makes your behavior far less determined by individual genes than any other species. Yes, genes are indispensable for the instructions to make proteins, but your behavior and experience cannot be explained by your individual genes. This means that your noncoding DNA endows you with a great degree of flexibility in how your genes are expressed. In other words, your self-care behavior can change which genes are expressed and which genes are not.

As the scientific community learned that the human genome is far more complex than expected, a new science called epigenetics emerged to explain how our genome is quite plastic. Epigenetics, meaning "above the genome," explores genes expression. It has revolutionized biological science, health care, and our understanding of how we came to be a species with complex mental capacities. Thanks to epigenetics, we know a lot more about how and under what circumstances different genes are turned on (expressed) and some are turned off (suppressed).

You may have a particular gene, but it may not be expressed because your environment and behavior suppress that gene or other genes that interact with it. Epigenetics explains how genetic material can be activated or deactivated in different contexts, such as your self-care behaviors. What's more, genes are expressed or suppressed, not by a simple on-or-off switch but more like a dimmer switch that adjusts in response to your diet, whether you exercise, sleep well, have quality relationships, and manage your stress effectively.

The interactions between your genome, behavior, and environment change your brain for better or worse. For example, the interactions between stressful environmental conditions, not getting enough quality sleep, and engaging in other unhealthy lifestyle habits adversely influence the expression of your genes, which can have detrimental effects on your brain, emotions, and clarity of thought.

Your brain possesses an array of short- and long-term memory capacities that in part are facilitated by epigenetic mechanisms for the regulation of neurotransmitters, hormones, and immune system molecules. If you believe that your environment is threatening, genes may be expressed to ramp up your sympathetic nervous system's fight-or-flight response or the neuroendocrine (hypothalamic pituitary adrenal [HPA] axis) stress pathways.

Psychologists have long pointed out that people who were neglected, abused, or insecurely attached to their parents tend to tolerate stress less. Now we know that epigenetic mechanisms are at play. For example, researchers have shown that people who are provided a nurturing environment early in their life turn on genes that give them greater stress tolerance than those who are neglected because those genes are turned off, leading to less stress tolerance. As a result, people who were nurtured early in life have a better thermostat for stress. They have an innate ability to turn off the stress response without even trying. They are essentially more durable in stressful situations. This thermostat for stress is provided by the epigenetic products of proteins, which are cortisol receptors. Neglected people are less likely to produce proteins associated with cortisol receptors. They have fewer cortisol receptors, which means that their neuroendocrine system has less of an ability to turn off their HPA axis, which produces cortisol. As a result, they may, at times, tend to experience uncontrollable stress.

If you are worried that you are one of those people who were neglected or abused and as a result suffered from epigenetic effects that I just explained, please do not feel stuck or doomed. Don't forget that genes can be turned on and off throughout your life. Following the recommendations in this book will help make up for these deficits.

Neurotrophic Factors—Your Brain Fertilizers

Growth substances play a significant epigenetic role in the health of your brain. A variety of substances cells called *neurotrophic factors*, protect and grow new brain cells and they appear to be activated through epigenetic mechanisms. Early nurturance is associated with the epigenetic expression (turning on) of a transcription factor called nerve growth factor (NGF), which binds to the cortisol receptor gene to increase cortisol receptors. In contrast, neglect or child abuse is associated with turning off NGF. As a result, neglected people tend to produce fewer cortisol receptor proteins in their hippocampus. Their stress response systems become hyperactive (harder to turn off), predisposing them to anxiety and fearfulness. For example, women who were neglected as babies tend to become stressed-out and neglectful mothers, too, continuing the cycle of neglect through the alteration of the NGF gene. They may even have offspring with the same alteration to their NGF gene.

You met brain-derived neurotrophic factor (BDNF) in the previous chapter, where I described how it plays a significant role in neurogenesis, neuroplasticity, and overall brain health. Unfortunately, some epigenetic influences of early life adversity can suppress the BDNF gene. The brain areas associated with this impairment include the hippocampus and prefrontal cortex, which are critical for higher cognitive functions such as planning, memory, and goal-directed behavior. Fortunately, you can stimulate the release of BDNF by aerobic exercise as I describe in Chapter 6.

Insulin-like growth factor (IGF-1) decreases blood glucose levels by helping deliver it to cells so that their mitos can generate energy. IGF-1 contributes to brain growth and can be epigenetically facilitated by prosocial circuits in the brain.

Though in Chapter 5 you will learn how the social factor is critical for overall brain health, the point here is that positive social experiences affect gene expression important for the health of your brain.

People who received nurturing tend to build resiliency networks in their brain such as more GABA receptor sites, which act to reduce stress and anxiety. They also have diminished levels of stress neurochemistry. In general, well-nurtured people are less anxious and more engaged in their environments, even during fear-inducing situations.

Telomeres—The Aglets on Your Chromosomes

In closing out this section on the plasticity of your genome, it is important to address one of the ways your genes can be damaged. Your chromosomes are capped with noncoding DNA called telomeres, from the Greek "end." Often analogized as aglets of shoelaces that protect them from unraveling, the telomeres protect your chromosomes (i.e., DNA) from damage. This vulnerability leaves genes more exposed to mutation (damage) and results in accelerated aging as well as the increased risk of many illnesses.

Your cells are constantly dying and being replaced by new ones through a process called cell division. When cells divide to make new ones, telomeres shorten. This is one of the reasons telomere length serves as a biomarker for health and longevity. Your behavior can impair your chromosomes by accelerating the shortening of your telomeres. Serious illnesses and poor self-care behaviors shorten telomere length.

The SEEDS factors may protect your genes by enhancing the health of your telomeres. They do this by promoting the release of an enzyme called *telomerase* that protects telomeres by adding nucleotides to telomeres. Whereas oxidative stress reduces telomerase activity, antioxidants increase it. Healthy self-care behaviors protect telomeres; not engaging in self-care shortens your telomeres.

Factors That Shorten Telomeres

- Metabolic disorders
- Cardiovascular disease
- Smoking
- Obesity (more than smoking!)
- Type 2 diabetes
- Social isolation
- Poor diet
- No exercise
- Poor sleep
- Alcohol and other drugs
- Chronic inflammation

Tyler and his brother were illustrating what a difference in behavior makes on a person. Lifestyle practices such as the SEEDS factors increase the activity of telomerase.

The Immune System in Your Brain

You may wonder why I have included a section on the immune system in a book on the brain health. Your immune system is not segregated from your brain to other parts of your body. It has a dramatic effect on your capacity to think clearly and to maintain energy, motivation, and a positive mood. In fact, you have specialized cells in your brain that are responsive to immune cells in other parts of your body.

When your immune system works well, it differentiates your cells from those that do not belong in your body. Your immune system, therefore, is by nature self-identifying so that it can protect you from what is not you. It keeps your brain safe, just like the rest of your body, from foreign substances. Normally, your blood–brain barrier protects your brain from harmful substances, but when there are threats to other parts of your body, the distress signals are sent to your brain. Because of this interaction, when your immune system is not working well, such as when it is turned on inappropriately, you can have trouble thinking clearly and may suffer from depression.

To get a better idea how your immune system works, let's first take a broad look at how it is organized. You have two basic divisions of your immune system: the innate and adaptive subsystems. As the name suggests, your *innate* system contains all the defenses that you are born with. It protects cells in your body from the threat of invaders that do not belong in your body and marshals an immediate defense. But its weapons are not crafted to meet the specific characteristics of a unique threat. That comes later with the *adaptive* immune system, which provides a more sophisticated and precise protection from specific new threats, such as viruses that you never encountered before.

Your adaptive system is so named because it adapts to new threats that you encounter throughout your life. It manufactures T and B cells, the latter of which create antibodies that develop in response to learning about the new invaders such as viruses. It also protects you from threats by charging up your innate system to fight harder. Without the innate immune system, your adaptive immune system does not possess the foot soldiers to do the majority of the heavy lifting needed to fight off invaders. Without your adaptive immune system, the innate immune system is not sophisticated enough to fight off more complicated invaders such as the COVID virus.

Inflammation is the universal response of your immune system to any danger to your body. Inflammation gets its name from the red flame-like swelling and the heat that occurs with an injury or infection. Think of inflammation as the yellow tape strung around a crime scene that protects it so that investigators can get in without anyone else coming in and messing with the evidence. Just like a crime scene, the purpose of inflammation is to restrict the area to only immune cells so that they can come in to inspect and deal with the danger. Inflammation promotes the opening up of blood vessels to let plasma (the fluid part of blood) bring immune cells into the damage area. This is why there is swelling around a wound.

Your innate immune system uses heat, such as fever, along with inflammation because microorganisms do not like it hot. Your immune repair cells do like it hot because it helps speed up your metabolism and enables wounds to heal faster. Meanwhile, the pain associated with inflammation motivates you to protect the area. Together with the loss of function, swelling, and heat, the pain gives you good reason to slow down and cease your activities so that you have time to heal.

When all these parts of your immune system are working well, they not only keep you alive but also protect your brain. However, malfunctions in your immune system can damage your brain. For example, while too little inflammation during an infection leaves your body defenseless, chronic inflammation can break down body systems and damage your brain. Chronic inflammation is associated with many diseases, including heart disease. Your brain is particularly sensitive to chronic inflammation, and its effects can lead to depression, cognitive deficits, and dementia.

Inflammatory Messaging

The language of your immune system is provided by cytokines. From the *cyto*, meaning cell, and *kine*, meaning movement, *cytokines* are proteins that move around your body conveying information about the state of your health and where immune cells must go to fight off invaders to protect your health. Pro- and anti-inflammatory cytokines come in many flavors and are released by a variety of immune cells, including macrophages, Helper T cells, and Killer T cells.

Your brain contains its own immune system response cells called glia cells (e.g., microglial cells and astrocytes). They release either pro- or anti-inflammatory cytokines depending on the challenges to your body. Microglia make up 6–12% of all the cells in your brain. They constantly monitor for potential threats to your brain by foreign invaders. When they identify danger, microglia release pro-inflammatory cytokines that promote inflammation in your brain. Sometimes the danger signals are psychological, such as when you are going through a stressful period, at which time your microglia cells may release pro-inflammatory cytokines. Chronic stress and ill health prime microglia so that they release pro-inflammatory signals more easily when they encounter danger again. In other words, chronic stress makes it more likely that the immune cells in your brain will be activated in the future and promote inflammation.

For their part, astrocytes also play a major role in your immune system in your brain by functioning as a point of interaction between cytokines and neurons through genetic transcription and synaptic plasticity. Astrocytes exchange signals with neurons, detect and react to immune signals, and release pro-inflammatory cytokines that signal peripheral immune cells. Astrocytes can perpetuate a chronic inflammatory spiral in response to the excessive release of inflammatory signals from microglia.

Inflamed Brain

Chronic inflammation is distinct from acute inflammation such as when you have an infection. Whereas acute inflammation is short-lived and is important for tissue repair should you get injured, chronic inflammation is destructive. It leads to a variety of pathological conditions such as depression and autoimmune and neurodegenerative diseases.

To understand how chronic inflammation is destructive to your brain, consider how it blocks energy from the areas that are inflamed. When your immune system is turned on in the absence of a foreign invader, it may even attack your own body, fighting your cells including those in the brain as if they are invaders. Chronic inflammation can make you feel and behave like you are sick. Your brain suffers, and so does your mental health.

Depression associated with chronic inflammation has been dubbed sickness behavior. For example, Sandra came to see me with complaints of low energy, difficulty thinking clearly, and mild depression. This is because those people like Sandra are afflicted with chronic inflammation. People like Sandra feel and behave as if they are ill. She was overweight and prediabetic. Her consistent complaint was feeling tired all the time, disruptions to sleep, and decreased social interests. She spent the evening eating comfort food, which was essentially composed of simple carbohydrates. Her anhedonia and deficits in learning and memory spilled over into her work environment. The downward spiral of depressive moods and lack of insight spread into poor job performance, which eventually made her feel worse after receiving a scathing evaluation from her supervisor.

Since Sandra felt ill, she acted as if she were ill. Her sedentary behavior and overeating inadvertently made her more depressed and feel even more ill. She thought that she needed to recoup or get over the illness by resting. Yet her sedentary behavior perpetuated chronic inflammation, which made her depression and cognitive fog worse. When she made a brief attempt to pull out of the spiral, she initially felt worse over the short term. So she stopped trying to break bad habits. Had she persisted long enough she would have discovered that over the longer term she would have felt better as she gradually decreased her chronic inflammation.

Symptoms of Sickness Behavior and Chronic Inflammation

- Anhedonia
- Depressed mood
- Cognitive deficits
- Loss of social interest
- Fatigue
- Low libido
- Poor appetite
- Somnolence
- Pain sensitivity
- Anxiety

Overall, chronic inflammation can result from poor self-care practices, obesity, and/or metabolic syndrome. The combination of all of these disorders contributes to insulin resistance, the risk of type 2 diabetes, and cardiovascular illness, which all contribute to more chronic inflammation in your brain. These combined effects to your brain are associated with psychological disorders such as cognitive impairments, anxiety, and depression.

One of the ways that chronic inflammation causes cognitive and mood deficits is by disturbing synaptic strength. There are high concentrations of receptors for pro-inflammatory cytokines located in your prefrontal cortex and hippocampus that can potentiate cognitive impairments, including poor memory and decision making. Excessive pro-inflammatory cytokines especially in your hippocampus can affect your memory by interfering with BDNF impairing your capacity for neural plasticity, neurogenesis, memory, energy balance, mood, and your efforts to rewire your brain.

Fat Cells, Chronic Inflammation, and Brain Fog

The body that you inherited from your ancestors cannot cope with the modern world of sedentary life, lack of exposure to sunlight, and junk food often low in fiber, processed, fried, and full of sugar, high fructose corn syrup, and saturated fat. Neither did they sit around on couches watching television or playing computer games.

Before 11,000 years ago, our ancestors survived by hunting and gathering vegetable matter. During periods when food was scarce, fat cells provided a backup source of energy. Fat cells are nature's way of storing energy. Of course, the amount of fat that they accumulated was minimal compared to most people today. And this extreme discrepancy is a major problem!

In the Western world today, we have stored fat cells—and at dangerous levels. For example, in the United States three-fourths of adults are overweight, and one-third of Americans are considered obese. These numbers are growing each year. The World Health

Organization estimates that two billion people in the world are either overweight or obese. Out of eight billion people in the world today, that represents a major pandemic. And the United States leads the world in this pandemic.

Now instead of storing small amounts of fat cells for backup sources of energy when food is not available, we are destroying what used to be a very efficient system for our survival. We flipped it upside down to our detriment, and our brain suffers. Consider that the excess amount of fat cells contributes to shrinking the brain. In fact, normally these are the areas of your brain that would help you get concerned about all this, including your hippocampus and prefrontal cortex.

This is not only a health crisis; it is a brain impairment crisis. It is no wonder that we have a pandemic of obesity, which the American Medical Association (AMA) now calls a disease.

The Centers for Disease Control and Prevention defines obesity as a body mass index (BMI) of over 30. The higher the BMI, the greater the chronic inflammation. Independent of age, if your BMI is over 30 you run the risk of a range of cognitive impairments associated with global brain atrophy, cognitive decline, and incidence of dementia. In other words, with increasing amounts of fat cells, there is a greater risk of all these brain health impairments.

Calculating Your BMI

How do you know that you are overweight—beyond looking in the mirror? The AMA defines being overweight and obese by using the BMI. It is calculated by your weight (in kilograms) divided by your height (in meters) squared. Though it is not a complete way to measure health, it is a good starting place. A BMI between 18.5 and 25.0 is considered normal. If your BMI is between 25 and 30.0, you are considered overweight. And if your BMI is over 30.0, you are obese.

A 24-year follow-up study in Sweden found that the greater the BMI, the greater the risk of developing Alzheimer's disease.

People with a higher BMI had a greater degree of atrophy of the brain. For every 1 point increase in BMI, the degree of brain atrophy was 13–16%. The location of those extra fat cells is also critically significant; belly fat predicts dementia independent of BMI. In other words, the larger your belly, the greater the risk of dementia. This health risk factor led to the concept that an apple shape body places you at a greater risk than a pear shape. In fact, one of the most significant risk factors for type 2 diabetes is obesity, and especially with fat above the hips. This makes excessive belly fat diagnostic of a variety of health problems, strongly associated with cognitive and mood problems.

Researchers in Korea found that an increase in BMI has an inverse relationship to cognitive ability as measured by the Mini Mental Status Exam. In other words, as the amount of fat cells increases, thinking ability decrease.

Extra fat cells are like decaying energy. They leach out pro-inflammatory cytokines, causing chronic inflammation. One type of fat cell is more dangerous than the other. Your subcutaneous fat cells are so named because they are right below your skin and located in abundance in your butt, belly, and breasts. The other type of fat cells is called visceral fat or organ fat, which cluster around your organs. In abundance, they are dangerous. One obvious symptom of excessive visceral fat is a large belly.

Belly fat generates inflammation in your abdominal cavity. Fat cells are not dormant and inactive storage units; it appears that they release the same inflammatory chemicals (such as pro-inflammatory cytokines) that your body releases when you have an infection or have been traumatized with injuries. Pro-inflammatory cytokines are associated with depression, and they lower the level of BDNF, the protector of nerve cells, the promoter of neuroplasticity, and neurogenesis.

In an extensive study done by my former employer, Kaiser Permanente, researchers examined more than 10,000 people who had been diagnosed with dementia to determine the relationship between BMI and dementia. They had been followed for 27 years and were evaluated for skin-fold thickness (belly fat) and BMI. The study found that men who had the highest skin-fold category at middle age had a 72% rate of dementia, and women in the same category had a 60% rate of dementia.

Being overweight—even worse, obese—causes a breakdown in multiple systems in your body. One malfunction, referred to as leptin resistance, makes it harder to reverse course and lose weight. Leptin is a hormone that tells your brain that you have had enough food. This means that you will be prone to continue eating though you are full, further increasing the risk of obesity and chronic inflammation.

Obesity not only causes chronic inflammation but is also associated with increases the risk of illnesses like autoimmune disorders, coronary heart disease, stroke, hypertension, sleep apnea, and type 2 diabetes. These inflammatory conditions break down many of your body's systems and are all associated with depression, anxiety, and cognitive impairments. Inflammation represents the common denominator for metabolic syndrome, obesity, cognitive impairment, and depression.

To understand the relationship between being overweight and inflammation, consider that not only do fat cells swell up but also are not cleared out efficiently when the dead ones are recycled. The cluttering up of dead cells alert immune cells such as macrophages to cluster around dead cells to engulf and digest them while simultaneously adding inflammation to seal off the area. Like a stagnant pond with muck building up because there are no streams coming in or out, fat cells decay and pollute your body.

Fat cells release proinflammatory cytokines. In other words, fat cells themselves are agents of inflammation. They can cause organ failure and inflammation in the brain. Having too many fat cells also deprives your brain of energy that would normally provide your neurons the capacity for thinking clearly and maintaining a stable mood. Whereas brain cells require energy to enable you to think, fat cells sap your energy and cloud your thinking.

While your brain cells contain far more mitos than fat cells, what available energy that you do have is drained away by working overtime carry around extra weight. Worse still, as you accumulate fat cells, your energy production decreases along with the number of mitos in your brain cells. Calling it brain fog is putting it mildly; it is *brain smog*. Unlike fog, which is not toxic and can be blown away by a continental wind, smog lingers and is toxic. This brain smog leads to exhaustion, depression, and trouble thinking clearly.

Excessive fat cells also block BDNF, which is one of the many ways that they contribute to dementia and depression. BDNF plays an important role in energy balance as it can reduce inappropriate hunger while it helps to increase energy output. This means that though your appetite increases, it can decrease your energy. Meanwhile, it blocks BDNF, which is critical for neurogenesis in the hippocampus and PFC, while it shrinks your brain.

Diabetes of the Brain

Along with the pandemic of overweight and obese people in the Western world, there has been a rise in the number of people at risk of developing type 2 diabetes. From this context, it is understandable why many neurologists are calling Alzheimer's "diabetes type 3" or "diabetes of the brain." This is because disruptions in brain metabolism underlie many types of dementia. Insulin resistance and type 2 diabetes are known to increase the risk of Alzheimer's and Parkinson's diseases and other dementias. In addition, dementias are associated with increases in free radicals, such as superoxide, low energy (ATP), inflammation, cell death, and neurotransmitter dysregulations.

Both a symptom and cause of major health problems, chronic inflammation and metabolic disorders make it difficult to rewire your brain, and they contribute to psychological disorders. For example, it is now well documented that not only are people who

develop type 2 diabetes prone to depression, but those people who
are depressed are more likely to develop diabetes. For these reasons,
the Western lifestyle with its unhealthy diet and little to no exercise tends to be quite destructive to the metabolism of your brain.
Chapters 6 and 8 talk about ways to add brain-healthy SEEDS to
your daily habits.

"Second Brain" Messaging Your Main Brain

Your gastrointestinal (GI) system or gut has been referred to as the
second brain. It includes a large group of neurons wrapped around
the walls of your GI system composed of 50 to 100 million nerve
cells—as many as in your spinal cord. Your gut maintains connections with the parasympathetic and sympathetic branches of your
autonomic nervous system. It receives signals to stimulate digestive
activity from the parasympathetic branch through the vagus nerve
and to inhibit activity from the sympathetic branch.

Roughly 90% of the signals conveyed through the vagus nerve
travel from the gut to the brain, whereas only 10% travel in the
opposite direction. In other words, feelings coming from your gut
are more prevalent than feelings extending from the brain to the gut.
In other words, "gut feelings" are sensed in the brain. Over a lifetime
your gut adapts to stress that communicate with gut microbes that
live near the gut wall. If they detect the presence of potentially dangerous bacteria, it can trigger a cascade of inflammatory reactions
in the gut wall in an effort to control pathogens.

Our ancestors periodically ate contaminated food, which caused
a responsive immune system in the gut to evolve and protect them
from infection, illness, and even death. The connectivity between
the gut and the brain became fine-tuned and responsive so that our
ancestors would feel that they ate something unhealthy. From this
perspective it is understandable that the gut makes up the largest
component of the body's immune system. If your gut's immune cells
were clumped together, they would be greater in number than those
immune cells in your thyroid, pituitary, gonads, adrenals, bone mar-
row, and circulating in blood combined. In short, your gut has more
immune cells than found in the rest of the body put together.

Your gut's abundant immune cells play a major role in signaling between its nerves and your brain about the state of your gut and body. In general these feelings are referred to as interoceptive information, or simply "gut feelings." This means that the term *gut feelings* is more than a mere metaphor. When inflammation—especially in response to stress—occurs in your gut, many of the sensors become more sensitive to normal stimuli. From synthesizing neurotransmitters and vitamins to activity in your immune system, what happens in your gut is signaled to your brain. This ongoing communication about the state of your gut to your brain affects your feelings, emotions, and even the clarity of thought.

Inflammation can contribute to a wide range of gut illnesses, including the aptly named inflammatory bowel syndrome (IBS), in which inflammatory signals travel to your brain and activate the microglia, which then respond to and release more inflammatory signals. Again, this means that inflammation in your gut can lead to inflammation in your brain.

Friendly and Unfriendly Bacteria

One of the most common causes of an inflamed gut is bacteria. Your gut contains more than 100 trillion micro-organisms, including bacteria, fungi, and archaea. If gathered together, they would weigh between 2 and 6 pounds. Outnumbering people on the planet by 100,000 times, these gut microbes perform many life-sustaining functions. The bacterial species that makes up *the gut microbiota* contains seven million genes, which means there are 360 bacterial genes for every one of your human genes. Because they are at home in your gut, only a small fraction of your body's genetic content is of human origin—which is why they have been referred to as *superorganisms*.

Your Mind–Brain–Immune System Communication

George Solomon, the father of psychoneuroimmunology (PNI), sat in my office over 30 years ago, discussing the landmark work that he and Rudolph Moos had done at Stanford decades earlier. PNI is the study of the mind–brain–immune connection. They were able to show that emotional stress exacerbated immune abnormalities, including autoimmune disorders. George described the immune system as the "mind's sixth sense."

Early studies in PNI showed that a person suffering from stress had a greater potential to catch the common cold. Chronic stress has been shown to dampen the immune system and is linked to a variety of diseases by increasing cortisol and changing the activity of Helper T cells. In some circumstances, stress can increase the potential that your immune system attacks your own cells and contributes to an autoimmune disorder.

Stress can decrease the ability to repair broken DNA and spike inflammation, including within the glial cells in your brain. Chronic stress can also cause epigenetic changes in the expression inflammatory genes in your immune cells, resulting in neuro-inflammation, which can occur even with illnesses like arthritis, chronic pain, fibromyalgia, and chronic fatigue syndrome. As a person like Sandra becomes more depressed, her physical illness increases, which leads to greater depression. Decreased stress tolerance, increased anxiety, and depression are associated with these chronic diseases, which combine to increase the effects of all of them together.

Insight into these interactions comes from the Dunedin Multidisciplinary Health and Development Research in New Zealand, which followed over 1000 people into adulthood. Those who had incurred childhood maltreatment tended to have elevated levels of inflammation 20 years later. The more severe the abuse, the more severe the level of inflammation. Another study, based on 37,000 subjects in the Canadian Community Health Survey, found that those suffering from posttraumatic stress disorder (PTSD) had significantly higher rates of cardiovascular disease, chronic pain syndromes, gastrointestinal disorders, respiratory diseases, chronic fatigue syndrome, and cancer, which are all associated with inflammation.

Overall, stress and inflammation tend to rise when your physical health is compromised. And that can happen through a variety of interactions such as by autoimmune disorders, excess weight, and increases in stress. Given that chronic inflammation can make it difficult to rewire your brain, you should minimize those factors that make inflammation more likely. There are many ways that chronic inflammation can begin and continue to plague you.

If free radical damage, mitochondrial dysfunction, and inflammation were not enough to impair your brain, epigenetic effects result from genes being turned on that you don't want on, and other genes turned off that you want off. Then you cannot produce proteins to repair your cells, your telomeres shrink, blood vessels stiffen and clog, and then crud builds up in your brain, killing your neurons. Fortunately, you can stop this downward spiral by adopting the SEEDS factors, discussed in Chapters 5 to 9. In Chapter 10, I will describe how your brain and its mind can affect all the systems described in this chapter.

3

Taming False Threats

Jane came to see me for help with her fear of public speaking. She had been asked by her employer to give a presentation on a new product line that her department had developed. She told me that she was chosen to make the presentation because she was one of the principal designers of the project. However, the thought of standing in front of 50 people made her fear that she would "make a fool" of herself.

I agreed to help her succeed and offered to go one step further: to help her become proficient at public speaking. She first said that she thought I was joking. Then she became curious.

Jane had suffered from frightening public speaking episodes in the past. One time in particular had made an indelible impression on her mind. It occurred moments after she was asked to report on her college class project. She remembers standing in front of her peers and freezing like a deer in headlights. After a few terrifying moments she rushed out of the classroom.

I told her that public speaking is one of the most common fears that people report in surveys. It is not a pathology. In fact, I too once dreaded public speaking until I realized that I must lean into the experience and get myself out of the way. Although she had the full-blown stress response associated with this fear, she could learn to modify it and eventually channel energy to rekindle interest in the project.

I suggested that we work together to rewire her brain so that her fears about public speaking could be neutralized. Her prefrontal cortex (PFC) could be trained to have better veto power over her amygdala. Then she would be better able to present her thoughts and feelings about the new product.

To begin to rewire her brain, Jane first needed to shift her *focus* to the enthusiasm that she had for sharing the project with others. This would engage her interest in the subject matter, which would help her get some distance from her overwhelming anxiety about standing up in front of people. The motivation to share her knowledge of the project would help to boost the neuroplasticity that was necessary for rewiring her brain.

When I told her about the importance of focusing and the other elements of FEED, she said, "All I can focus on is all those people watching me trip over my words!"

I explained that she could choose to focus on a constructive part of speaking in front of people. She could shift her focus from the speaking performance to her enthusiasm for the subject matter. This was simply the first step in activating her prefrontal cortex to calm down her amygdala, which was overreacting with false threat.

Since Jane was a principal designer of the new product, there was an opportunity to tap into her knowledge of it. She had to make a concerted *effort* to fuse positive emotions into the task ahead of her. By describing her product to various individuals before her presentation, she could tap into this reservoir of enthusiasm.

I asked Jane to explain the project to me. As she did, her face lit up and her voice became more animated. I pointed this out to her. At first, she was surprised. Then she said, "Well, you're just one person, not a crowd of strangers!"

"True," I replied, "but you sure got me interested, not just by the details of the project but also by how you described it. The people you'll be talking to already have an interest in the subject."

I encouraged her to make a strong effort to practice with her family and her friends at least five times before the next appointment. When she returned, she told me that each practice presentation had been more useful.

I reminded Jane that those people weren't computer engineers like her upcoming audience. She was surprised that she managed to generate interest in people who might not want to learn about the subject matter at all. She also became more at ease when talking about the subject each time she spoke to a small group of people.

On the day before her presentation, Jane experienced a surge of anticipatory anxiety as she imagined herself in front of strangers. As planned, she shifted her focus back to the subject matter of her talk and managed to kindle neuronal networks that represented excitement in telling others about it. By combining her positive feelings about the project with the practice of presenting the information to friends and family, she linked up the neurons that were associated with talking about the project.

Jane managed to get through the first part of her talk by again making a concerted effort to stay focused on her enthusiasm for the project; she also confronted her anxiety instead of running from it. I had taught her that leaning into this effort was critical because exposure to the anxiety-provoking experience while staying focused on the subject matter would allow her to break through a false alarm barrier. She, like many people, had simply avoided public speaking. Consequently, the barrier had become bigger for her. Now she was able to get through the barrier. During the last part of her presentation, she was on a roll. It wasn't that speaking in front of large groups was becoming effortless—that came later. However, she had a taste of how less threatening public speaking was than she had thought it would be.

After the presentation, Jane congratulated herself for having challenged her old fears. She was amazed that she had gotten through the experience with a boost in confidence instead of what she feared: humiliation. She even had the further reward of receiving compliments from some of the audience about her inspiring command of the subject matter.

When we discussed her success, I suggested to her that she continue to practice speaking about her project. Her initial response was that she had "gotten through it, so why would I want to risk all that I gained by putting myself out there again?" I told her that in order to rewire her brain so that public speaking would no longer incite fear and would remain *effortless*, she had to be *determined* to repeat her efforts.

With this in mind, Jane accepted the invitation to speak about her project again. During that presentation, a computer engineer in the audience asked a question that she had never considered. Instead of clamming up and becoming defensive, she thanked him for the good question and told him that she would get back to him. She was actually excited to get back to him later with the answer. His question helped her team make important changes to the project. Thus, talking to the audience about the project served as a means by which to gather useful information.

Jane had to remain determined to stay with her gains in public speaking and to follow through on other opportunities to speak in front of people. It wasn't long before her supervisor asked her to speak at another meeting. Despite all her gains, she told me that she had "done my bit" and wanted to decline. I reminded her that this was another opportunity to share her enthusiasm for the project and hear useful ideas from the audience.

Other opportunities to speak came later, and they were just what she needed to get to the feeling of effortlessness when speaking in front of people. By developing the determination to stay with the practice Jane tore down her wall of anxiety that she had associated with public speaking. She rewired her brain so successfully that she was even sought out for public speaking events to express her enthusiasm for her project.

You might not want to become a public speaker. I didn't. But I found that sharing my enthusiasm for what I was learning helped me continue to push myself to learn more. I'm sure that there are other things you might not have tried because you feel uneasy about them. There might also be bad habits that you want to break and good habits that you want to develop. You can rewire your brain to succeed at your goals.

Jane's story represents some key points about how to tame your amygdala. Her effort to feed her brain with the challenge of public speaking illustrates the following key points about dealing with stress and anxiety:

- Excessive anxiety often results from false alarms.
- Moderate anxiety is actually useful for neuroplasticity.
- You can tap into your parasympathetic nervous system and calm yourself down.
- You must avoid avoidance.
- Increasing exposure to what makes you anxious reduces anxiety in the long run.

Stress and False Alarms

Anxiety has a lot to do with unrealistic feelings of threat and fear. Jane feared embarrassing herself and drawing social ridicule. Fear sets an alarm in your threat detection circuit to feel overwhelmed by any hit of danger. You may suffer from anxiety symptoms such as shortness of breath, rapid heartbeat, and worrying. When the alarm stops and it may become apparent that there was really nothing to fear, you are able to say in retrospect that it was a false alarm. Dealing effectively with anxiety requires you to turn off a false alarm or keep it from turning on.

People who came to my anxiety class often said that once they get a clear picture of what's going on in their brains, they feel more hopeful that their anxiety can be mastered. The fear of what was happening to them evaporated by this knowledge. You, too, can minimize your anxiety level by understanding how it is triggered in your brain.

Threat detection is triggered, in part, by the amygdala. Ideally, your amygdala and your orbital frontal cortex (OFC) maintain a harmonious relationship. For many people, this healthy relationship is built on warm and nurturing relationships early in life and is maintained throughout life. In my anxiety class, I explain the importance of taming the amygdala.

In addition to functioning as a relevance detector for your experiences, the amygdala can also serve as an alarm button, becoming activated for false threats as well as genuine threats. This is possible because of the reciprocal relationship between the amygdala and the OFC. Sometimes when your amygdala is overactive, it can overpower your OFC. But you can rewire your brain so that your OFC can tame your amygdala and be available for positive responses too. I say *tame* rather than *shut down* because you need the amygdala. It contributes to a wide range of responsiveness, not just threat detection. You don't want to shut it down; rather, you want it to work for you.

Fast and Slow Tracks

Your amygdala reacts to the emotional intensity of events and situations; when the situation is potentially dangerous, it activates the threat detection system in your body. This is sometimes called the fight-or-flight response. This alarm system is automatic; that is, it happens before you have time to think about it. When our ancestors encountered a predatory animal like a lion, it was best to react immediately and not stand around thinking about the lion, admiring its beauty, or wondering why it was bothering them instead of tracking down some tasty antelope. Thus, the fast track to the amygdala kept our ancestors alive.

In fact, there are two principal ways to activate your amygdala: the slow track or the fast track. The slow track goes through the cortex and hippocampus. This means that you can think about things before you become fearful. This is both good and bad: good because you can remind yourself that there is nothing to fear; bad if you develop irrational fears.

The Immediate Response Circuit

The fast track to activate your amygdala can trigger your sympathetic branch of your autonomic nervous system into action and can potentially contribute to anxiety or panic. Your amygdala can sound the alarm before your cortex knows what's happening. This means that you can *feel* threatened before you even think about it. Within a fraction of a second, the amygdala can signal part of our brain called the locus coeruleus to release norepinephrine to spark impulses throughout your sympathetic nervous system.

A fast-acting fight-or-flight response is very effective in the wild. All mammals have this lifesaving capacity.

The rush of adrenaline that you experience prepares your body to get moving by increasing your heart rate and your breathing so that you can send more oxygen to your muscles. Adrenaline binds to your muscle spindles, intensifying the resting tension so that your muscles can burst into action. The blood vessels in your skin constrict to limit any potential bleeding if you are wounded, and your digestive system shuts down to conserve energy. Saliva stops flowing (so your mouth becomes dry), and the muscles in your bladder relax to conserve glucose.

During a period of high stress, your brain may narrow to a singular focus on the stressful situation at hand. You don't sit back and speculate about the meaning of life when you are stressed. Instead, you narrow your focus and devote all your energy to deal with the threat. Sometimes, however, this shift away from the higher-thinking parts of your brain to the automatic and reflexive parts of the brain can lead you to do something too quickly, without remembering that this is what happens when you are overwhelmed with anxiety. In an extreme situation, such as when you are having a panic attack, you might rush off to an emergency room for treatment for a heart attack—not because you are actually having one, but because you jump to the extreme conclusion that you are.

Your Sustained Stress System

Some people suffer from extended periods of stress that morph into edgy feelings of anxiety. Their stress detection system is in overdrive. Your amygdala also signals your hypothalamus, which is responsible for many metabolic processes. This signals the pituitary gland, which signals the adrenal glands to release adrenaline and later cortisol. This system is called the *hypothalamus-pituitary-adrenal* (HPA) *axis*.

Your hypothalamus releases cortical-releasing hormone, prompting your pituitary gland (a small gland at the base of your brain) to release the adrenocorticotropic hormone (ACTH) and activating your adrenal glands. These glands dump epinephrine (adrenaline) into your bloodstream, which jolts your system to increase your breathing, heart rate, and blood pressure. Then they release cortisol, which makes available glucose from stores in your body to give your body energy for a sustained challenge.

Short-term, cortisol facilitates dopamine, which keeps you alert and activated. However, cortisol can be corrosive to the brain and the body if it stays activated too long. With excessive and prolonged cortisol, the levels of dopamine become depleted, and this makes you feel awful and tense at the same time.

Cortisol is actually very useful. If you encounter stress that requires a prolonged response beyond a quick flight-or-fight response, your body needs a way to keep you alert. Your HPA axis works to get cells to release fuel (glucose) to make energy by your mitochondria. Epinephrine (adrenaline) immediately converts glycogen and fatty acids, but when the stress is longer-lasting, cortisol takes over. It works through the bloodstream, so its effects are slower than that of adrenaline.

Cortisol works more systemically than adrenaline does. It triggers the liver to send more glucose into the bloodstream and blocks insulin receptors in nonessential organs and tissues. This allows the glucose to work as fuel, giving you maximum energy to deal with the threat. You don't have a lot of glucose floating around, so cortisol works to "shake the branches" for cells in your body to release whatever glucose is available to make more energy.

One of the many problems associated with chronic stress and high levels of cortisol is that parts of your brain bear the brunt—especially the hippocampus. Your hippocampus has cortisol receptors which under normal circumstances act as a thermostat to help to trigger cortisol production to shut off, much like a thermostat. However, when cortisol production is excessive and prolonged, the receptors become impaired. The hippocampus then begins to atrophy—and along with it your memory capacity.

Unfortunately, the reverse happens for the amygdala. Instead of atrophy, it is hypersensitized by an increase in cortisol. From an evolutionary perspective this makes sense because when our early ancestors were stressed by something like dangerous predators, they needed to be hyperalert and not focus on anything else but the danger. Because the amygdala can become hypersensitive, excessive danger can make you jumpier and more anxious. This is one of the reasons war veterans with posttraumatic stress disorder (PTSD) will hit the floor and cover their head when they hear the loud blast of fireworks. Before they have a chance to think about it, the blast sounds like a bomb exploding or a gunshot. Their amygdala triggers the fight-or-flight response—a false alarm.

Just like chronic stress, when you experience severe trauma the once-cooperative partnership between your hippocampus and your amygdala tends to be dominated by the amygdala. This is because the hippocampus is assaulted by excess cortisol and glutamate when the amygdala is pumped up. Cortisol and glutamate act to excite the amygdala, and the more it is excited, the more easily it is triggered.

Since your hippocampus provides the context for your memories, your ability to put stressful events into perspective becomes impaired. The amygdala, in contrast, is a generalist. When it gets excited, it doesn't care about the context. Any loud noise sets off the fight-or-flight response.

Stress and the Impaired Memory Systems

Just as excessive and prolonged cortisol can be destructive to the hippocampus, so can a surplus of the excitatory neurotransmitter glutamate. Cortisol initially encourages LTP by increasing glutamate transmission in the hippocampus. This too makes evolutionary sense, because when our ancestors were stressed by something, such as a particularly dangerous area near a lion's den, they needed to remember it. However, in the complex modern world, this tendency locks us into rigid or fixated patterns. You can't forget what stressed you, and more glutamate helps you to remember.

Too much of a good thing can cause bad things to happen. Like excess cortisol, excess glutamate damages the hippocampus by allowing electron-snatching calcium ions into cells, which creates free radicals. If you don't have enough antioxidants in your system, free radicals can career around and punch holes in your cell walls, rupturing the cells and potentially killing them. Dendrites, the branches of a neuron that reach out to other neurons to receive information, begin to wither back into the cell body. Thoughts and emotions become more rigid and simple. Your decisions may become inflexible instead of adaptive to changing situations.

Fortunately, there are ways to shut down false alarms before they become destructive. One way to do it is supported by the pioneering research of Joseph LeDoux of New York University. LeDoux has shown that one area of the amygdala, the central nucleus, is particularly involved in the snowballing effect of fear and anxiety. The central nucleus links nonthreatening stimuli with presumably threatening stimuli. For example, you could associate a bridge with death or talking to a stranger with humiliation.

Another connection to the amygdala, sometimes referred to as the *extended amygdala,* is technically called *basal nucleus stria terminalis* (BNST). The BNST contributes to unpredictable threats. These fear- and stress-related responses involve CRF, which modulates its excitability. BNST and amygdala communicate via CRF, and norepinephrine signals BNST to promote anxiety, especially diffuse threats. It organizes fear responses that poorly predict when danger will occur, no matter the duration.

Fortunately, you can test the situation through the power of your PFC. Your BNST neurons stir up fear to threats when they are typically ambiguous and unpredictable.

Neutralizing Anxiety

By approaching what makes you anxious, you also activate the left prefrontal cortex, which can decrease the overreactivity of the amygdala. The right prefrontal cortex is often overactivated in people with anxiety disorders. The left prefrontal cortex is also more action-oriented, whereas the right prefrontal cortex is more passive and withdrawal-oriented. Furthermore, the left prefrontal cortex promotes positive emotions, whereas the right prefrontal cortex promotes more negative emotions.

Thus, you have the capacity to turn off the fight-or-flight response and the false alarms. The left prefrontal cortex and the hippocampus work together to tame the amygdala and shut down your sympathetic branch of your autonomic nervous system and your HPA axis. Taking action and doing something constructive can shut down the feeling of being overwhelmed, which is generated by the over-reactivity of the right prefrontal cortex.

Stress is a fact of life; it's not something that you can or should totally avoid. If you try to escape all stress, when you encounter even a mild stressor or even the threat of stress, you will feel extremely stressed. Rather, stress should be managed and used to accomplish your goals. Some stress and anxiety serve as useful motivators. Without a little stress, you wouldn't get to work on time, complete projects efficiently, or drive within the speed limit.

Mild stress can be fun. Not everyone can experience the same level of fun from mildly stressful experiences. I have enjoyed mountain climbing, skiing down a steep slope, and traveling, but the mountains that I climbed were not beyond my ability and the countries I've visited have not been under safety advisories. Your brain needs a little stress to remember important events and situations; your job is to learn how to regulate the stress. A little stress helps to consolidate memories. No stress means boredom—no alertness or excitement. This means that you won't remember what you are experiencing. Too much stress, however, narrows your focus and is not helpful for learning.

Jane rewired her brain by using a moderate degree of anxiety. She had already experienced feeling overwhelmed with excessive anxiety, and she had done what she could to avoid public speaking. That avoidant behavior, ironically, simply increased her anxiety.

As I explained in Chapter 1, neuroscientific research has shown that a moderate degree of stress is optimal for neuroplasticity. Too much or too little stress is not useful in this regard. Thus, rather than shy away from stress, you should confront it and make it useful. Consider the following skiing analogy: Leaning back on your skis increases your chance of falling, but if you lean forward just a little, you'll have more control of your skis—even when you are skiing down a very steep slope!

Think of it this way: Being bored, overconfident, and lazy about studying for an exam prepares you to fail. Being panicked about it also leads to potential failure. The balance between too much and too little stress is optimal for learning and memory: the inverted U (i.e., the Yerkes-Dobson curve). The inverted U means that moderate activation (i.e., stress or anxiety) keeps your brain alert, generating the correct neurochemistry to allow your brain to thrive and promote neuroplasticity and neurogenesis.

Moderate Stress

With a moderate degree of stress, levels of cortisol, CRH, and norepinephrine bind to the cell receptors that boost the excitatory neurotransmitter glutamate. When the glutamate activity in the hippocampus is moderately increased, there is a corresponding increase in the flow of information and associated neuroplasticity. The more often a message is sent along the same pathway, the more easily it will fire the same signals and use less glutamate—making the cells fire together so that they wire together.

The most efficient way to deal with stress is to strive for the moderate path. The main point here is that you shouldn't try to run away from anxiety; you should face the anxiety head-on and learn to manage it. By managing it, you'll promote a healthy, thriving brain.

Your Autonomic Nervous System

Your autonomic nervous system has two opposing parts: your sympathetic and parasympathetic systems. While the sympathetic nervous system excites you, the parasympathetic nervous system relaxes you. In extreme situations, the sympathetic nervous system triggers the fight-or-flight response. You might think it strange that the term *sympathetic* is for a system that makes you charged up. The name of this system can be traced back 2000 years to the concept of sympathy, first used medically by the Roman physician Galen to mean "connection between parts."

The branch that counterbalances the sympathetic nervous system is called the parasympathetic nervous system. The name *parasympathetic* means above (para) the sympathetic. It helps to lower your heart rate and slow your breathing rate. For this reason, it is called the rest and digest system as it functions to conserve your body's natural activity and relax once an emergency has passed.

A balance between your sympathetic nervous system (which activates you) and your parasympathetic nervous system (which calms you down) allows you the flexibility to respond to situations appropriately. Sometimes you need to be quite alert and afterward need to calm down. These systems—along with the circadian rhythm, nutrition, exercise, relaxation, and meditation—can help you to be calm and positive.

Sympathetic Nervous System	Parasympathetic Nervous System
↑Heart rate	↓Heart rate
↑Blood pressure	↓Blood pressure
↑Metabolism	↓Metabolism
↑Muscle tension	↓Muscle tension
↑Breathing rate	↓Breathing rate
↑Mental arousal	↓Mental arousal

Different breathing patterns promote different emotional states. Your breathing rate speeds up when you are experiencing stress. The muscles in your abdomen tighten up and your chest cavity becomes constricted when you breathe too fast. If you tend to breathe very quickly, you may be like some people who tend to talk very fast and not give themselves a chance to breathe. As they go from one sentence to another, they stir up anxiety in themselves. The neutral topics that they talk about become laced with anxious thoughts stoked by their fast breathing. The increase in anxious feeling states is connected to the same neural networks that promote anxious thinking.

Most people breathe 9 to 16 breaths per minute at rest. Panic attacks often involve as many as 27 breaths per minute. When your breathing is accelerating, you can experience many of the symptoms associated with a panic attack, including numbness, tingling, dry mouth, and lightheadedness. This is because your cardiovascular system includes both the respiratory system and the circulatory system. Rapid breathing will make your heart rate speed up and can make you more anxious.

If you slow your breathing down, your heart rate will slow down to promote a more relaxed state. However, to learn to relax, you'll have to make an effort to develop some new habits, such as the way you breathe. Since one of the most common symptoms of panic is shortness of breath, you'll have to learn to breathe differently. Physiological changes occur in your brain and body during hyperventilation or breathing too fast. If you're prone to panic attacks, you tend to overrespond to these physiological sensations and to breathe even more quickly.

Hyperventilation

When you hyperventilate, you inhale too much oxygen, which decreases the carbon dioxide level in your bloodstream. Carbon dioxide helps to maintain the critical acid base (the pH level) in your blood. When you lower your pH level, your nerve cells become more excitable, and you may feel anxious. If you associate these feelings with uncontrollable anxiety, this can spur a panic attack.

The excessive dissipation of carbon dioxide leads to a condition called *hypocapnic alkalosis*, which makes your blood more alkaline and less acidic. As a result, you may have a vascular constriction, which results in less blood reaching your tissues. Oxygen binds tightly to hemoglobin, which results in less oxygen being released to the tissues and the extremities. The paradox is that even though you inhaled a lot of oxygen, less is available to your tissues. Hypocapnic alkalosis leads to dizziness, light-headedness, cerebral vasoconstriction, which leads to feelings of unreality, and peripheral vasoconstriction, which leads to tingling in your extremities.

Avoiding Avoidance

A paradox occurs when you avoid what you fear because your fear then grows. This is counterintuitive, because when you avoid what you fear for a short time, your fear does decrease. Over a longer period, however, avoidance allows your anxiety to build. For example, let's say that you are anxious about going to a dinner party because you fear talking to strangers. For a brief time, avoiding the evening immediately diminishes your anxiety momentarily. However, if you avoid the next dinner party invitation, and then the next and the next, you stir up even more anxiety than you experienced before. Because of your avoidance of those dinner parties, you have made your anxiety about talking to strangers worse than it was at the start.

You have to try to work against avoidance, even though it seems to immediately make you feel better. I call this challenging the paradox or simply avoiding avoidance. Replace avoidance with moderate exposure to what makes you feel anxious, and you eventually become habituated to them, and your anxiety will fade.

The earlier example of a Ukrainian war veteran with PTSD can illustrate this point. When he came back to civilian life, he avoided situations that made him anxious. Ironically, his anxiety got worse. His therapy involved exposing himself to situations that are not dangerous but made him mildly anxious so he could tame his amygdala. His hypersensitivity lessened with each time he heard fireworks and other loud booms, and nothing bad happened. Eventually he began to hear the explosion of fireworks instead of exploding buildings. He slowly re-associated the sounds of the loud booms with entertainment. The taming process can go on even without his cortex (i.e., his thinking process) being involved. When he says to himself, "Wow, those are spectacular fireworks. There's nothing to get panicked about!" the taming occurs more quickly.

The following types of avoidance contribute to anxiety:

- Escaping stressful situations that are not dangerous
- Avoiding any situation that makes you nervous
- Procrastinating about engaging in an anxiety-provoking situation
- Using safety behaviors such as using medication

Escape behaviors consist of the things you do in the heat of the moment in response to anxiety-provoking situations. You impulsively escape the situation to avoid feeling anxious. Suppose you are in a crowded room and begin to feel anxious. Fleeing the room to avoid feeling anxious is an escape behavior. Your anxiety increases over time because your tolerance of it decreases. If you escape instead of allowing yourself to adjust to even a little anxiety, you'll eventually feel extremely sensitive to the slightest hint of anxiety. This is called *anxiety sensitivity*.

Avoidant behavior includes the things you do to stay away from anxiety-provoking experiences. Let's say that a friend invites you to meet her at the home of one of her other friends for dinner. You decide that going to the other friend's home would make you anxious, so you don't go. That's an avoidant behavior. Consequently, your long-term anxiety will increase, because when you avoid situations that make you anxious, you never allow yourself to learn that those situations are tolerable and often enjoyable.

Procrastination means that you put off things because you think (erroneously) that it's easier on your stress level. For example, you put off going to the dinner, waiting until the very last moment to finally go. When you wait and wait until the last possible moment, you build up anxiety as you hold off. It's like you are pressing the gas pedal and brake at the same time. You're subtly teaching yourself that the situation *was* worth putting off until the last moment, because when you finally arrived, you were indeed nervous and tense. Holding yourself back from an anxiety-provoking situation builds up even more anxiety than you experienced initially.

Safety behavior involves doing something or carrying things to distract yourself or give yourself a sense of safety. Suppose you go the dinner and begin to feel anxious. To prevent yourself from becoming more anxious, you begin to fiddle with your watchband to draw your focus away. That's a safety behavior. Safety behavior allows you to hang in there and not escape, but eventually the behavior becomes a nervous habit, and by engaging in it you're telling yourself that you're too nervous to face whatever is presumably causing your anxiety.

All these forms of avoidance are ineffective methods of dealing with anxiety because they keep you from habituating to that which makes you anxious so that you can neutralize the anxiety. Avoidance makes it next to impossible to learn to overcome the anxiety.

Because avoidance gives you temporary relief from anxiety, it serves as a powerful short-term reinforcer. It is therefore difficult to resist. The more you avoid what makes you anxious, the more elaborate the forms of avoidance can become. If avoidance is taken to the extreme, you can even become agoraphobic, afraid to leave your home. Once you begin avoiding, it's difficult to stop.

Avoidance is difficult to avoid for the following reasons:

- It works to reduce anxiety for a short amount of time.
- The more you engage in avoidance, the harder it is to resist engaging in even mildly anxiety-provoking situations in the future.
- It promotes superficial logic to avoidance, such as, "Why wouldn't I avoid something that makes me anxious?"
- You get a secondary gain from it, like extra care, because people around you are sympathetic.

Another way that you might try to avoid anxiety—but that actually increases it—is to try to rigidly control it. An obsession with being in control can lead to avoidance. By trying to control every experience to avoid anxiety, you put yourself in a mode of always trying to anticipate the future so that you can steer yourself away from the *possibility* of any anxiety. Here's where your avoidance can become rather elaborate. When you anticipate what *might* happen, you brace yourself for any hint of anxiety that you might never have experienced.

The more you retreat, the more you will think that you must retreat. First you are vigilant only about what you previously felt to be anxiety-provoking, but soon you will be vigilant about what *might* be anxiety-provoking. You limit yourself to activities and situations that you are certain will not be anxiety-provoking. When you encounter a little anxiety in a situation that you thought would be anxiety-free, you begin to avoid *that* situation in the future. Soon the range of your activities shrinks dramatically. As your world shrinks, the things that trigger anxiety increase. If you take it to the extreme and become agoraphobic, you won't want to leave your house because you will have grown to fear everything outside.

Defusing the Worry Circuit

Worry is a form of cognitive avoidance. Since no one can be certain about anything, when you worry about even the uncertainty, it can lead to anxiety. Worry serves only to search for certainty to try to calm your mind. This form of avoidance stirs up the "worry circuit" in the brain, and you end up imagining the worst.

Your amygdala and BNST cannot tolerate ambiguity. This leaves a lot of room to worry because nothing is certain. The worry circuit stirs up the amygdala, which increases your sense of threat, and the overactivity of the amygdala preoccupies the OFC, which tries to figure out why you feel anxious.

Inability to tolerate uncertainty kindles the worry circuits. This is the dilemma of my client Lina, who worried about the uncertainties in her life. Her excessive worry stoked up feeling anxious so that her worries contributed to overreacting to stress, only to create more anxiety. With more free-floating anxiety, Lina worried more because she felt uneasy. And so worrying perpetuated the tendency to worry, as a feedforward loop. Lina's worry loops fed her intolerance to uncertainty combined with poor problem-solving and positive beliefs about worry. Her worry attempted to problem-solve about possible future negative events. She tried to think herself out of discomfort only to find more uncertainty and discomfort. Worry is both consciously and unconsciously self-reinforcing.

One of the self-reinforcing aspects to worry for Lina was that the more she worried, the more she had to worry about. She searched for ways to verify that things would be okay. She often asked her husband for reassurance that this or that particular concern was unjustified. He tried to be kind and reassure her that the concern was nothing to be worried about. This well-meaning reassurance only fed her insatiable worry loop. He provided only short-lived comfort by addressing her specific worries instead of the overall tendency to worry. By resolving and reassuring her that a specific worry was not worthy of concern, she moved on to another worry. This pattern of his reassurance and her continued worry was replicated in the therapeutic encounters she had with our interns. In response to the natural tendency to sooth and reassure that intern offered, Lina moved on to a different concern to worry about. Therapy only became effective when Lina was encouraged to learn to accept and appreciate that there is no such thing as absolute certainty.

I cautioned our intern that she was not doing her any favors by explaining that there is certainty in life. By helping her to acknowledge and accept that there is no absolute certainty, she began to break out of the worry loop. Our intern learned that like others plagued by excessive worry, Lina's difficulty dealing with uncertainty fed her worry loop. This tendency was directly associated with an intolerance for ambiguity. Since she tended to select threatening interpretations of ambiguous stimuli, therapy was focused on developing her tolerance for ambiguity. By learning how to deal with ambiguity through exposure to and development of an appreciation for ambiguity she built a stronger PFC. She also came to call that skill a characteristic of maturity or "wisdom."

An Orienting Circuit

Since the amygdala functions as an orienting subsystem for the rest of the brain, alerting other systems to gather information and learn from the situation, it serves as part of an integrative system that crosses categorical boundaries such as emotion, motivation, vigilance, attention, and cognition. When not moderated by the PFC it impairs the process of tolerating uncertainty and ambiguity and causes free-floating anxiety.

If you are seduced into trying to reassure yourself that specific worries are unwarranted, ironically this effort serves to support your worry loop. Excessive worrying is sometimes referred to as the *doubting disorder*. If you try to avoid even a slight doubt, your worry loop fuels self-perpetuating worries. Encountering ambiguity and uncertainty is unavoidable because you cannot be sure how things will work out. You will always be vulnerable to worry if you cannot accept ambiguity and uncertainty.

Lina was hypervigilant, scanning her environment for potential danger and avoiding rather than approaching stressful situations. She overread the potential stress and overresponded to it with intense anticipatory anxiety, which tied up her thoughts with personal concerns and led to worry.

Boring the worry circuit helped Lina tolerate uncertainty. It involves a variant of cognitive behavioral therapy (CBT) referred to as *scheduling worrying time*. In Lina's worry hour, she carried around a notebook so that as worries occurred throughout the day she wrote them down. Then between 5 and 6 o'clock each evening, she opened her notebook and devoted the entire hour to reflecting on all the worries. Eventually her worries became boring or alternatively as ambiguities that she found interesting. This method helped build more connectivity in her prefrontal cortex through exposure to ambiguity. Eventually she learned to accept various degrees of ambiguity as harmless and interesting. In the process her OFC learned that ambiguity is inherent to the richness of life.

The goal is to observe the worries uncritically and label them as merely worrisome thoughts without trying to solve them. It is rare that a person fills up the entire hour without strong encouragement to do so. Borrowed from the contemplative traditions, this method promotes detachment of the thought from the feelings of anxiety. Transforming an anxious thought from thought-emotional *fusion* to *thought diffusion* is illustrated in the change in statement from, "Oh, that thought makes me anxious," when there is no distance between an anxious thought and the feeling of anxiety to, "Oh, that's an anxious thought." This statement identifies the thought as merely a thought—nothing to get anxious about. Such thoughts flit in and out of consciousness unless they elicit an emotional charge. When they fuse with emotion, overactivating the amygdala, they perpetuate anxious thoughts. Labeling these emotions reduces anxiety, detaching the emotion from thought and labeling it as a mere thought.

When you apply nonjudgmental attention and acceptance to your worries, a paradox occurs: the worry circuit calms down. Thus, if you are prone to worry excessively, instead of engaging in the details of what worries you, simply observe. This technique is used in contemplative attention and mindfulness meditation.

Changing Your Narrative

Your PFC—and particularly its foremost section, the dorsolateral prefrontal cortex dlPFC—decides, through its powers of attention and emotional regulatory skills, what is important and what is not. Your hippocampus provides the context for any memories that are associated with the situation. When you're walking through a park one evening and you notice through the corner of your eye a large, hunched figure, you may immediately brace yourself for a mugger. Your fight-or-flight response kicks into gear. That's your sympathetic nervous system in action. Then your PFC directs your attention to the figure. Your hippocampus helps to remind you of the context of the figure and the shrubs along the path. As you look closer, you see that the figure is just a shrub. Your PFC tells your amygdala, and your sympathetic branch of your autonomic nervous system for the fight-or-flight response to calm down.

The perspective with which you describe each experience can potentially rewire your brain. In fact, this is one of the methods of psychotherapy. The more you describe your ongoing experiences in a particular mood and different perspective, the stronger the neural circuits that represent those thoughts will become. Your narratives can be positive or negative. For example, if you find yourself constantly telling yourself, "This is hard," or, "I wonder whether

I'm going to survive," or "It looks like this is going to turn out badly," it's time to reframe the way you approach the situation from something intolerable to eventually tolerable.

Your ongoing narrative is organized by general levels of thought: automatic thoughts, assumptions, and core beliefs. On the surface are your automatic thoughts. These are like short comments to yourself that momentarily flash through your mind. They are a form of self-talk that you use to navigate throughout the day using your default mode network. You produce a variety of automatic thoughts, such as when you walk into a room full of strangers you might say, "I don't like this," or "Oh no! People I'll have to meet." Both automatic thoughts can contribute to increased anxiety. Your automatic thoughts can be rewired in your brain to represent more adaptive self-talk. You could say, "Oh great. New people to meet. This should be interesting."

Your assumptions, which are positioned midway between your automatic thoughts and your core beliefs, act as a kind of translator between the two. They aren't as fundamental as core beliefs, yet they aren't as superficial as automatic thoughts. Like your automatic thoughts, your assumptions can be rewired by reflecting reality instead of your worries. Assumptions are one of the prime targets of CBT, which aims to restructure a person's thoughts to reflect adaptable and constructive thinking problems. For example, previously in the roomful of strangers you might say, "I'm not good with strangers," or you could say instead, "I may be a little shy, but I find meeting new people interesting."

Your assumptions can serve as theories that help you to cope with your core beliefs, which are broad generalizations about yourself and how the world works. When these beliefs are associated with anxiety, they paint you into a corner psychologically, so that whatever you do, you're faced with an insurmountable challenge—one that will always fail.

Negative core beliefs can contribute to anxiety. For example, you might have a core belief that you have a "broken brain" or that you have "bad genes" so that you cannot make use of any kind of help. Negative core beliefs keep you away from any expectation of relief from anxiety. They set you up to fail because you leave yourself no hope. For example, you could believe that "I'm incapable of forming new relationships," or you could cultivate a core belief such as, "I'm a good person, and when people get to know me they agree."

With core beliefs that meet the challenge that you face, your automatic thoughts and your assumptions will eventually adjust to your new self-image. And if you work on them simultaneously with your core beliefs, the two shallower levels can be integrated to work effectively in your favor.

In short, these automatic thoughts, assumptions, and core beliefs should encourage engagement instead of avoiding what makes you anxious leading you to restrict your activities, which makes your anxiety generalized, which then prompts more avoidance, and promotes more generalized anxiety, which in turn stirs up even more avoidance. As you can see, it becomes a vicious cycle.

The key to taming your amygdala is to break this vicious cycle. You must make sure that you expose yourself to what you were fearful of in the past. By keeping your behavioral options open to anxiety-provoking experiences, you allow yourself to be flexible and resilient in changing situations. By exposing yourself to what made you anxious in the past, you can learn to recondition yourself and habituate to the situation.

Almost a century ago, Franklin Delano Roosevelt said, "There is nothing to fear but fear itself." That insightful phrase describes anxiety in a nutshell. When I have used it with clients, they have not only often laughed but also nodded with recognition of the wisdom. In fact, for them it was more than just a wise statement. They lived it. First, they feared fear, then they faced their fears, and in the process they found that there was nothing to fear.

4

Shifting into Action

Megan came to see me after a prolonged period of feeling sad. Although she denied having many of the symptoms associated with full-blown depression, she said, "When things don't go right, I crawl into my shell, and it's hard to crawl out again." She described the shell as a "dark and gloomy place."

She said that her husband asked her to see a psychologist because "he was tired of my pessimistic attitude and what he described as my endless negative comments."

"Is his description accurate?" I asked.

"Sort of. But, hearing him say that put me in a blue period," Megan replied. "He was right, and he said that he was tired of propping my mood up all the time."

"What do you do when you're feeling down?" I inquired.

She gave me an ironic smile. "Not much."

"You get more passive and feel bluer?" I asked.

"Yup," Megan said, as if she knew that there was a twisted logic to this pattern that I would understand. She explained that she had learned from her parents that "when they heard any sort of criticism or something went wrong, they'd get quiet until somebody pulled them out of it."

"Can we say that your passivity in response to anything going wrong makes things worse?" I inquired.

She reflected for a moment. "Well, honestly, until my husband said that he was tired of it, I didn't know I was doing it."

We talked at length about how passivity increases depression. I described how her brain responds to passivity and simultaneously spurs depression. The left PFC promotes positive feelings and taking action, and the right PFC promotes passivity and negative emotion.

"So, he propped you up," I observed.

"Yeah, I guess I was lifted with all his optimism. But he said that he's tired of doing all the work while I drag my feet and complain," Megan admitted.

"Are you tired of it?" I asked. "Because if you're not motivated to change your behavior, whatever we work on together will be just going through the motions. In fact, being frustrated enough with your situation might be a positive thing. In fact, to be able to rewire your brain, you'll need to be fully engaged, and committed to action."

"From what you're saying," Megan concluded, "I ought to thank him for saying that he'll stop doing things for me. Okay, it's time to make some changes."

This agreement was only the first step. The idea of making the changes sounded good, but actually making the changes took some work. It was just too easy for her to fall back into her old habit of being passive and thinking negatively.

Megan came to understand that her tendency to be passive represented how underactive her left PFC had become. She needed to kick-start it by taking action, however small a step it seemed, to get her left PFC engaged.

I also taught her to use the FEED method. By labeling her passive behavior, she could identify how it worked against her best interests. I explained that this first step helps her identify the behavior that makes the situation worse.

When Megan found herself becoming passive and sinking into negative emotions, she would say to herself, "Whoops, those negative thoughts mean that my left PFC is going to sleep again. I need to do something to give it a wake-up call."

The tendency to revert to her old habits occurred when something went wrong. It was her habit to shift into a pessimistic attitude and ironically make the situation worse. By using the FEED method to slowly shift her pessimism to optimism, she was able to rewire an attitude and not cultivate a negative mood to spoil the day.

Megan learned that the emotional state she was in at any given time influenced her perceptions, thoughts, and memories. That is, the mood she was in would color all her experiences. This is because all the cells that fire together to create the mood also fire with other neurons to create thoughts and memories. The more that you are in a particular mood, the more prone you'll be to be in that mood. Think of it as a gravitational pull.

This tendency can occur spontaneously and can spiral out of control if you don't make an effort to pull yourself out of it. Let's say that you're rushing to your aunt's house for a dinner that you don't want to attend. You're driving through rush-hour traffic when you suddenly notice that the gas gauge reads almost empty. Now you're really feeling rushed and sulky. As you pull into a gas station, you notice how many cars are lined up at the pumps. To make matters worse, some people who are pumping gas are taking their time, washing their windshields, and even leaving their cars to go to the restroom.

You're already in a bad mood, and now you imagine your aunt getting upset with you for being late, so your bad mood deepens. The more you think about your aunt's disappointment, the worse you feel. There are so many things that you would rather be doing at the moment, and waiting for people to move on so that you can get to the gas pump is not one of them. These feelings intensify the firing of the neural networks that support the bad mood.

The woman who has been pumping gas in front of you is finished, but she leaves her car at the pump and rushes into the station to buy some snacks. You angrily pull up to a different pump. Why didn't she pull into a parking space after she finished pumping her gas? Didn't she realize that there were people waiting behind her?

As you are finally pumping your gas, she walks back to her car, carrying an iced drink, and hands it to her child, who is sitting in the backseat. She left her car at the pump for a drink! You glance at the child, see that he has no hair, and realize that he must be undergoing chemotherapy for cancer. In a flash, your spindle cells kick in with the insight of how you have been in a pathetic self-perpetuating bad mood. You experience a deep sense of empathy for her and her child.

The child spills the drink all over the seat and begins to cry. His mother tries to comfort him as she wipes up the mess. You rush into the store to buy the child another drink. When you return and hand it to the boy, he responds with a smile.

As you finish pumping your gas, you reflect on how these two people helped you to snap out of your sulky bad mood. You decide to go to your aunt's house with a renewed sense of compassion and selflessness.

This little vignette illustrates how easy it is to drift into a bad mood. Once the neural networks begin firing together, they recruit other neurons to keep the bad mood going. As you feed the bad mood with sulky thoughts, it becomes deeper and harder to shake. These bad moods can go on for hours or days at a time. Some people are plagued by them for months or even years at a time.

If you tend to be in a particular mood more often than not, we can say that this mood forms a chronic foundation for your experiences in life. It's the background emotional current, or the center of gravity in your life. Most of your experiences are based on it and revolve around it.

Let's say that during the past few months you have been sad because of the death of your mother. The emotional tone that is created by this sadness recruits related memories and feelings that resonate with it. You may even tell yourself, "I'm going to stay with these sad feelings, because it's a way to honor her."

Yet if you cultivate the sadness, perhaps even thinking that you are releasing it, you're keeping those neurons firing together and thus cultivating a chronic foundation of sadness. More often than not you will feel sadness and will think, remember, and behave in ways that cultivate that emotional tone.

The longer you stew in a low emotional state, the greater is the probability that those neurons will fire together when you are sad and will therefore wire together. As a result, this will become the chronic default mood. Sadness and the thoughts and feelings that revolve around that sadness self-perpetuate.

I am not saying that you should suppress your feelings of grief. Sadness is a normal and natural reaction to losing someone close to you. The point is that you need a balance. You have to move on with your life in addition to acknowledging the feelings of sadness.

If you have a chronic emotional tone that is sad, depressed, or angry, it might seem like a scratched record. The needle on the turntable gets stuck in the scratch, and the same lyrics play over and over. This is the origin of the phrase "sounds like a broken record." You have to get up and bump the needle over a few grooves to make the song stop repeating itself. You need to find ways to "bump the needle" if your emotional foundation is sad, angry, or depressed.

Here are several ways to rewire your brain to promote positive moods, covered in the following sections, and they all should be practiced simultaneously:

- Priming positive moods
- Full spectrum light
- Aerobic boosting
- Constructing positive narratives
- Wiring positive thinking
- Social boosting
- Taking action
- SEEDS (covered in Part 2)

Priming Positive Moods

You can start to rewire your brain by priming a positive mood through acting as though you are in a good mood when you're not. Let's say that you've been sad recently and have been pulling back from your friends. Maybe you've said to yourself, "I don't want to put on a happy face." The common phrase "Fake it till you make it" applies to priming. You should force yourself to call a friend and go out to lunch when you don't feel like it. Once you are at lunch, even just smiling can activate parts of your brain associated with positive emotions. You need to jump-start these circuits with action. What I mean by jump-start is analogous to how we can start a car that has a manual transmission, yet its starter is broken. We put it "in gear" and push it before "popping the clutch to start the engine." The same goes for your mood: kick into action. Do something constructive.

Your Reward Circuit

The reward circuit in the brain involves three principal areas: the nucleus accumbens, the striatum, and the PFC. The nucleus accumbens is a peanut-sized structure that thrives on dopamine and is involved in pleasure and thus emotion and memory. It evolved to keep us engaged in behaviors that are critical for our survival, such as looking for food and mates. Because it is a pleasure center, it can be hijacked in addictive behaviors. The striatum is involved in movement, and because of its rich dopamine connections with the accumbens and the PFC, it serves as an interface between our emotions and our actions. The PFC, as I noted, is involved in problem-solving, planning, and decision-making.

The accumbens–striatal–PFC network connects pleasure, movement, emotion, and thinking. Thus, the reward circuit links what you do with rewards. When, for example, you lose a sense of pleasure, the accumbens is deactivated. When you are sluggish in your movements, the striatum is deactivated by less dopamine. If you have poor concentration, the PFC is deactivated.

Without knowing that brain systems are involved, cognitive-behavioral therapists have encouraged depressed people to increase their activity level and have found that these people become less depressed. Behavioral activation, as this is called, appears to trigger the same rewards circuit that involves the accumbens, the striatum, and the PFC.

Thus, trying to put yourself out there helps you lift depression. In contrast, passivity is linked to sad feelings, and the right hemisphere. The left hemisphere, in addition to processing positive emotions, is associated with action. Taking action helps people to feel less depressed, whereas inaction and passivity create sad feelings. People who are depressed underactivate their left PFC. If you are prone to feeling down more than up, activating your left PFC by doing something constructive will help you to shift out of the chronic low emotional foundation.

Hemispheres and Emotion

The following correlations have been made between hemispheric asymmetry and depression:

- Evidence from neurology indicates that a left-hemisphere stroke (making the right hemisphere dominant) has a *catastrophic* effect and causes the person to become very depressed, whereas a right-side stroke has a laissez-faire effect and causes much less depression (making the left dominant).
- The relative inhibition of the left PFC and the relative activation of the right PFC are associated with depression.
- The left PFC is associated with positive emotions and is action oriented.
- The right PFC is associated with negative emotions and is passivity, avoidance, and withdrawal.

(continued)

(*continued*)

- Language, making interpretive sense of events, and generating positive and optimistic emotions are all products of robust left hemispheric functioning.
- Instead of putting details into context, depressed patients are overwhelmed by a global negative perspective. The right hemisphere favors global thinking.
- Behavioral activation is one of the principal therapies for depression.

Sometimes you need a dose of detachment to move yourself beyond negative thoughts and emotions. In other words, you need to learn to take things less seriously. Humor promotes neuroplasticity, and it is a wonderful treatment for what ails you. If you are sad, humor serves as a brief nudge from one mood state to another. Avoid tear-jerker dramas because they promote a tearful mood. Try watching comedies to help you detach from negative thoughts and feelings. Comedies promote a lift out of the sad mood you were in and move into another, happier state. In this sense, humor is a soothing method of detachment. The wisest type of humor is maintaining humor about yourself, as I describe in Chapter 10.

Full Spectrum Light

Many depressed people keep the drapes drawn because they don't want to let the outside world in. Not only does withdrawal promote depression and overactivity of the right hemisphere, but when you do it without natural light your depression also will get worse. This is a bad strategy because it cuts them off from natural light and changes the biochemistry of the brain. Low levels of full spectrum light have been associated with depression.

Your brain picks up signals from the retina of whether it is dark or light outside and sends that information to the pineal gland. If it is dark, the pineal gland will secrete the circadian rhythm hormone melatonin, which is sedating. If it is light outside, your pineal gland won't secrete melatonin. In Chapter 9, I describe the role of melatonin in your circadian rhythm for sleep. You don't want melatonin on board during the day. It is very similar in chemical structure to serotonin. When there is an overabundance of melatonin, it competes with serotonin for the same receptor sites, and the serotonin level decreases. Low serotonin is one of the many factors correlated with depression.

Low full spectrum light (natural light) is associated with people who are suffering from seasonal affective disorder (SAD). People with SAD often find themselves becoming more depressed during the winter, when there are fewer hours of daylight. A disproportionate number of people in the northern latitudes or in the extreme southern latitudes suffer from SAD because of the overcast skies and shorter days in the winter. Therefore, if you're depressed, you should maximize your exposure to natural full spectrum sunlight. One of the treatments for SAD is to sit under a full spectrum light. Sunlight is better, of course, but if you live in an area with low levels of light in the winter and you suffer from SAD, check into getting a full spectrum electric light.

To take advantage of the benefit of light chemistry, when possible maximize the natural light that you receive during the morning to ensure that your circadian rhythm is not disrupted. With full spectrum light, also important is a dose of vitamin D, which is important for your immune system and brain, as I discussed in Chapter 2 and will pick up again in Chapter 8.

Aerobic Boosting

A study of a quarter million people from 60 countries found that having a medical condition increases the risk of also having depression by 30–60%. With two medical conditions the risk of depression increases to 80%. Dealing with one or more serious illnesses is stressful and depressing, but the immune dysregulation also plays a major role in depression.

Risk Factors for Depression

These risk factors for depression also increase inflammation:

- Medical illness
- Psychosocial stress
- Sedentary lifestyle
- Obesity
- Diminished sleep
- Social isolation
- Diet (e.g., simple carbohydrates)
- Smoking and secondhand smoke
- Air pollution
- Winter for those with seasonal affective disorder

As I described in Chapter 2, chronic inflammation is strongly associated with depression. The association between depression and chronic inflammation has been consistent in studies of people across the life cycle. Depression often involves the stress-induced release of epinephrine and norepinephrine, which stimulate the release of proinflammatory cytokines. A syndrome called sickness behavior, which is associated with inflammation, also contributes to depression. Sickness behavior including fatigue, social withdrawal, disturbances in mood, cognition, and immobility all contribute to depression. Sickness behavior is essentially depressive behavior.

Chronic Inflammation, Neurotransmitters, and Depression

Inflammation alters the levels of dopamine, norepinephrine, and serotonin through a variety of pathways that reduce the availability of their amino acid precursors, such as tryptophan necessary for serotonin synthesis. Low levels of these neurotransmitters represent just one of the many inflammatory contributors to depression and anxiety. Proinflammatory cytokines also have significant effects on the hypothalamus and the hippocampus, which can play a role in sickness behavior. Sickness behavior, characterized by disturbances in mood, cognition, and neuro-vegetative behaviors, can mimic major depression.

You cannot climb out of the pit of depression without energy. And as I noted in Chapter 2, your mitos are the source of energy. If you do not use biological energy (ATP) you cannot make it without generating free radicals. In fact, to make energy you must use it or you will end up losing it. If you do not use your biological energy (ATP) it's harder to generate more of it. You also need to keep your mitos healthy and kill off the weak ones. The birth of new mitos is called biogenesis. Recall that not only do you fail to make more energy if you do not use it, but you also create free radical damage if you do not use it. So, this is more than a use-it-or-lose-it phenomenon but rather lose-more-if-you-don't-use-it. And you need energy to keep from falling into depression.

One of the most powerful ways to generate energy and minimize chronic inflammation is exercise. Exercise has numerous positive effects, which is why it is one of the five healthy factors encoded in the mnemonic SEEDS. It boosts your mood in a variety of ways. Ironically, exercise boosts your energy reserve even though it takes energy to generate the energy.

Exercise enhances oxygenation of the blood. As noted, oxygen is one of the main raw materials that your mitos use to generate ATP. You need good circulation to get the blood supply with its raw materials to your brain cells. So, it is no wonder that when blood is transported to your brain, you feel alert and calm. Since your muscles are endowed with a rich blood supply, exercise promotes better blood flow to the muscles and results in an energized feeling; so does stretching. By stretching, you force or pump the used and deoxygenated blood back to your lungs and freshly oxygenated blood is pumped back to your muscles. Stretching promotes refreshed and invigorated muscles and the release of tension.

Exercising forces an increased output of norepinephrine, which revs up your heart rate. This increased output of norepinephrine also occurs in your brain. A higher level of norepinephrine can boost your mood as illustrated by the fact that some antidepressant medications work by increasing the transmission of norepinephrine. Study after study has shown that exercise is an antidepressant. It is humbling to mental health professionals that exercise is as effective at alleviating mild and moderate depression as psychotherapy, antidepressive medication, and psychotherapy with medication combined. In fact, norepinephrine in addition to exercise upregulates the neurotransmitters such as serotonin, norepinephrine, and dopamine that are targeted by the range of antidepressive medications.

Exercise does not have to be confined to a specific method, such as running. You can get an aerobic boost by climbing the stairs, raking the leaves, or taking a brisk walk. Research has also shown that exercise is one of the easiest ways to promote neurogenesis, as I described in Chapter 1. For now, just remember that when you combine exercise with changing the way you think, you powerfully boost your mood.

Constructing Positive Narratives

As I have explained, the two hemispheres function differently. Your right hemisphere is more holistic and emotional and when overactive tends to promote withdrawal. Your left hemisphere, though more linear and action oriented, is also the interpreter of your experiences. It tends to put a positive spin on how you interpret your experiences. Interpreting and labeling have a significant effect on your mood. Psychologists call this a narrative.

Your left hemisphere utilizes language and puts your narratives in a linguistic form. Since your left hemisphere tends to promote positive moods, if you maximize a positive spin on your narratives, you promote rewiring with a positive perspective.

Think of yourself as the narrator of your life. For example, perhaps you are facing a challenge because your old neighbors moved out and new neighbors have moved in. You considered your old neighbors to be irreplaceable. The new neighbors, meanwhile, have a completely different lifestyle. You can construct a positive narrative that describes how you are now being given an opportunity to get to know people you have never met before. Although it was sad to see your old neighbors go, your new neighbors present a new interpersonal adventure. You'll rise to the occasion to embark on this new adventure.

You modify your memories each time you remember them. This is because when memories are recalled they are influenced by the mood and the conditions that exist during your recall. Your left hemisphere can activate and change those memories with a positive spin. It also helps you to cultivate a positive narrative about what you will remember. Your two hemispheres must work like equal partners. Your right hemisphere is important for the subjective essence and the gist of a situation. It sees the whole picture, but it needs the input from your left hemisphere, which provides details and a positive spin.

Thinking and Mood

Positive thinking patterns can have a powerful effect on your mood. Research has illustrated how changing your thinking patterns can affect your brain and thus your mood. Brain-imaging studies have shown different patterns of brain activity with different types of treatment for depression. Cognitive behavioral therapy (CBT) activates the hippocampus, whereas the anti-depressant medication lowered the activity of the hippocampus. CBT appears to turn down the overactivity of the OFC, which can be involved in ruminations. CBT cuts through the negative thinking and replaces it with realistic thoughts that quiet down the corrosive ruminations.

The new positive and realistic thoughts are coded into memory through the hippocampus, but this does not necessarily occur with antidepressants. Also, after a person stops taking the medications, there is a rebound of depression. In contrast, when CBT is stopped, people remember what they have learned.

Wiring Positive Thinking

There is a two-way street between your moods and your thoughts. This is why changing the way you think is very important for alleviating depression. The goal is to change your dysfunctional thoughts so that you can change how you're feeling. If you are depressed, you probably get bogged down by cognitive traps, or beliefs that promote negative moods. These cognitive traps distort reality. There are many cognitive distortions, too many to list extensively. Here are some of the most common ones:

- **Polarized thinking:** black and white, all or nothing, good or bad, wonderful or rotten
- **Overgeneralization:** taking one unfortunate incident that occurred at work and jumping to conclusions about your entire life
- **Personalization:** interpreting every glance or comment made by someone as a negative reflection on you
- **Mind reading:** negatively assuming that you know what other people are thinking
- **Shoulds and should nots:** making rigid and inflexible rules that provide little flexibility to adapt to today's complex social environment
- **Catastrophizing:** perceiving any event as a major catastrophe or a sign of one on the way ("Oh, no, a red light! I might as well not even go.")
- **Emotional reasoning:** basing opinions on how you feel
- **Pessimism:** seeing a negative outcome for most events

Since the first edition of this book, a variety of improvements have been made in the therapeutic treatments of depression and anxiety that built on the old CBT models. Together I call them the metacognitive models. Instead of outright "restructuring thought patterns" the emphasis is on changing the way you experience them. For example, instead of having a depressing thought and then saying, "That is depressing," simply labeling the thought as a thought puts distance between the thought and the emotion. By observing it as simply a thought, it can pass away.

If any of the previous cognitive distortions apply to you, you will need to modify them so that you don't paint yourself into a depressing corner. By using what CBT therapists call *cognitive restructuring*, you can train yourself to change the way you think. There are several methods of thinking that can help you to resist negative thinking and moods and rewire your brain, including:

- **Thinking in shades of gray:** This perspective counters black-and-white thinking. By considering all possibilities between the two extremes, you allow yourself to adjust to a reality between extremes.
- **Context checking:** Here you adjust your opinions and perceptions to the context of the situation rather than just going with a preset opinion.
- **Optimism:** You consider every situation as an opportunity.
- **Detaching:** You disconnect yourself from repetitive negative beliefs.
- **Externalizing problems:** When something unfortunate happens, consider it a problem to be resolved rather than a reflection of your worth.

The key to making these methods work for you is to practice them often and consistently. By applying the FEED method to each of these thinking methods, you can dissolve depressive moods and thoughts.

Megan, whom you met at the beginning of this chapter, learned to shift from a pessimistic frame to an optimistic one. Optimism is one of the most important aspects of emotional intelligence. By developing, cultivating, and keeping an optimistic perspective, you can weather many storms of misfortune. Optimism provides you with an attitude that promotes durability and resiliency. I'll have more to say about optimism in Chapter 10 because it is so fundamental to your mental health.

Social Boosting

We humans are fundamentally social creatures. Your mood can be lifted by support from other people. Ironically, when you're down in the dumps, you may want to withdraw from people. Don't forget that withdrawing from people overactivates your right prefrontal cortex, and you need the action-oriented left prefrontal cortex to be activated to feel better. From your first few breaths as a baby, your brain craved positive bonding experiences with your parents, and later this was repeated with others. Your OFC became wired to the quality of bonding experiences that you had, and it prepared you to try to repeat the same type of emotional relationship with others.

Though I will get the social factor in greater detail in the next chapter, the important point here is that there is an antidepressant effect when your connection with people is positive. When your relationships are negative, you go through withdrawals, not unlike withdrawal from drugs. Your OFC is rich in natural opiates, and positive feelings of closeness with another person help these natural opiates to activate your OFC. Separation from an intimate partner and the subsequent feelings of withdrawal may be the result of those opiate receptors losing excitation.

The neurotransmitter dopamine is activated when you are attracted to another person; this leads to anticipated feelings of pleasure. Then the neurohormone oxytocin is activated simply by feeling close to touching and cuddling with your partner. Thus, it is biochemically and neuronally comforting to have close relationships. Positive relationships lead to positive emotions. Because social connections are so important for your health, Chapter 5 is devoted to its benefits.

When you are feeling down, you should maximize your dose of social medicine to help yourself feel better. Though you may say that you don't feel like being around other people when you feel down, but just as you take your medicine when you're ill, you should take a healthy dose of social medicine because it will help you to feel better.

Taking Action

Life was going along fairly well for Brenda. After graduating from college, she managed to get a good job as a registered nurse in a community hospital. She married a bright and funny man named

Brett, and soon they had a son. Her sisters told her that she seemed to have an ideal life compared with them. Brenda was the most attractive of the three sisters. When she was growing up, she always had a boyfriend and was pursued by other boys. Her sisters, in contrast, went through much adolescent angst in response to rejections and shifting friendships during their high school years.

Nevertheless, Brenda was the most pessimistic and least durable of the three sisters. She complained often, and her sulky moods seemed to control the social climate no matter who she was with at the time. Her two sisters dealt with various challenges through their lives—difficult marriages, health problems—but they seemed to be optimistic that things would get better as long as they tried to make them improve. While her sisters learned by effort to adjust to challenges, Brenda let others accommodate her.

Brenda had few, if any, major challenges in her life. Everything seemed to go smoothly, which is what she had learned to expect as she grew up. Her first major bump came at work. She had worked for 7 years in a credential office, where the stress was low, but she complained that it was high. She worked under a supervisor who gave her stellar performance evaluations. Then she was transferred to the intensive care unit, and her world suddenly turned upside down. For the first time in her life, she encountered significant stress. She encountered a charge nurse whom she thought was the most controlling and critical person she had ever met.

Brenda was given a performance evaluation that pointed to areas where she needed to improve; these were areas in which she thought she had been doing quite well. She perceived these criticisms as harassment, so she met with the nurses' union and explored how to file a grievance. The union representative told her that although he would help her to file the papers for the grievance, the hospital was gearing up for a National Commission on Quality Association (NCQA) review because the administration had been told that it was out of compliance. The NCQA review had everybody under the microscope, and top performance was necessary.

Brenda responded, "Are they looking for a scapegoat? Because if they are, I won't put up with it!"

"No, actually. You aren't the only one who received this kind of evaluation," said the union representative.

"Well, it feels like it," she said, and walked out of the office feeling bruised and uncertain if she should file the grievance papers.

By the time Brenda returned home that night, she had decided that quitting was her best option. She would ask her husband to work overtime until she found a new job. Her husband looked glum when she walked in the door. "So you've heard, huh?" she asked.

"Heard? Well, yeah! They said that the layoff will occur immediately," he said.

"How dare they!" she exclaimed. "I didn't even file the grievance. I was just thinking about it."

Brett stared at her, trying to connect her response to what he had said.

Then it hit her like an earthquake. He wasn't talking about her; he was talking about himself. She couldn't quit now.

It was hard for Brenda to comprehend that Brett was feeling dejected because she was so upset about her own job situation. Now she felt trapped. Her plans of quitting suddenly were impossible in light of Brett's layoff. Instead of feeling empathy for him, she felt a confusing sort of anger.

Going back to work the next morning was hard. Since Brenda had decided to quit and then found out that she couldn't, she felt hopelessly trapped. She began to feel depressed. The more she thought about the conflict, the stronger her feelings of hopelessness and depression became.

She dragged herself through the next work week as if she were on slow-motion autopilot. Her ability to care for her patients began to suffer. By the end of the week, her friend Molly had to remind her to go back in and check a patient's blood pressure. It was Brenda's responsibility to stay on top of such routine tasks, but the combination of the self-pity that she was cultivating and the resentment she felt for management was dampening her ability to function. Her ability to think clearly was colored by her new mood and her sense of meaninglessness about her work.

Soon Brenda found herself resenting the patients because they somehow represented the hospital management that she had come to resent. She was relieved to be off for a weekend. Unfortunately, she didn't use the weekend to refuel herself. Instead, the weekend served to drag her down even further. First, she turned down an opportunity to go to a dinner party on Saturday night. Then she told her husband to take their son to the park so that she could be alone. She closed the drapes, sat on the couch, and stewed about her situation. Her food intake dropped, and she drank a few glasses of wine at night to "get my mind off things."

The weekend only kindled the neuronal patterns that cultivated depression. Her shift to passivity led to greater activity in her right hemisphere. By the next week she was even more depressed.

Brenda slogged through another week with the same depressive pattern brewing. Molly approached her with the concern that Brenda's patient care was suffering. Instead of using this as a wakeup call to become more attentive to patient care, Brenda responded by feeling worse about herself.

At that point she realized that she needed to do something to break out of this downward spiral. Brenda came to me a few days later, suffering from a mild depression. She said that she needed a "quick fix" and wanted an antidepressant medication. I offered instead to help her adapt to the situation at work and to boost her mood at the same time. Antidepressant medications usually take as long as a month to begin to work, that is if they do.

"What about Valium?" she asked.

"You're a nurse," I replied. "You probably know that it's very addictive and that one of the side effects is depression. You could change your brain chemistry immediately by cutting out the wine and forcing yourself to eat three balanced meals per day. Also, maximize natural light and walk for at least a half hour per day."

I explained that she needed to maintain a balanced diet because her body makes neurotransmitters from specific amino acids that she consumes in her food. Also, her neurotransmitters GABA and serotonin were decreased because of the wine she was drinking.

I'll explain these factors in greater detail in Chapter 8. The bottom line for Brenda was that she needed better neurochemistry, not worse.

I explained that when her depressive pattern began, her passive and sulky attitude contributed to brain circuit activity that perpetuated her depression. Brenda needed to take action to break out of the passive mode that overactivated her right PFC and to shift instead to doing something to activate her left PFC. She therefore had to do some things that she didn't want to do to get out of the emotional rut she had cultivated.

It was evident from her history that she was used to having things go easily for her. As a result, Brenda had not developed the emotional intelligence to deal with the challenges that she now faced. She needed to become more durable for the bumpy road of life. She had developed a brain to deal only with a smooth road. Consequently, when she hit one of the few bumps in her life, she experienced it as catastrophic.

One of the cognitive distortions we confronted immediately was that Brenda had come to expect things to be too easy. Her passivity mode had developed because things had come so easily for her. She didn't need to try because things usually turned out well without her making any effort. In fact, she even went into nursing because it was "easy to find a job."

It was evident that Brenda was a warm and compassionate person. This was one of her talents as a nurse for which her peers and patients appreciated. I knew that we needed to tap these emotional skills to deal with this and subsequent challenges in her life. Her compassion represented the cognitive and emotional bridge we could use to establish a connection between the patients and the hospital's effort to pass the accreditation review.

I asked her to describe the patients that she was currently treating in the intensive care unit. She told me about an old man with congestive heart failure whose family lived out of state and had called only once to check on him. There was a man with multiple injuries from an auto accident. There was also a single mother of a 5-year-old who was being treated for complications from surgery for ovarian cancer.

As Brenda continued to tell me about other people, I could see a stream of warmth and compassion rekindling in her. After she described the mother, her eyes welled up. Then she looked like she was having an epiphany that in comparison to that woman, her "trauma" was extremely petty. She glanced back at me with a flash of guilt and then reconstituted herself.

I asked her to reconnect with those patients before our next session and report back to me on their progress in treatment and how they were doing emotionally.

"What's that got to do with why I came to see you?" Brenda asked.

"You need to remind yourself why you are working there," I replied. "Then we can connect that with how you can cope with the administrative changes."

What I didn't tell her yet was that her homework assignment would serve multiple functions. It would help her to detach from her exaggerated sense of hurt that fueled her negative reaction to her supervisor's evaluation, and it would enable her to refocus on the hospital's mission to care for people. She needed to rekindle motivation for her work.

When Brenda returned for the next session, there was more color in her face. The angry sullenness was gone, and her voice was soft and warm. After hearing about her patients, I asked how the rest of her colleagues were doing as they tried to prepare for the reaccreditation and care for their patients at the same time. Here I was implicitly asking her to develop a greater context for her perspective.

"It's been hard," she said. "They're all stressed out."

"And your supervisor?" I asked.

"Especially her. She looks very run down," she noted sadly. Then Brenda reverted to her old victim mode. "But she didn't have to treat me that way."

I acknowledged that her supervisor wasn't perfect. This seemed to free her up to recognize that her supervisor was under tremendous pressure from the administration to get everyone in line. Brenda's supervisor had quite a challenge on her hands. This discussion helped Brenda to move from black-and-white thinking to a perspective with shades of gray. As we discussed what the hospital was going through, she was able to externalize her problem.

Initially, Brenda was able to change by first *focusing* on the need to shift to other moods. However, focusing alone didn't make it happen. She needed to make an effort to change her behavior until it became *effortless* to be in a new mood. Because she didn't want to make the effort, because her chronic low emotional foundation demotivated her, the extra effort was critical. Thus, she had to do things that she didn't feel ready to do.

Next, I helped Brenda learn to *focus* on how and when she began to drift into a sulky reactive mode and to make an *effort* to shift into action. By tapping into the empathy that she had for her patients and let that serve as the central motivating force. Consequently, she restructured her effort to support the accreditation process so that she and her colleagues could be free to treat the patients as they deserved to be treated.

I explained that a moderate degree of stress is useful to make neuroplastic changes. Brenda's negative evaluation spiked her stress level enough to stimulate the necessary changes for her to get out of the passive (right PFC) mode and shift to an active (left PFC) mode. These changes helped to prepare her for the bumps that will inevitably come later in her life.

Brenda's Action

Brenda learned to channel her anger about her situation into taking action to change it. When you can do something about what angers you, the situation can potentially change. Research suggests that anger stirs motivation. Use it constructively to rebalance your efforts to feel more positive about your situation in life. Rather than feeling helpless about your situation, doing something constructive primes positive emotions. It will be easier the next time you need to take action.

If you are down in the dumps or just plain depressed, taking action gets you going and makes you feel better. I often say to people who are down in the dumps that the best prescription for depression is action. Passivity indirectly promotes feeling bad. But you won't immediately feel the connection between your passivity and feeling bad. Being passive might immediately seem to be a good way to make yourself feel better because you're "conserving energy." But the truth is that being passive doesn't pay off in the long run. Even if you can get someone else to do things for you, there are major negative emotional consequences. Passive-aggressive people tend to be more depressed than active people. They drift into a pessimistic mode because they sit back and let other people do for them what they can do for themselves.

When you FEED your brain so that you can get out of an emotionally depressed period, first *focus* on the mood that you would rather feel. This focused attention will help you to be aware of the difference between the more positive mood state you want to be in and the negative one that you would like to abandon.

Next you must make an *effort* to do things that will move your mood to a more positive one—from passivity to action, from your right PFC to your left PFC. You must make a rigorous effort to do what you don't really want to do, for instance, going to dinner with your friends even though you'd rather stay home alone because you are in a bad mood. You must make an effort to prime positive moods, take action, and construct positive narratives. By wiring positive thinking and ensuring that you're reconnected socially, you can make the new mood last.

The need to focus comes into play again when you drift back into your old mood. Be alert so that you notice each time you begin to drift back into a passive and negative mood. You'll have to make a concerted effort to do many of the things I've described. Eventually your efforts will change the default mood into a positive one. Soon you will begin to feel at ease with your new, more positive mood, and it will become *effortless* for you to remain in that mood.

You may begin to enjoy things so much that you sit back and passively wait for the next series of good things to happen to you. If you sit back too long, you'll run the risk of reverting to the old pattern. This could happen quickly if an event or a crisis arises that makes you upset. This is when you need to be *determined* to stay with your new strategy to ensure the previous three steps of feeding your brain.

If you stay determined when an unfortunate incident occurs, you can weather the storm despite the complications of fierce winds. This resiliency depends on a sense of optimism that the plan will work, as we will expand upon in Chapter 10. You need to remind yourself that the previous steps helped you to feel good before. Now you must stay in practice to make sure that this is your new emotional foundation. Being in a positive mood is not only more pleasurable; it's also more practical. If your moods tend to be positive, you'll be more likely to think about possibilities instead of limitations and bad outcomes.

Part 2

The Five SEEDS Factors

5

The Social Factor

Marc came to see me after his thyroid test results came out negative. He had asked his primary care physician for the test because he thought he might have hypothyroidism, a condition characterized by a low level of the hormone thyroxine. Its symptoms include low energy and mild depression.

His primary care physician thought that Marc might be depressed. He knew for sure that Marc was terribly lonely. In fact, he told me that Marc frequently went online to research medical conditions so that he could justify an appointment for a medical checkup. The real reason for the appointments was to come in and chat about the conditions. "It's like he views me as his best friend," the doctor said.

When I sat down with Marc, he acknowledged that he had no friends besides his acquaintances at work and the people he played bridge with online. Even with the latter, he never actually developed much of a relationship. At work, he never went out to lunch with people or took walks with them, and he certainly did not see them outside of work. I asked him if he was lonely.

"No, no, I'm fine by myself," he said unconvincingly. Then Marc told me that he had never been married and had dated only a few times though he was 42 years old. "Relationships are too complicated. I like to keep it simple and live alone," he insisted.

I pointed out that he went to his physician on many of his days off and that those visits were his only social contacts.

"Well, he's a good friend," he said, then realized that he had implied more than he intended.

"It sounds like you need some friends." I suggested.

"I've got all I need," he replied.

"You mean your doctor?" I asked.

"Did he complain about me?" Marc looked hurt.

"Not at all," I answered. "He's concerned about you and thinks that your loneliness is making you feel ill."

"That's nice of him to care," he said, looking comforted. "But it's not necessary." He tried to recompose himself.

"It feels good when people care about you, doesn't it?" I inquired. Marc shrugged his shoulders, looking as if he didn't know how to answer.

I told him about the findings from a huge body of research that people who have close personal relationships experience fewer health problems, live longer, and are less depressed and anxious.

"That may be so for some people, but not for me," he claimed.

"Yet you've had some symptoms associated with having few social contacts, such as those you thought were connected to hypothyroidism, even though you do not," I pointed out.

His eyebrows shot up. Marc seemed more receptive to hearing more now, since he had symptoms correlated with loneliness. I suggested that one way to rule out the connection between his symptoms and the possibility that he was lonely would be to see if increasing his social contacts would reduce his symptoms.

His immediate answer was no. Then I told him about the parts of the brain that thrive on social contact. I noted that those parts of the brain could help him deal with stress more effectively and boost his immune system so that he would become ill less often.

This information about his brain seemed to open the door to his at least thinking about finding out more about this connection with his health. Then it dawned on him that he might soon be encouraged to extend himself in ways that would be out of character. "Even when I was growing up, I didn't have many friends," he noted. "What am I supposed to do?" He seemed to be trying to convince me that his brain was hardwired for loneliness.

Marc described his emotionally distant family environment when he was growing up. His emotional attachment to his parents was avoidant, and he had few positive interpersonal experiences from which to draw. I described the process of neuroplasticity and explained how he could rewire his brain to learn to be more comfortable in social situations. "It's never too late to develop new skills," I said.

"Just the thought of it makes me feel uneasy," he admitted.

We talked for some time about how people can make changes at any point in their lives. Despite the fact that he had a lifelong history of no intimate connections to people, it was still possible to change. After some encouraging and comforting words, I pointed out that to make gains, he must do what he didn't feel like doing, which involved stepping way out of his comfort zone.

Marc indicated that he understood what he needed to do rationally and intellectually but that he still had anxiety about extending himself socially. It was too broad a jump for him to go from socializing at work to extending himself in a social situation with little structure. The thought that he could be thrust into a social situation in which people congregated for the primary purpose of getting to know one another was overwhelming. Therefore, we started by structuring time that involved doing something constructive with other people like learning a new subject. He registered for an activity that interested him: a computer class at the local community college.

After a few weeks, Marc acknowledged that it felt good to be with a group of people who were together by choice instead of for a paycheck, as at work. He so much enjoyed learning about computers that he bought extra books on the subject and read them.

Eventually, a few of Marc's classmates asked him for help with their computers. This motivated him to show up early so that he could be available to them. As spring break approached, he told me that he dreaded the week away from his fellow students.

Then one of his fellow students, a woman named Karen, suggested that they meet at the local cafe with their laptops during the spring break week. This suggestion made him feel both anxious and excited. He managed to respond by saying, "No problem."

I asked why he would say "No problem," using a negative when replying in the affirmative. Instead, why not say, "Sure, that sounds great?"

Marc was surprisingly frank. "I guess I was worried that if I had sounded too positive, Karen would have thought I was hitting on her."

"Are you attracted to her?" I asked.

He blushed, then looked at his watch.

"Women don't want remoteness," I explained. "Let her know that you are enjoying the time that you spend with her."

He shifted around in the chair, looked at me sheepishly, then nodded that he would try.

At our appointment the following week, Marc looked like a different person. He was energized, there was color in his face, and he was beaming.

I asked, "So what's new?"

"Life," he responded, as if I would immediately understand.

I did. "Does Karen feel the same way?"

"Maybe," he answered. "She wants to get together at the cafe again this weekend, even though class is back in session."

Marc and Karen began meeting for coffee on a regular basis. Soon she began introducing him to her friends. Eventually he told me, "It's like a family I never had." During that month, his visits to his physician dropped to zero. I asked him about his doctor, and he said, "I don't need him. Whoops, I said that, didn't I?"

"Let's call what you're experiencing social nourishment," I suggested.

Marc told me that not only was he enjoying his "new family," but that he also felt exhilarated with the time he spent with Karen. Yet he worried that if he told her that he felt more for her than friendship, he would lose her and all his new friends.

"Sometimes you have to take risks in relationships," I told him, "and I think you're ready."

During our next session Marc told me that they had had their first "real date" and that he would "always remember every moment of it."

My visits with Marc became sporadic after that. He told me that he would call if he needed me, then he chuckled.

Marc is not alone. Although we are frequently online, emailing, texting, and calling on the phone, the time we actually spend with one another person has decreased. Compared with just a few hundred years ago—when our ancestors were socially immersed in their communities, villages, and extended families—we are in virtual communities shielded from one another but linked by our electronic devices. This lack of social connectedness leaves us starving for warmth and grasping for a vicarious version of it through TV shows and movies. Multidimensional relationships of the past have given way to one-dimensional and disconnected relationships. If you need help with your computer, you call tech support located "offshore" and talk to a person who has been trained to lose their accent so that you will feel comfortable and more likely to trust them.

Despite these trends, study after study has shown that positive relationships are good for your health (particularly your immune system), whereas poor or no relationships are bad for your health. Chapter 2 noted that this field details the interface among the immune system, the mind, and emotion. The positive effect of the social factor affects your brain as well as many other areas of your body.

Health Benefits of the Social Factor

The following list shows the many health-related effects of the social factor:

- ↓Cardiovascular reactivity
- ↓ Blood pressure
- ↓ Cortisol level
- ↓ Serum cholesterol
- ↓ Vulnerability to catching a cold
- ↓ Depression
- ↓ Anxiety
- Slowing down of cognitive decline
- Improvement in sleep
- ↑ Natural killer cells

What's going on here? How do your relationships have such an impact on your body, including your brain? Consider first that we are the species that is born most premature. A colt and calf are born from their mother, and within minutes' walk around. We are born totally defenseless, and so carried around by our parents for a year before we begin to walk and talk. Then we are "brought up" by our parents for almost two decades. During that time, we are marinated in the emotional and cultural climate of our family and social environment. It has profound effects on your brain, genes, and immune system.

The interaction between those socially sensitive parts of the brain that thrive on social interaction wire up when you bonded with your parents. If those relationships were positive, you developed an ability to control your emotions. When your relationships are supportive, you feel comforted, and these brain systems become wired so that you can also comfort yourself. This is because these brain systems are connected to parts of the brain, such as prefrontal cortex, and to the parasympathetic nervous system, which helps you to calm down your amygdala in the face of stress.

Spindle Cells

Your brain contains a unique type of neuron called spindle cells known for their spindly shape, unique size, and highly connected quality. These spindle cells have long axons that transfer immediate and emotionally compelling insights.

The human brain has many more spindle cells than our closest ape relatives possess. At birth humans have approximately 28,000 spindle cells, growing to 184,000 by age 4, and 193,000 by adulthood. By comparison an adult ape has 7000.

Because they are about four times larger than other neurons and have such long and thick dimensions, they are believed to make high-velocity transmission possible. Hence the *snap* in *snap judgment*.

Supporting the capacity for empathy and insight are your OFC and the front of the cingulate cortex, which are rich with spindle cells. These areas are thought to be involved in our emotional reactions to others, especially the instantaneous feelings of empathy. Hearing a baby cry, for example, makes you feel empathy for that baby. These parts of your brain are also related to your capacity for love because they activate when you find a person attractive or see a picture of a person you love.

The discovery of spindle cells has illuminated how people have the ability to make effective snap decisions involving emotion and interpersonal experience. These neurons are able to connect divergent information quickly and efficiently. They provide a unique interface between your thoughts and your emotions. As such, they aid your ability to maintain sustained attention and self-control. They provide you with the flexibility to make quick but complex problem-solving decisions in emotionally stirring situations. Spindle cells can't function well if they have little to work with interpersonally.

(continued)

(*continued*)

> Spindle cells are rich with serotonin, dopamine, and vaso-pressin circuitry, intimately connected to mood, social ties, bonding, expectation, and reward. They form connections between the cingulate cortex and the OFC. The front portion of the cingulate cortex contains many spindle cells that connect diverse parts of the brain and are involved in bonding and social communication. They provide a means to grasp an intuitive sense of the emotions of another person, enabling us to make snap, intuitive judgments that are fused with emotion and social sensitivity.

The neurohormone oxytocin has many receptors on your vagus network. When you feel close to other people, your vagus is active, which also activates your parasympathetic nervous system. In other words, being close to those that care for you can calm you down. If you are ill and suffer from chronic inflammation it is harder to feel close to others.

Your orbital frontal cortex (OFC) thrives on social interaction. When these neurons are activated effectively, you experience fewer psychological problems and better mental health. The bonding experiences you have had with your parents from the beginning of your life have affected your brain. Your later relationships then modify those neural connections. Positive relationships enhance your sense of well-being, whereas negative relationships undermine your sense of well-being.

We know that neurochemicals such as oxytocin are not only involved in childbirth and bonding but also become activated in intimate relationships. Higher oxytocin levels help to blunt pain and make us feel comforted by other people. For this reason, oxytocin is referred to as the "cuddling hormone" in the mainstream press. When oxytocin is activated by close personal contact, your parasympathetic nervous system becomes activated through contact with receptors on your vagus nerve system (Table 5.1).

Table 5.1 The Systems of the Social Brain

Neurotransmitters	Brain and Nervous System
Oxytocin	Ventral vagus
	Orbital frontal cortex
Dopamine	Amygdala
Vasopressin	Insula
Neuropeptides	Cingulate cortex
Neuropeptides	Mirror neurons
Serotonin	Spindle cells

These systems provide you with the opportunity to form rich and multidimensional social relationships. Consequently, there are many forms of social communication. One of the most basic is based on touch.

Touch

The skin is the largest organ in the human body. It contains two different types of receptors: (1) those that help you to locate, identify, and manipulate objects; and (2) those that help you to connect with other people through emotion. This socially sensitive function facilitates mental and physical health and longevity.

Touching and being touched have served many important evolutionary functions. In other primates, for example, mutual grooming promotes social cohesiveness and bonding. Touching expresses reassurance and affection. Partly for this reason, being touched by someone else is more pleasurable than touching yourself. Not only does it enhance bonding or sensuality, but it also feels better because it is unpredictable.

Touching and being touched promote biochemical changes in the brain. The release of the neurotransmitters dopamine, oxytocin, and endorphins occurs with caressing, comforting, and soft touching; this promotes closeness with a person that is touching you as well as feelings of well-being. Touching has also been associated with lower levels of stress hormones and enhanced brain cell survival.

Touching has been shown to enhance the immune systems of people who are suffering from various illnesses as well as the immune systems of the people who are caring for them. For example, therapeutic back massage enhances the immune functions of people who have cancer. Touch positively tempers the aberrant behavior of people of all ages. Depressed or aggressive adolescents have benefited from touch, and agitated elderly people in nursing homes are calmed by hand massages.

The Effects of Nurturance and Its Deprivation

Caring for and being cared for by others have powerful effects on your brain from birth to your death. A graphic example of how the lack of nurturance can affect the brain occurred in Eastern European countries before the fall of the Soviet Union. After the repressive regime of Nicolae Ceausescu was overthrown in 1989, more than 150,000 children were found languishing in Romanian orphanages. They were malnourished and neglected, and many were dying of infectious diseases. Typically, one person cared for 30 or more children. The children were fed and kept clean but otherwise received minimal care. The orphans often resorted to such primitive methods of self-stimulation as head-banging, incessant rocking, and hand-flapping. They exhibited multiple developmental delays because they missed human contact during critical developmental periods.

Infants less than a year old who were placed in these orphanages for more than 8 months had higher cortisol blood levels (an indicator of significant stress) than orphans who were adopted within the first 4 months of their lives. The cortisol levels of children who were institutionalized beyond 8 months continued to increase. This means that the longer they were deprived of nurturance, the greater were their stress levels during childhood.

As middle-class European, Canadian, and U.S. families began to adopt some of these children, they were faced with the daunting problem of managing the tragic effects of early neglect. Several studies have examined how these children have adapted to their adoptive families and how they have fared poorly in school. For example, Michael Rutter compared 156 Romanian orphans who were adopted by British families at age 3 and a half and compared them to 50 nondeprived children who were adopted before 6 months of age. All the children were followed longitudinally and were examined for a variety of behavioral problems. The adoptees were more likely to exhibit behavior problems such as ADHD, autistic-like behavior, and other cognitive impairments. These problems were more likely to occur among children who left the orphanage after their second birthday. The children who left the orphanage prior to 6 months of age resembled the nondeprived children adopted in Britain.

The risk of developing behavioral problems increased for the children who were adopted after 6 months of age from an orphanage and was greatest if they were adopted after age 2. During the first year of life, a baby thrives on nurturance or is stunted by the lack of it. The effects on the brain have a profound bearing on how successfully the children will adapt to the world later in life.

The British study was one of many that illustrated the powerful effects of being deprived of nurturing, especially early in life. A similar story occurred in Canada, where researchers found that the children who had spent at least 8 months in an orphanage had significant developmental problems, whereas those who spent less than 4 months there did not suffer the same degree of impairment.

Similarly, the orphans who were adopted by U.S. families continue to show many of the same symptoms of their early social deprivation. They have been described as being stoic, being uninterested in playing, tending to hoard food, and having difficulty crying or expressing pain. Brain scans reveal that key parts of their brain, associated with controlling emotions and engaging other people, were underactive.

Why, you may ask, did I bother to describe this sad story about orphans. It is because it illustrates how fundamentally critical our social connections play a role in our brain health. Being deprived of nurturing can cause significant neurochemical abnormalities.

Bonding, Deprivation, and the Brain

Being separated at birth from mothers results in persistent abnormalities in the production and normal functioning of neurotransmitters, including alterations in the following:

- The expression of dopamine transporter genes
- The dopamine-mediated stress response
- The expression of serotonin receptors
- The expression of benzodiazepine receptors
- The infant's sensitivity to opioids
- The cortisol receptors related to stress response

Think of how the factors listed earlier play a critical role in managing stress and feeling comforted. They provide a major part of your critical infrastructure of your sense of well-being. This network is wired over a lifetime. For example, the research on babies of depressed mothers has shown that these infants behave as if they too are depressed, even in the presence of nondepressed adults. Maternal depression causes multiple deficits and developmental problems in children, including not only behavior problems but also neurological and immune system deficits. Infants of depressed mothers have a wide range of problems. For example, infants of depressed mothers have displayed increased aversion and helplessness and have vocalized less. They have had higher heart rates, decreased vagal tone, and developmental delays at 1 year old.

Attachment and Gene Expression

Though lack of early nurturing can damage the brain, a growing body of research introduced in Chapter 2 shows that nurturance has a protective effect on the brain gene expression and thus on psychological development. Among the brain systems that benefit from nurturing are the hippocampus and its receptor sites for stress hormones such as cortisol. With early nurturance, cortisol receptors multiply and provide a negative feedback loop, like a thermostat. When stress hormones filter into the brain, these receptors on the hippocampus trigger a shutdown in the production of cortisol, as if to say, "I've had enough of that stress hormone; no more is needed." However, when there are too few receptors, a different response is triggered, as if to say, "I can't turn off the stress! It's too overwhelming!" The negative thermostat provided by this gene expression keeps stress low as a result of nurturance.

Despite the importance of early nurturance, you can still gain benefits from nurturance throughout your lifetime. If you were lucky to receive enhanced nurturance early in your life, it gives you a head start in gaining from all the benefits of social connections. Through the power of neuroplasticity and gene expression, you can enhance and enjoy the benefits of the positive nurturance or, like Marc, repair the limitations you've acquired from poor nurturance.

The Epigenetics of Bonding

When nurtured, you are more likely to nurture others. For example, the initial research was on rat pups and showed that the rats that were cared for best grew up to do the same for their offspring, but the rat pups that were not well nurtured grew up to neglect their pups. The researchers arranged it so that the less attentive mothers raised the offspring of nurturing mothers, and vice versa. The rat pups born to the inattentive mothers but raised by attentive mothers grew up to be indistinguishable from the biological offspring of the nurturing mothers. They were significantly less fearful when put in unfamiliar surroundings, just like those who were born of and raised by nurturing mothers. The opposite occurred when the biological offspring of nurturing mothers were raised by inattentive mothers. They grew up to be anxious and fearful adults.

(continued)

(*continued*)

Researchers have also found that the gene that produces the glucocorticoid receptor (cortisol in humans) in the hippocampus is twice as active in rat pups raised by nurturing mothers as in those raised by inattentive mothers. It appears that receiving nurturance causes an increase in a molecule that increases production of the glucocorticoid receptors in the hippocampus. That gene produces more receptors, which provide an enhanced thermostat and resistance to stress. In other words, nurturance turns specific genes on. This means that if you were nurtured, your brain went through structural changes that help you manage stress. This doesn't mean that you won't experience stress. It just means that you have gained greater resiliency than people who did not receive as much nurturance.

Bonding and Attachment

Having secure and mutually nurturing relationships helps you form the basis for good mental and physical health. If you haven't experienced those types of relationships yet, there's still time. While on one hand the genes you were born with may have less effect on you than nurturing does, on the other hand those genes may be expressed differently based on the quality of nurturance that you received. If you are fortunate to have experienced secure relationships, you can build on them.

Bonding forms the foundation for your communication skills. Psychologists refer to the quality of relationships as attachment styles because they represent the degree to which you feel comfortably attached to your caregivers and other people since childhood. Early bonding begins before the development of language, and many of the basic attachment patterns are formed during the period of right hemispheric dominance, which is during the first 2 years. The right hemisphere continues to play a dominant role in appraising and establishing the emotional meaning of your interpersonal experiences.

The amygdala, too, plays an important role in mediating early attachment relationships. Highly connected with other brain areas, the amygdala stamps the incoming stimuli with emotional relevancy in a very quick, good-and-bad manner. The amygdala does this with stimuli coming from within you as well as with the external stimuli that come in through your ears, eyes, and skin. Along with the right hemisphere, the amygdala appraises the emotional relevance of facial expressions and tone of verbal communications that you received first from your caregivers and now in your relationships with others.

Developmental psychologists have used a variety of methods to explore how early attachment relationships play a significant role in the type and quality of your relationships later in life. For example, Mary Ainsworth described the attachment types as secure, avoidant, and ambivalent types. Her student, Mary Main, now at the University of California at Berkeley, identified the disorganized type. Attachment researchers maintain that infants don't construct their attachment patterns by themselves; rather, they do it in response to their perceptions of their parents' behavior. The child's attachment behavior correlates quite well with the behavior and communication style of the mother. A mother's responsiveness to her baby can take a variety of forms, such as the following:

- Parents of securely attached infants accurately interpret the infant's communications, responding quickly and consistently to the child's needs in a "good enough" manner.
- Parents of children with an avoidant attachment style tend to remain unresponsive to the child's distress, discouraging crying and promoting separation.
- Parents of ambivalently attached infants behave inconsistently, being sometimes tuned in and sometimes indifferent to the child's state of mind.
- Parents of children with a disorganized attachment style tend to be abusive, impulsive, and depressed.

Thus, your attachment style developed in intimate context, based on the behavior of those around you. You may be asking yourself if the attachment style you developed by the time you were a year old tends to be a highly durable personal characteristic that remains evident later in your life. Longitudinal studies have shown that one's attachment style persists into adulthood 68–75% of the time.

Since attachment patterns tend to be long-lasting, what chance is there to rewire your brain to change those patterns? In a study of the degree of rewiring that is possible even with the most deprived, Michael Rutter (whom you met earlier on the English and Romanian adoptees study team) looked at healing early attachment traumas through enriched environments. Researchers drew the cautiously optimistic conclusion that to some extent, even with the extreme effects of early deprivation, a person can overcome the ill effects with good, quality relationships later in life.

If you had a poor attachment pattern initially and don't work to rewire your brain to change it with positive relationships, what chance is there that you will pass it on to your own children? There is growing evidence that the way a parent responds to their baby is based on the parent's own attachment style. Many studies have looked at the application of attachment research to adults. Mary Main and colleagues created an assessment of adult attachment called the Adult Assessment Interview. Its classification of the parent predicts the child's security or insecurity 75% of the time. This appears to hold true even when the parent is assessed before the child's birth.

If your brain was initially wired through a secure attachment, you may tend to feel relatively secure later in life. Research suggests that 55% of adults fall into this category. You are likely to feel worthy of affection and care, enter relationships with reasonable ease, become close and feel comfortable in these relationships, and expect your partner to be emotionally available and supportive in hardship. Your self-esteem may be relatively high, and you tend to be resilient, optimistic, intellectually curious, and open to new ideas. When misunderstandings result in arguments, you can more easily resist feeling rejected or insulted.

If, however, you are among the approximately 20% who are anxious in your adult relationship and worry that your partner doesn't really love you, you may feel unworthy, clingy, and prone to obsessive preoccupation, as well as addicted to something. You may worry about abandonment and are prone to jealousy.

If you're among the approximately 25% of the adult population with a dismissive attachment style, you may be uncomfortable in intimate relationships and have a hard time trusting a partner. You might not share your feelings and even be consciously aware of them. This is how Marc started out. Yet, as I described earlier in this chapter, he took risks, and it paid off. Had he not, his relationship with Karen would probably not have happened.

Indeed, if you had an insecure attachment experience as a child, you may tend to see the world and those around you with defensiveness and mistrust. It can be hard to maintain a sense of self-esteem, and you may be prone to pessimism. When those around you are imperfect and say or do things that are imperfect, it may be hard for you to forgive them and move on.

According to a large analysis of the Adult Attachment Inventory studies, insecure attachment is correlated with anxiety and mood disorders later in life. In contrast, secure attachment is correlated with a lower incidence of psychological disorders than in the general population. However, whether or not you were securely attached as a child, you can still rewire your brain to build a sense of security that will support positive relationships. It will require that you, like Marc, feed your brain by exposing yourself to social situations that might initially feel a little risky. He did it, and so can you.

Challenging yourself to go beyond your comfort level is easier than it initially seems. In preparation for increasing your social relationships, imagine yourself communicating successfully with others. This will stimulate some of the same neurons that you'll be using when you engage in social interactions. By using a technique called *priming* you can trust others even when you have not trusted them in the past. For example, priming has been used successfully with Arab and Jewish students in Israel. Positive images and associations of a sense of security are primed in people before they interact with others who normally would have seemed unsafe.

Consider the West–Eastern Divan Orchestra consisting of musicians from the Middle East, including Israelis and Palestinians. It was founded in 1999 by the conductor Daniel Barenboim and academic Edward Said and named after an anthology of poems by Goethe. The cultural history of opposition these young musicians had learned initially, melted away not only to cooperate but to play beautiful music together.

You can also use priming successfully if you are anxious or avoidant by disposition. Positive attachment images and associations can be primed even by using words such as *love, fortune, hug*, and *support*. By boosting thoughts of caregiving and positive attachment, you can increase your feelings of compassion and warmth toward others. As a result, you will probably feel less distress around other people and greater connection to them.

To reap the gains of social factor, you'll need to take risks like Marc and expand your sense of security in relationships. The greater your efforts, the greater your rewards. If you're lonely, think of it this way: you have nothing to lose by putting yourself out there socially.

The Social Factor and Empathy

The neurobiology of empathy helps you responds to a person who appears sad and dejected. You feel sad along with that person. Talented actors cultivate this empathetic system so that you can vicariously experience the trials and tribulations that they experience on screen. Your attachment style is primed by exposure to attachment themes in the movies, especially when they are emotionally powerful.

The capacity to engage another person and imagine what he or she is thinking and feeling develops in our early latency years. *Theory of mind* (ToM) is a process by which you try to understand and predict the behavior of others. You probably developed aspects of it by age 5. The neural foundation of this capability is the same one that you use when you are planning your future. It bolsters your capability to formulate responses to the behavior that you anticipate in others.

Goal-Directed Social Connectedness

Goal-directed behavior and planning for the future are functions of your prefrontal cortex (PFC). It is no wonder that during evolution, the expansion of the PFC dramatically differentiated our species from other apes. Specific neurons in your PFC and in other parts of your brain are highly social. The subgenual anterior cingulate cortex (sgACC) modulates emotional processing and is associated with empathy.

As the social world of our ancestors became more complex, a more complex brain evolved to support those social skills. The cortex developed rich layered feedback loops and enhanced skills to inhibit instinctual and automatic responses to social situations. The capacity for a balanced appraisal of the social context and the complexities of each situation had tremendous survival value, not only by controlling aggression but also by increasing the chances of reproductive success and survival in complex social settings.

During evolution, the demands on communication increased with population growth and resource competition. The advantages of enhanced gestural communication, in turn, may have contributed to further social development through the imitation of gestures. Social and emotional capacities evolved through vocal communication and sounds that emerged as a sort of protolanguage, which gave a huge competitive advantage to our species over others and vastly expanded the human potential for empathetic and intimate relationships.

Mirror Neurons

The discovery of *mirror neurons* has shown that parts of your brain are acutely sensitive to the movements and intentions of others. The early work on mirror neurons involved monkeys and focused on an area of the frontal lobe that is associated with expressive movements; in the human brain, this is called Broca's area and is important in speaking. For our species, the transition from phonetic gestural communication to actual words paralleled the expansion of the frontal lobes and the mirror neuron system. An illustration of the link between imitation and mirror neurons is that just listening to someone talk activates the listener's tongue muscles.

Mirror neurons may also have evolved through vocal communication and sounds that emerged as a sort of protolanguage, which gave a huge competitive advantage to our species over others and vastly expanded the human potential for empathetic and intimate relationships.

Mirror neurons therefore may have played a key role in the evolution of our species. As the social world of our evolutionary ancestors became more complex and favored more sophisticated dimensions of social situations, a more complex brain developed that supported these social skills. The cortex developed rich layered feedback loops and enhanced powers to inhibit instinctual and automatic responses to social situations. The capacity for a balanced appraisal of the social context and the complexities of each situation had tremendous survival value, not only by controlling aggression but also by increasing the chances of reproductive success in complex social settings. Mirror neurons allow you to mirror another person, or to feel what they feel without even thinking about it. For example, when a friend yawns, have you ever found yourself yawning immediately afterward?

Theory of Mind—Knowing the Mind of Another

The brain areas associated with social connectedness networks can become deactivated with loneliness. One such area, the temporal-parietal junction, which is associated with cognitive empathy, can actually atrophy. This intersection between the temporal and parietal lobes in the right hemisphere can develop greater complexity as you try to understand the thoughts and feelings of other people. Cognitive empathy represents this skill and develops with ToM. There are several areas in the brain associated with ToM, including the amygdala, the insula, and the front of the cingulate cortex.

The right OFC decodes mental states, whereas the left OFC reasons about those states. These are some of the major aspects of your ToM skills:

1. Self-related mental states
2. Goals and outcomes
3. Actions

ToM skills give you insight into what another person is thinking or feeling. You can't truly communicate effectively without these skills. People differ in their level of sophistication of ToM skills, and people with autism have few or no ToM skills. You can work at expanding your ToM skills as you cultivate the talents of seeing the world through the eyes of others. Therapists work to perfect these skills throughout their careers.

Experiencing empathy and compassion for others cultivates compassion for yourself. Here we see "giving is receiving" as a brain-based truth. Together with the anterior cingulate, the anterior insula provides the capacity for empathy, which comprises the awareness of our own bodily state. In other words, feelings from our body are intertwined with feelings about another person. Insensitivity and selfishness are essentially bad for your brain and your mental health. Even witnessing altruism can boost your immune system. There is a good reason compassion and loving relationships are therefore good for your brain and your mental health.

Love

Why is falling in love so blissful? Why did Marc look so alive after he got to know Karen? Throughout history, many theories about love have contributed more to mythology than to clarity. Take, for example, the concept of the soul mate, which stems from Plato's proposal that there is another "half "out there in the universe that "completes" each of us. Although there is much debate on whether opposites attract or repel, there is a way of understanding what happens in your brain when you are falling in love. Examining what happens in your brain does not devalue love; as I have stated several times in this book, the brain and the mind are two parts of the same picture. Whatever happens in the mind changes the brain, and vice versa. When there is chemistry between you and another person, there is chemistry *within each* of you when you're together. This "good chemistry" occurs because of the way you behave toward each other.

Falling in love is a blissful experience with a powerful rush of euphoria partly because your pleasure center is activated. For example, during the infatuation phase, your dopamine system is charged up. From the first sight of your new partner, your PFC works with the dopamine system to help you attend to this attractive person. This enhanced attention triggers your brain to release more dopamine and tells your hippocampus to remember this attractive person. The more dopamine, the greater the chance that you will probably remember the first time you saw the person.

Your attachment history corresponds to your unique method of regulating your emotions in intimate relationships that play a major role in how connected you feel to other people. These tendencies further influence the effort you make to reach out to this person to hopefully enjoy a balanced relationship. By making an effort to take a risk, it enables you to move the relationship ahead for mutual enjoyment.

Love's Chemistry

The following aspects of the "chemistry of love" give you those blissful feelings:

- At first sight, your PFC says, "Pay attention! This person is attractive." This triggers your brain to discharge dopamine.
- Your hippocampus records this memory of first sight.
- Your nucleus accumbens (Grand Central Station for pleasure and addiction center) is activated with dopamine. When you are separated too long from the one you love, you experience something akin to withdrawal symptoms.
- The *septal region* (another pleasure center) is activated after dopamine triggers the excitement. This area is also activated during orgasm.

- You and your partner run the risk of developing a tolerance for dopamine. After the initial rush, there tends to be less dopamine released. Both of you will have to create novelty to stimulate continued dopamine release.
- Followed up by the release of oxytocin, you feel soothed and comforted by each other

The first few dates are infused with pleasure because your pleasure center (nucleus accumbens) is activated by the neurotransmitter dopamine. This is the same pleasure center that is activated by dopamine via drugs, gambling, pornography, and anything else that can become addictive. Some people don't activate the rest of their brain systems and can't move on to a more mature form of love. They are addicted to falling in love, so they move on to another relationship because they are constantly looking for that initial rush of excitement.

When the septal region is activated, you generalize a positive feeling to other experiences. For example, when you spend time with your partner on a sunny day, that day seems full of energy and color, fragrance, and warm people. Any flaw in your partner is glossed over or seen as an endearing characteristic. Everything is fused with hopeful anticipation. The things that normally bother you don't. Your brain essentially recruits memories and associations that make all experiences positive.

Since dopamine circuits thrive on novelty, you and your partner can risk becoming distant with one another, losing excitement, and becoming bored. To prevent this dulling of your relationship, you can charge up your dopamine system by doing novel things together, like traveling and going out on romantic dates. The feelings of pleasure from these new experiences will spill over into your relationship by kindling the dopaminergic system.

To maintain positive and secure attachment feelings for an extended period of time, you'll have to stimulate the neurochemistry in your brain that fosters long-term bonding. Fortunately, your brain has the neurochemistry potential to make long-term bonding a possibility. Oxytocin facilitates close relationships. Oxytocin helps to create a bond between people who are forming an intimate relationship. Your oxytocin level rises when you have warm physical contact with someone you are close to and with whom you feel safe.

A Bonding Hormone?

Oxytocin functions as a neuromodulator, which means that it orchestrates the activities of other neurotransmitters and helps to enhance or dampen the effectiveness of synaptic connections. It is sometimes called the cuddling or the commitment neurohormone because it facilitates bonding in all mammals. Animals with a relatively high amount of oxytocin are monogamous. The classic example is the prairie vole, which mates for life. Oxytocin is released in women during labor and breastfeeding, and it is released in both sexes when nurturing children, cuddling, making love, and having an orgasm.

In romantic relationships, dopamine triggers excitement, and oxytocin triggers feelings of warmth and attachment. You can modify the chemistry of your relationship to deepen your long-term commitment. For example, when oxytocin is combined with dopamine (which occurs when excitement is rekindled through novel experiences), a long-term sense of love and commitment arises that feels exciting, safe, and fulfilling. It is my hope that this is what happened to Marc and Karen.

If you make the effort to expand and deepen your social and intimate relationships, you will enjoy the vast benefits of the social factor. Do it in conjunction with the other SEEDS factors. For example, you can go out on hikes or vigorous walks with friends. That is what I am doing this afternoon. Afterward, we will sit down for a nutritious dinner and share interesting ideas and things that we are learning, for the education factor.

6

The Exercise Factor

Matt was depressed and complained that he was not able to focus attention the way that he had in the past. He said, "All the stress of the patrol cop position is gone since I've been reassigned to a desk job." However, he found himself feeling "zoned out." To remedy his mental fatigue, he guzzled a six-pack of soda. Though he was fatigued, he tossed and turned in bed. The sleep deprivation only added to his mental fatigue.

His sergeant at police headquarters suggested that he take more breaks and walk during them. Matt responded with, "If I had the energy maybe, but I don't." The sergeant corrected him by reiterating what he had learned at the health seminars that I presented to the entire department. He said, "It is a use-it-or-lose-it kinda thing."

Matt tried to correct the sergeant with another authority, a previous president of the United States who stated that exercise was a waste of energy. The sergeant knew better because this president was famous for uttering other absurd statements.

The sergeant is right that exercise is critical for brain health. To prove it, he ordered Matt to take walks during his breaks. At first Matt objected and called the union rep in to protect him from this order. The union rep said, "What? You're being offered extra breaks. Take them!"

Why was the sergeant right? What is it about our bodies that require exercise? To answer these questions, we must look to our ancestors and how they survived.

Centuries ago, our ancestors moved their bodies much more than we do today. This is because our ancestors engaged in many physical activities just to stay alive. As hunter-gatherers, they moved 10 miles a day. Very few people do that today, other than in their car or on a train. We have the same body, but we are not doing what our bodies evolved to do. This means that we are disabling our bodies and in turn our brains.

The Physical Activity of Our Ancestors

The typical activities of hunter-gatherer correlate to these modern-day forms of exercise:

- Slow cardio: 5–10 miles a day of low-intensity walking
  - Hunter gatherers cover 5–15 miles per day. Persistence hunters cover in excess of 30 miles/day.
- Resistance training: lifting, throwing, and carrying objects
  - Encompass functional movements such as pushing, pulling, sprinting, and jumping
- Interval training: periodic bursts of high-intensity activity
  - Brief bouts of sprinting alternating with walking or jogging in pursuit of prey

Some years ago, at a Kaiser Permanente conference on the benefit of walking, a University of British Columbia professor of internal medicine said that not exercising regularly was worse than "smokodiabesity"—smoking plus diabetes plus and obesity. Today we say that sitting is the new smoking. In fact, many studies have shown that the more time you spend sitting, the more likely you are to develop a host of chronic diseases such as cardiovascular disease.

Prolonged sitting, especially while commuting or in a high-pressure job, can put you at risk for chronic inflammation by allowing your muscles to remain persistently inactive.

Your muscles make up a third of your body weight. Moving them vigorously causes them to release myokines, which are messenger proteins that serve as potent anti-inflammatories. When you move them vigorously, your muscles can act like glands, synthesizing and releasing myokines, which are substances that support your metabolism, circulation, and bones and control inflammation. In other words, exercising—moving your muscles vigorously—dampens down chronic inflammation. And as you learned in Chapter 4, chronic inflammation is one of the most often causes of depression. Since exercise is an anti-inflammatory behavior, it is an antidepressant. Yet there is more to its powerful effects. Read on.

Imagine an old-fashioned hand pump we used before we had faucets. Now think about the act of a brisk walk: your calves act like pumps to help prevent blood from building up in your legs. Sitting for extended periods of time tends to allow blood to accumulate, potentially causing inflammatory swelling and clots in your veins. Brisk walking pumps the blood back into circulation.

In fact, the word *exercise* was adapted from the Latin verb "exerceo," meaning to work, practice, or train. It is only in recent history that the word has come to mean a physical activity that we do to stay healthy.

Exercise promotes a healthy immune system. In fact, vigorous exercise enhances the effectiveness of natural killer cells, which are your weapons that find and destroy cancerous cells. In fact, moderate to vigorous exercise has been shown to lower the risk of a variety of cancers such as colon and breast cancer.

Build Back Stronger

Vigorous exercise can make your muscles tired, and that is good for them. Over the short term the strain may feel uncomfortable, but over the long term they not only get stronger but also boost your metabolism. Some people complain that exercise makes them tired;

I respond by saying that's a good thing. In fact, you should want to get tired when you exercise because then you know you're gaining from it. You're pushing your body beyond its comfort level to strengthen it.

Regular exercise builds back the muscles that you exert, and your muscles get stronger with exercise. Exercise promotes a stress-and-recovery process that strengthens the body and the brain. The build back stronger goes beyond what biologists call homeostasis (returning to a normal baseline). Instead, vigorous exercise and the build back stronger process provide allostasis (the anticipation and preparation of future exercise). Consider how building back stronger happens when you use dumbbells. As you add more weight and work out each day, you will build strength, bone density, and stronger muscles.

Build Back Stronger Cells

At the cellular level, this stress-and-recovery process occurs by:

- Oxidation
- Metabolism
- Excitation

Oxidative stress occurs in the cells during the conversion of glucose into energy that enables the cells to burn fuel. Waste by-products are produced when glucose is absorbed into the cells. As I described in Chapter 2, mitos (the energy factories of your cells) turn the glucose into *adenosine triphosphate* (ATP), the principal type of fuel that a cell can burn. This conversion process produces mild levels of useful free radicals. In addition, the cell produces protective enzymes as internal antioxidants that mop up the waste products.

Metabolic stress occurs when the cells can't produce enough ATP. It's as if they run out of gas. This happens because glucose can't get into the cell or because there is not enough glucose. Finally, *excitotoxic stress* (a condition destructive to neurons) occurs when there is not enough ATP to keep up with the increased energy demands of excessive glutamate activity.

Exercise promotes repair mechanisms that deal with the different types of stress. These repair mechanisms promote recovery and strengthen the entire body, including the brain. Exercise also raises the stress threshold of cells. This stress-and-recovery process goes beyond strengthening to actually rebuilding on multiple levels. For example, vigorous exercise rebuilds muscles in a rip-and-rebuild process. The short-term microdamage to muscles triggers brief inflammation, swelling, and soreness. This stimulates growth because the microdamage stimulates muscle cells to turn on a cascade of genes that make proteins to increase the number and thickness of muscle fibers.

One of the wear-and-tear processes that generally occurs to your body as we age is the result of reaction oxygen species (ROS), commonly known as free radicals. As I described in Chapter 2, these free radicals, when excessive, can cause damage to your cells, tissues, and organs. When you breathe, the oxygen is combined with glucose and used as fuel to produce biological energy (ATP) to power all your cells. It can be a messy process, especially if your diet is poor and you do not exercise.

Here is how it happens: When your mitos produce energy (ATP), unpaired electrons (free radicals) can leak, stealing electrons from other molecules. This oxidation burns and destroys molecules and cells. Think of how oxidation causes metal to rust or an apple to turn brown after it's been cut and left on the counter too long. When free radical levels are high, the damage to your cells, your cell's DNA, and the mitos themselves can result in low energy, illness, and accelerated aging. Since your brain is one of the high-energy consumers in your body, free radical damage to your brain cells can cause thinking problems at best and dementia at worse. To keep your energy levels high and your free radical levels low, you need a healthy diet, and you also need to use the energy (ATP) your mitos produce. This is a use-it-or-lose-it process. If you don't exercise, your mitos will generate less energy. And worse yet, like a dam with leaks, your dying mitos spew out free radicals.

In his book *Exercised*, Daniel Lieberman describes how after vigorous exercise your resting metabolism (RMR) tends to remain elevated for hours. This is sometimes called *afterburn*. For example, I write these few pages the day after a vigorous day of skiing, which I can feel as a burning sensation in my upper thigh muscles. Mild stress mechanisms including cortisol increased because we were challenged with some very steep mogul runs through the trees. My friends are expert skiers, and I am but an imposter or fool to follow them. My heart rate sped up to mobilize my energy reserves, and they quickly consumed calories as they pumped out waste. Compounds that had compromised my cell's functions such as weak mitochondria leaked out free radicals, which killed them off, making room for new healthy ones to develop. Today, my muscles are still slightly sore, but my rest-and-mend system has slowed my heart rate, lowered my cortisol, unleashed an anti-inflammatory response, repaired DNA mutations, and damaged proteins. Exercise elevates messenger RNA and recycles new mitos to build up muscles. All this gave my brain the boost it needed for a day of writing about, well, the brain. This afterburn is healthy as long as I avoid becoming sedentary and overconsuming unhealthy foods during the rebuilding process.

During vigorous exercise we reach a limit to how much energy we can obtain from oxygen. For example, when I hike the trails near my house, I use more oxygen the faster I go until I reach my maximal oxygen uptake, or VO2. That's when I begin to pant, and my muscles begin to burn. I need glycolysis when I reach my VO2 to supply additional fuel to my muscles.

Glycolysis

Glycolysis is the breaking down of glucose. The term comes from *glycol*, meaning "sugar," and *lysis*, which means "breaking down." During glycolysis, enzymes snip sugar molecules in half, which liberates the energy from those bonds to charge to ATPs. Recharging ATPs from glucose can happen without oxygen which can only supply short-term energy beyond the small supply of stored ATP.

During exercise, the leftover halves of each sugar molecule, known as pyruvate, tend to accumulate faster than cells can handle. When pyruvate builds up to intolerable levels, enzymes convert the pyruvate into lactate along with a hydrogen ion. The lactate is eventually used to recharge ATPs. But the hydrogen ions make muscles increasingly acidic, making them painful and burn. Aerobic metabolism makes up to 18 times more ATP than glycolysis and can last a whole lot longer. However, it takes more time to generate stored ATP and glycolysis for immediate action.

If you were a couch potato and weighed 180 pounds, it would take 1700 calories to keep you alive. Your resting metabolism (RMR) is a measure of your metabolism to keep all your organs, such as your brain, functioning while you do nothing but "rest." From your RMR, add in the energy you need to do anything beyond keeping your organs functioning, like walking out to your car, going shopping, or washing the dishes. The total daily energy expenditure (DEE) represents the calories you need for all those activities plus keeping your organs functioning. On average if you weigh 180 pounds and use another 500 for those activities, you would use 2200 calories per day. This means that more than half of your calories are used just to keep you alive and your brain functioning.

Your PAL

Scientists have developed a way to measure our energy expenditure with a metric called the physical activity level, or simply PAL. You can calculate your PAL by the ratio of how much energy you use in 24 hours and divide it by the amount of energy you would use if you did nothing. If you are a couch potato, your PAL would be around 1.4. If you exercise once a day for 1 hour, your PAL would be in the range of 1.7 to 2.0. Though there is some variation for hunter-gatherers, the average for men is 1.9 and 1.8 for women. This means that if you can get about 1 hour a day of exercise, you are getting close to the norm of our ancestors.

Exercise provides an immediate relief for the physical and emotional symptoms associated with stress. Exercise relaxes the resting tension of muscle spindles, and this breaks the stress-feedback loop to the brain. By breaking up this stress-feedback loop, you cue your brain that your body isn't stressed anymore, so it must be okay to relax.

Brain Building

Just as no exercise can lead to the atrophy of your muscles and feeling weak, so does the lack of productive behavior lead to losing the brain circuits that help you to feel like doing things that make you feel better.

You have neurotropic molecules that help protect and grow neurons in your brain. The one that has received the most attention is called brain-derived neurotropic factor (BDNF). As I explained in Chapter 1, it helps facilitate neuroplasticity and neurogenesis. This magic is organic fertilizer for your brain. It represents one of the best ways to jump-start neuroplasticity and neurogenesis. However, it is not available without some effort. While aerobic exercise facilitates its release, being a couch potato, eating junk food, and growing excessive fat cells block its release.

Vigorous and long-duration exercise has been associated with the release of BDNF, which promotes neurogenesis in the hippocampus. In fact, people with Alzheimer's disease who exercise can slow down the progression of their symptoms. This is because the area of the brain that undergoes neurogenesis is the hippocampus, the very area that is significantly impaired in Alzheimer's disease. Exercise-induced BDNF release is thought to help astrocytes take care of other brain cells and their connections. Astrocyte damage has been identified as one of the contributors to Alzheimer's disease.

Exercise was once thought to benefit health simply because it helped circulation and the heart. The term cardio refers to boosting your cardiovascular system. When you engage in aerobic exercise, more oxygen and blood are delivered quickly throughout your body. Exercise pumps more oxygen through the brain, which increases the health of the small blood vessels called capillaries. This means that your heart and blood vessels get stronger and more elastic. They do so with the aid of a substance called vascular endothelial growth factor (VEGF) that helps your blood vessels expand and maintain flexibility.

Getting fuel to the cells is critical, and exercise is a method by which to construct and enhance the blood vessels. VEGF comes to the rescue by building more capillaries in the body and the brain. VEGF increases the permeability of the blood–brain barrier, which allows substances vital to neurogenesis into the brain during exercise. Consider how this benefits not only your body but also your brain. In addition to the importance of your arteries feeding the brain with nutrients, you have tiny blood vessels called capillaries doing the same all over your brain. If they get stiff and rigid, they may pop, leaking out blood and killing cells in the area. VEGF keeps them flexible and provides nutrients.

Meanwhile, you need to keep your blood vessels from clotting. Exercise raises good cholesterol (HDL) and lowers bad cholesterol (LDL) as well as not allowing fats called triglycerides to build up. In other words, by exercising you keep your plumbing system in your brain less prone to clotting, which minimizes the risk of stroke and aneurysm.

Without exercise, you run the risk of development of metabolic syndrome and type 2 diabetes. Here's how it happens: Stress causes your hypothalamic pituitary axis to secrete cortisol, which shunts sugars and fats that accumulate in your body out into your blood stream. Large amounts of insulin flood your body to deal with the flood of glucose. Your insulin receptors grow dull because they cannot deal with the onslaught. This makes you crave sugar and fat-rich food. In addition, you store extra fat cells. All of this promotes obesity, type 2 diabetes, and chronic inflammation.

Exercise is an essential way to minimize the risk of cardiovascular and metabolic dysregulation. One mechanism that helps is insulin-like growth factor (IGF-1), a hormone released by your muscles when there is a need for fueling the cells during a physical activity. As the name implies, it increases the growth of receptors for insulin.

Since glucose is the major energy source in the brain, IGF-1 works with insulin to deliver it to the brain cells to make energy (ATP) and manage glucose levels to minimize the risk of developing diabetes. It teams up with BDNF, which increases in the brain during exercise, and together they activate neurons to produce more serotonin and glutamate. Although chronic stress increases cortisol and lowers IGF-1, exercise reverses that tendency.

Gene Expression and Exercise

Exercise has also been shown to stimulate several genetic processes that enhance the health, longevity, and immunological functions of the brain. Exercise-stimulated transcription—the genetic process of constructing RNA from DNA—aids neuroplasticity, including the stimulation of BDNF, which enhances memory and promotes neurogenesis in the hippocampus.

Fibroblast growth factor 2 (FGF-2) is critical for neurogenesis and has been associated with the reduction of anxiety and depression. Exercise induces FGF-2 and its mRNA in the hippocampus. FGF-2 is a potent regulator of cell growth and differentiation and is critically important in normal development, tissue maintenance, wound repair, and angiogenesis in somatic stem cells. It helps tissues to grow in the body, and while it is in the brain it aids in neuroplasticity.

When blood circulation increases during exercise, the BDNF that gathers in reserve pools near the synapses is unleashed. During exercise, IGF-1, VEGF, and FGF-2 push through the blood–brain barrier, through the web of capillaries, through the tightly packed cells that screen out intruders such as bacteria. These three hormones work with BDNF to increase the molecular processes that sharpen cognition and memory.

Exercise, especially if it takes place in a new and stimulating environment, is an effective way to promote neurogenesis. Learning is critical because the development of new neurons takes place in the section of the hippocampus that is involved in new learning and memory. Thus, physical exercise and learning work together to stimulate neurogenesis. Exercise makes new stem cells, and learning prolongs their survival. Exercise can help your brain networks facilitate learning, but the benefit occurs after—not during—exercise. This is because during high-intensity exercise, the blood is directed away from the PFC to enable the body to deal with the physical challenge. Because the PFC is the brain's brain—the center of executive functions—it is necessary for learning. After you finish exercising, the blood shifts back to your PFC, and with it you get an increased capacity for focus.

Stem cells can divide into neurons or glial cells through a process enhanced by exercise. However, exercise alone won't sustain the new neurons. Exercise plus an enriched environment will allow you to keep the new neurons. In other words, you need mental exercise in addition to the physical exercise to maintain the new neurons. As long as you aren't overeating, aerobic exercise can help you burn visceral fat (organ fat) as well as use sugars and lower inflammation. Meanwhile, your body boosts energy by biogenesis (the building of new energy factories—your mitos). And it builds new brain cells through the release of BDNF. You can't take a pill for all of this!

Stress, Anxiety, and Depression Relief

A "runner's high" is based on the idea that when you exercise vigorously you get a shot of brain chemicals that make you feel euphoric, along with a cornucopia of neurotransmitters, neurohormones, and neuromodulators that are elevated after a dose of exercise.

One of the first brain chemicals to be identified and later to gain a big reputation are *endorphins*. These endogenous opioids are nature's way of helping you cushion pain and discomfort from the strain of your muscles after the intense exertion. Another player in this chemical cocktail was not on the radar screen until recently. Endocannabinoids are molecules that your muscles use to communicate with other tissues and organs. Their effects—enhanced by exercise—on health and performance include increased glucose uptake, improved insulin action, and mitochondrial biogenesis. They play a major role in this euphoric afterglow from intense exercise.

Brisk walking is one of the easiest ways to get your dose of exercise. It can be done anywhere and anytime. When you're stressed and feeling anxious take a quick dose of exercise to calm yourself down.

One way to decrease stress levels is to exercise in the late afternoon, when stress chemistry may be abnormally high and when there normally should be a natural lowering of stress neurochemistry. This timing of your exercise will help your sleep because low levels of stress chemistry promote sleep later in the night, as I will describe in Chapter 9. Also, elevated cortisol, especially in the evening, contributes to insomnia. To lower cortisol and improve sleep try late afternoon or early evening exercise.

A study of 1.2 million people showed that regular exercise lowered the incidence of mental health problems from 12 to 23% compared with sedentary people. Multiple studies have shown that exercise is effective in treating depression and generalized anxiety. Exercise is the best antidepressant, and there are good side effects, not bad side effects!

Aerobic exercise can have an anti-anxiety effect. The physiological changes that occur by exercising can overpower the negative effects of the physiological contributors to anxiety. For example, in one study, the subjects were injected with CCK-4, a chemical that can induce a panic attack even in healthy adults with no history of panic. Thirty minutes of aerobic exercise prior to the injection of CCK-4 lowered the panic scores, whereas resting before the injection did not.

Exercise promotes lower blood pressure by increasing the efficiency of the cardiovascular system. As your heart rate increases, your heart produces a hormone called *atrial natriuretic peptide* (ANP). It tempers your body's stress response by putting the brakes on the HPA axis stress response. ANP does this by going through the blood–brain barrier and attaching to receptors in the hypothalamus to tone down the HPA axis activity. Meanwhile, other areas of your brain, including the amygdala, produce ANP. ANP works against the corticotropin-releasing hormone (CRH), which is part of the chain of neurochemical processes that induce the stress response and eventually result in the release of cortisol by your adrenal glands. In this way, ANP eliminates one of the main contributors to anxiety. It also stems the flow of epinephrine (adrenaline) and lowers the heart rate, defusing another trigger for anxiety. All this ANP activity helps you feel calmer.

Exercise and Stress Reduction

Exercise also contributes to stress reduction by:

- Providing a distraction
- Reducing muscle tension
- Building brain resources (neuroplasticity and neurogenesis)
- Increasing GABA and serotonin
- Improving resilience and self-mastery
- Mobilizing motivation to engage in productive behavior

Exercise should be part of the overall strategy of preventing and treating general anxiety and PTSD. Exercise increases the levels of neurotransmitters that promote anti-anxiety and antidepressant effects. One of the ways it does this is by increasing the neurotransmitters GABA and serotonin. Simply moving your body triggers the release of GABA, your brain's primary inhibitory neurotransmitter. So-called anti-anxiety medications like the benzodiazepines target GABA receptors to calm you down, but those medications have terrible side effects, including depression, and they are very addictive. Once you remove the medication, the anxiety symptoms return—and at an increased level. In fact, they increase anxiety sensitivity.

Exercise is as or more effective than many pharmacological treatments for depression. Many psychiatric medications target one neurotransmitter system, such as serotonin, norepinephrine, or dopamine. But exercise upregulates a wide range of neurotransmitters such as serotonin, dopamine, norepinephrine, the cannabinoids, GABA, and glutamate.

Serotonin is one of the many neurotransmitters that have been associated with depression and anxiety when it is at a low level. Extremely elevated levels of serotonin are associated with ecstasy and more moderate levels with others. Serotonin has received a lot of attention in the last several decades because of a class of anti-depressants called selective serotonin reuptake inhibitors (SSRIs). An increase in serotonin occurs when your body breaks down fatty acids to fuel your muscles. These fatty acids compete with the amino acid L-tryptophan (the precursor to serotonin) for a place on the transport proteins that increase fatty-acid concentration in the bloodstream. Once L-tryptophan pushes through the blood–brain barrier, it is synthesized into serotonin. Serotonin also gets a boost from BDNF, which increases with exercise. So give it a kickstart by exercising even when you don't feel like it.

Dopamine is one of the neurotransmitters that becomes more active with exercise. As is a major part of your reward system, dopamine is released from the ventral tegmental area (VTA) of your brain into the nucleus accumbens—the pleasure center of your brain. When this happens, you will be motivated to do whatever you did to get that effect again. By the way, this reward circuit can get hijacked with addictions. Why not harness the dopamine circuit for something that is good for you? However, if you are obese or have not been exercising regularly, you probably have fewer dopamine receptors than people who do exercise. This means that you need to try a little harder initially to get your dopamine network up and run-ning again. Exercise rehabilitates these neurotransmitter systems so that you can benefit by their antidepressant and anti-anxiety effects.

Get Moving

Getting started always sounds good in theory but when it actually comes down to doing it, you may procrastinate. We sometimes engage in regular exercise only when it's convenient.

Even just *thinking* about exercise activates some of the same neuronal systems in your brain. Mental practice not only creates changes in the brain but also improves physical performance. The same parts of the brain are activated during mental practice and actual physical practice. This finding led researchers to see if mental practicing improved physical performance down the line. They found that 5 days of mental practice followed by 2 hours of physical practice improved performance as well as 5 days of physical practice did!

These findings support the long-held belief in sports psychology that visualizing and mentally rehearsing one's performance can improve performance on the playing field. This is true regardless of the sport. Although you may find that the faster you can imagine doing something, the faster you can actually do it, there are limitations to what is possible. This is because your mind and brain are two aspects of the same process. For example, if you are right-handed, you'll be better at both imagining moving and actually moving your right hand than at imagining and moving your left hand. This constraint occurs even if you have had a stroke and one side of your body is weaker. The unaffected side is as quick in imagining moving as in moving. This is because you are using the same brain systems.

The benefit of exercise on learning has garnered the attention of some state education departments. The California Department of Education has shown that students with higher fitness scores also have higher test scores, and it has also shown an overall positive influence on memory, concentration, and behavior in the classroom.

Most health care organizations recommend that their patients exercise on a regular basis. Do at least 150 minutes of moderate exercise or 75 minutes of vigorous aerobic exercise a week, and supplement that with two sessions of weight training. In case you are not clear on how to determine what type you are getting, moderately intense exercise is defined as 50–70% of your heart rate and vigorously intense exercise is 70–80% of your maximum heart rate. Based on these recommendations, epidemiologists have calculated that this level of exercise will reduce your risk of premature death by 50% and lower your chances of heart disease, Alzheimer's disease, and various cancers by 30–50%. Now that is pretty outstanding medicine!

The important thing is to get started and make it part of your daily routine. Give yourself at least a minimal dose, and then build on that. For example, to get to my mailbox I must walk a mile and a half (round-trip) and a 400-foot elevation change. I build on that minimal dose of exercise with 160 pushups, core exercises, and dumbbells, and then hike up the trail on the ridge where I live.

Take advantage of wherever you live. When I lived in San Francisco, I took advantage of the many hills. Sure, it is a city, but there are sidewalks. Now I record my distance, which is measured with my iWatch. If I lie about anything, I am only lying to myself.

7

The Education Factor

Sylvia was a 55-year-old mother of three who came to see me with complaints that her employer was asking her and colleagues to receive additional education to learn a new computer software program. She insisted that she was "too tired" to learn anything new. Then she looked at me horrified and said, "I just saw a TV show on Alzheimer's. Maybe I've come down with it?"

Sylvia was indeed quite busy, but she didn't have Alzheimer's. She was holding a job as a bookkeeper for a furniture wholesaler, which she described as stressful. During the first 15 minutes that she was sitting in my office, she received two text messages from her daughters. Despite the fact that we were meeting for the first time, she felt compelled to read the messages and text back. Each time, she turned to me afterward and asked, "Now, what were we talking about?"

Sylvia told me that she barely had time in the morning to make coffee before her daughters needed something from her and she had to get them out the door to school. I asked her if she had time for breakfast. She laughed and responded, "You're kidding, right?"

As she described the rest of her day, it quickly became evident that her typical day was disorganized. She told me that she had recently lost a few accounts for new orders with furniture stores because of her failure to learn the new computer system. Her supervisor put her on probation after the last time. That's what prompted her to come in to see me.

Early in her life, Sylvia was a very attentive and focused student who earned good grades. Now, like many other people she had a tendency to veg out by getting lost in social media. So that's where our work began. We began to structure Sylvia's day so that she was present with whatever she was doing at any given time. She relegated text messaging and looking at social media to a specific time of the day. She learned to *focus* attention on each task until it was completed. With enhanced effort to attend to the present moment, her working memory began to function better so that she could code information into her long-term memory.

Sylvia had to get over the simplistic notion that her learning capacity was something to be either lost or found. Education requires a range of skills that she left dormant. Like muscles that atrophied from lack of use, her brain was not challenged and there was little new wiring. She complained that it was too late in her life to learn anything new and that she had already had all the education she needed. I told her that education is ongoing, without which the connections in her brain wither and the old knowledge becomes less useful. Our plan entailed utilizing all the SEEDS factors together. She could not learn anything new without a healthy diet, sleep, and regular exercise.

As soon as her diet had improved and she had made a concerted *effort* to structure her day so that she was better able to focus on one task to completion, her stress level dropped. Sylvia said, "I'm not on edge all the time. It feels strange!" She was not yet gaining confidence in herself. She needed to learn to challenge herself. "It's like I'm slowly getting my brain back again," she said during one of our sessions. Sylvia described how she wasn't intimidated by the computer classes. It seemed easier and at times even *effortless* to remember things.

However, just as Sylvia began to look forward to learning more, one of her daughters made the varsity basketball team. She had the desire to attend not only the games but also the practices when she wasn't working, which abruptly halted her progress. She reverted to her old habits, saying, "I've learned enough in my life." When I reminded her that she could better support her daughters if she got back to the training program.

"Of course you could go to the games," I said.

She nodded knowingly and resumed where we left off. To develop durable educational skills, she had to be *determined* to stick to her effort, even when there were distractions.

As Sylvia learned to organize her time, she noticed that her long-term memory for new knowledge improved. These educational skills were used to develop memories based on associations. She learned to organize what she wanted to remember by linking each item, image, or piece of information into a coherent series of associations. Once she learned that her brain worked best to construct memories based on associations, she was more willing to make the effort to form the associations.

I taught her a series of mnemonic tricks to form associations. These became fun games, about which she said, "Who would ever have thought I'd be rewiring my brain by playing memory games?"

Cognitive Reserve

In the world of neuropsychology, we have described the benefits of building up cognitive reserve. This means that with ongoing education you build up more synaptic connections in your brain that act as a reserve in case you suffer from brain impairment. Also, as you age, your brain stays youthful longer. Many studies have shown that lifelong learners age slower. It is not only because they are more adaptive and resilient but also because they rely on many brain networks as backup so that they can continue to rewire their brain. Cognitive reserve represents structural changes to the brain, which will promote greater longevity.

The power of education to boost cognitive reserve and delay dementia was well illustrated by a study known as the Nuns' Study. Researchers at the University of Kentucky's Sanders-Brown Center on Aging performed autopsies on deceased elderly nuns. The most highly educated nuns had more branches and connections between their neurons. They also seemed to have suffered the least from the symptoms of dementia.

People with more education can sustain greater neuronal damage than people with less education and still not show the symptoms of that damage. For example, one study showed that approximately 25% of older individuals showed no symptoms of Alzheimer's disease when they were alive, but their autopsies found that they had Alzheimer's-related brain pathology. Thus, despite the fact that their brains showed the classic Alzheimer's plaques and tangles, they functioned as well as those whose brains did not have Alzheimer's plaques and tangles.

One measure of neuroplasticity during aging is how you process information. As you age, your brain shifts to emphasizing different processing areas. Researchers from the University of Toronto have shown that people between the ages of 14 and 30 tend to emphasize the temporal lobes (on both sides of the brain) when performing cognitive activities. The more educated the person is, the more they use this lobe. A different pattern is evident in people over 65. When they are given the same cognitive tasks as younger adults, they tend to emphasize the frontal lobes. The more education they had, the more they used the frontal lobes.

Memory—The Basis of Learning

Perhaps you're like Sylvia and the 90% of people who would like to improve their memory. A national survey found that 9 of 10 people complain that they have faulty memories. A majority of the people who were surveyed reported that they have gone into a room to fetch something and forgotten what it was by the time they arrived. Could most of us be experiencing declining memories?

As Sylvia discovered, memory is not a thing to be lost or found. Memory skills can be cultivated or left to atrophy. In today's society, social media, instant messaging, and mass media bombardment combine to erode our attention and our memory skills. To improve your memory skills, you have to resist having your attention fragmented. You can still use your smartphone at select times, but not constantly, and you'll have to be present, focused, and organized.

There's a lot you can do to improve your memory, but there are also limitations. The following are some ways to improve your memory:

- Improve your attention skills.
- Learn how to use the different types of memory.
- Use associations such as mnemonic tricks.

The following are some of the limitations:

- You cannot pay attention to several things at once and remember everything with great accuracy. This is why you can forget to look for the correct road signs while you're driving if you're talking on your cell phone at the same time. Fortunately, many US states and other countries are making it illegal to use a cell phone while driving.
- Don't expect to improve your memory without effort. Memory is not something you have or don't have. It must be exercised to be enhanced.
- Don't assume that you will remember everything you've ever experienced. Memories are not frozen in time like indelible snapshots. They are constantly revised as you recall them, or they fade away if they are not used again.

Attention and Working Memory

Attention also serves as the gateway to memory. Attention is critical for redirecting the energy in your brain and promoting neuroplasticity. You might forget all the details of what a friend told you during a conversation at dinner if you were only half listening to what they said. But if you place emotional importance on the next conversation you have with them, you will listen more attentively and remember it later.

Your PFC directs attention and tells the rest of your brain what is important and what to learn. Neuroplasticity and memory require that you open this gateway. As a key part of the PFC, the dorsolateral prefrontal cortex (dlPFC), which you met in Chapter 1, is responsible for maintaining working memory. Your working memory is called *working* because the short-term memories it holds relates to what you are working on in the moment. Throughout the day you go from one experience to another, using your working memory to focus on the completion of each task or experience. You hold on to these experiences for up to 30 seconds as you weave a sense of continuity from one experience to the next. For instance, while reading a page in a book, are you able to hold in mind the information from the first paragraph when you reach the next paragraph so that you can build knowledge?

If something draws your attention that you want to remember, the neurotransmitters dopamine and norepinephrine help heighten your attention; they say, "Remember this information." The feedback between your dlPFC and your hippocampus encodes information from working memory into long-term memory. Working memory is the route to long-term memory. If working memory is impaired, long-term memory will experience a dearth of new information. If the road to long-term memory through working memory is blocked, new information can't get through.

Working memory can be disrupted in a number of ways. Since attention and concentration are so closely tied to working memory, any distraction, such as getting a text message, can hamper working memory. If you're distracted by an e-mail about a colleague abruptly leaving the company for a new job, you will probably forget what you were holding in your working memory because your attention shifted to that other provocative piece of information.

The initial demands of a good memory are as follows:

- Attention is the key. The door is locked without it. You must be engaged to remember.
- The more relevant a piece of information is to your life, the stronger the memory will be in long-term storage.
- Emotional engagement strengths memory.

When I use psychological tests that measure working memory, I measure someone's ability to pay attention. If I give a person psychological tests that measure various other types of memory and find that they are deficient, I must try to rule out working memory as the cause. The bottom line is that if you don't pay attention, you won't be able to move a short-term memory into long-term memory.

Education requires layers of memory. It is helpful to understand all the different types of memory so that you can put them to use by skillfully weaving them together to learn. Cultivating memory skills and education are two sides of the same coin. Forming memories requires neuroplasticity change in your brain. The benefits of education are the result of forming and strengthening synaptic connections.

The Types of Long-Term Memory

There is a limit to how long you can hold in mind information in your working memory, but your long-term memory is not bound by a time limit because long-term memories are stored throughout the brain. If you are 95 years old, you still may remember how you played with your family dog, but you may forget the name of your friend's dog if they introduced several other topics right after telling you.

Long-term memory is an archive that can be and often is modified. This is because you are always encountering new information that may change your perspective. When you recall the memory and add in the new information, the memory is reconsolidated. This is partly what happens in psychotherapy.

If you recall something about your past such as events, details about who was there and why, images of how people looked, or content of what people said, it's called *declarative memory*. This is because you declare it into consciousness. Declarative memory, sometimes called explicit memory recall, has many forms. Your recall of explicit language-based information is called *semantic memory*. Overlapping memories about your past events are referred to as *episodic memory*. These types of explicit memory are distinguishable as follows: If you remember getting a badly scraped knee, that's episodic memory. If you remember the facts about an injured knee, then describe it with words, such as scraped and infected, that's semantic memory.

Habitual styles of moving, such as riding a bicycle or writing your name, are called *procedural memory*. Some people call this muscle memory. Generally, you can think of this type of memory as movement habits, such remembering how to ride a bicycle or type at your computer keypad.

You possess two broad memory systems: *explicit* and *implicit*. This distinction is important for your understanding of how to cultivate your memory skills. Explicit memory involves facts that you declare into conscious awareness. Implicit memory involves procedural skills and emotional memory that are generally nonconscious. They are remembered implicitly and play out in your behavior without declaring them, such as habits. The components of the two kinds of memory are shown in Table 7.1.

Some implicit memories, such as emotional memories, are acquired rapidly, such as being traumatized by assault, whereas others can be formed over an extended period of time such as through adaptability to a particular family expression. Still others are formed when particular events occur such as when you are listening to a song. Later when you hear that song you might feel the same emotions. Procedural memories, such as the learned ability to play the cello, are acquired only with painstaking repetition.

The fact that you are able to read this book automatically and relatively effortlessly (unless you're distracted) indicates that you have procedural memory. Because of procedural memory, you could even read a page without any of the content entering your consciousness. In other words, you "read" the page without remembering what you read.

Table 7.1   Components of Explicit and Implicit Memory

Explicit Memory (Declarative)	Implicit Memory (Nondeclarative)
• Semantic	• Procedural
• Episodic	• Emotional

This is a result of procedural memory, which you acquired for reading when you first struggled with understanding letters and words.

Procedural memory contrasts with various types of explicit memory in some important respects. It allows you to recall how to repeat specific skills and habits such as reading, typing, and riding a bicycle. In procedural learning, you remember *how to do* things without thinking about it. With enough practice, procedural memory allows you to perform different actions or processes automatically and unconsciously.

The Almond and the Seahorse

Deep within your temporal lobes are two structures that are involved in memory. The major explicit memory structure is called the *hippocampus*, the Greek word that was Latinized for "seahorse" because of its shape. Researchers have discovered the birth of new neurons, or *neurogenesis*, in the hippocampus. As I noted in Chapter 1, it was previously believed that neurogenesis was not possible. The discovery of the birth of new neurons in this part of the brain that lays down new memories highlights the importance of cultivating your memory skills to rewire your brain.

A structure in your brain involved in implicit memory is called the *amygdala*, named after the Latin word for "almond," *amygdalon*, because of its shape. The amygdala is a relevance detector. It can be triggered by intense states of threats, and it assigns emotional intensity to the incoming information or by a quick glance from a very attractive person or by your boss glaring at you. It does not tolerate ambiguity. See Figure 7.1 for an image of the amygdala and hippocampus, deep within the temporal lobes.

(continued)

(continued)

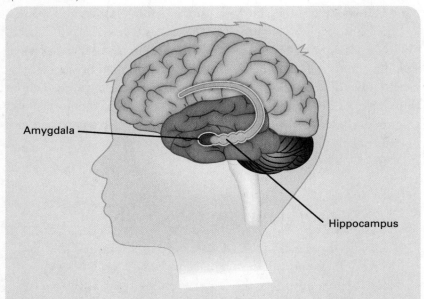

Figure 7.1   The amygdala and hippocampus

The hippocampus and the amygdala are involved in explicit and implicit memory, respectively. You use your explicit memory when you try to remember what you read last night, when your next dental appointment is, or the name of a familiar-looking flag outside a building. These are facts, dates, words: pieces of information. It is this type of memory that people often complain they are losing.

Your hippocampus is responsible for encoding explicit memories. If it were destroyed, you would literally not remember yesterday. That might sound good if yesterday was distressing. With no memory of the past your life would be a disaster. Not only would you make the same mistakes over again, but you would not be able to make decisions about the future. You need to understand the mistakes of the past to plan for success in the future.

The Man Who Lost His Explicit Memory

Henry Molaise was one of the most famous patients in the history of neurology and neuropsychology. His condition taught us a lot about the hippocampus and explicit memory. Henry lost the ability to consolidate new explicit memories after he had brain surgery as a young adult. At age 7 years, he had a bicycle accident that resulted in a traumatic brain injury and medically intractable seizures. A neurosurgeon removed Henry's right and left hippocampus in 1954 to try to control the seizures, before the role of the hippocampus was well understood. After this surgery, Henry could not remember events from earlier in the day. If he was introduced to a person with whom he chatted amiably and the visitor then left the room for a few minutes and came back, Henry would not remember having ever seen the person before.

Henry did, however, remain capable of remembering events from before surgery and forming procedural memories. For instance, he could be taught a certain movement and when asked to make that movement again later, could do so with greater facility than when he first learned it, but he would have no recollection of having ever performed the task before. In other words, though he lost the capacity for explicit memory, he retained the capacity for implicit memory.

Through many evaluations of Henry, neuropsychologist Dr. Brenda Milner discovered that the hippocampus is centrally involved in laying down and retrieving explicit memories of past experiences. The hippocampus is necessary for consolidating an explicit memory about a situation that arises in your current life.

The health of the hippocampus plays a central role in aging. Without good health later in life there is a gradual atrophy of the hippocampus. In worst-case scenarios, many Alzheimer's patients lose declarative memory while, like Henry, retaining parts of their procedural memory. They continue to perform procedural memories out of habit while having an increased difficulty remembering recent facts about their lives.

A variety of illnesses and poor lifestyle habits can impair your hippocampus. Chronic inflammation caused by obesity, alcohol abuse, and chronic stress have all been shown to be associated with hippocampal shrinkage.

Emotional Learning

Emotionally significant events are more likely to be remembered in the long run because they are not only more personally meaningful but also associated with higher levels of arousal. Emotional events stir a physiological reaction, including an increase in the level of blood glucose, which promotes the process of memory consolidation. Emotional events resonate in your mind, creating neuroplastic change and enhancing memory consolidation. If you want to remember something, become emotionally involved in it.

Fast and Slow Tracks

The emotional memory's neural networks can often be associated with the experience of threat detection. As I noted earlier, classically conditioned threat responses to auditory and visual stimuli are fast and mediated by the subcortical pathways that connect the thalamus (the central router of the brain) to the amygdala. As researcher Joseph LeDoux of New York University noted, "This circuit bypasses the cortex and thus constitutes a subcortical mechanism of emotional learning." LeDoux pointed out that the experience of fear is constructed by higher parts of the brain (the cortex). The slow track interprets it as dangerous and based on the context of the situation. You do that with thought, not emotion alone.

Despite the importance of the amygdala in emotional learning, it appears to play a less significant role in most declarative memory processes. The cortex, in contrast, is unnecessary for the acquisition of conditioned threat detection, but it is essential for the extinction of conditioned threat. In other words, fear can be conditioned without your awareness but cannot be eliminated without it. The cortex is also critically important in taming the amygdala to conquer fear and anxiety.

The amygdala helps you by stirring enough fear in you to make you pull off the road, but it also made you oversensitive to rainstorms. The problem is that this threat detection system is activated even when you don't need to be fearful. In other words, sometimes it is turned on when it would be better to have it turned off. Chapter 4 described how you can tame your amygdala so that it doesn't become overactivated when you need to stay calm.

The power of emotional conditioning varies based on your state at the time. If your norepinephrine level is high, as is the case in anxiety-provoking situations, conditioning occurs more rapidly and also lasts longer.

You typically have few explicit memories of the first 3–5 years of your life. Sigmund Freud inaccurately referred to this phenomenon as *infantile amnesia*. He assumed that early memories are repressed into unconsciousness. However, you haven't forgotten memories; rather, these implicit memories are not conscious, and they are emotional reactions to situations that trigger them. The implicit memory system develops before the capacity to encode explicit memories.

Your amygdala activates generalized responses to your environment. You need your hippocampus to provide contextual information about the situation to determine if there really is any danger present. Your amygdala mobilizes your entire brain–body system through its interactions with the sympathetic branch of your autonomic nervous system (fight-or-flight response) and the hypothalamic pituitary adrenal axis (HPA axis). You can store episodic memories even when emotional arousal is not a component of an incident. When you are once again in that emotional state, you are more likely to remember explicit material that is congruent with that state. In other words, if you want to remember explicit facts, get yourself into the implicit emotional state that you were in when you originally learned these facts.

Implicit memory is the basis for your emotional predispositions. For example, as I explained in Chapter 3, if you tend to withdraw when dealing with social stress, it is likely to remain a bad habit unless you work hard to make changes. In situations in which fear conditioning and procedural learning can occur simultaneously, you may have acquired emotional habits and conditioned physical responses to dangerous situations as a child that were outside your awareness. For example, if someone in your family tended to use a particular angry tone of voice, later in life simply hearing that tone and seeing a person make an abrupt movement may make you flinch before you know why.

Many of the habitual emotional responses and behavioral patterns that you consider an integral part of your identity are implicit memories. Because they are habitual, they are not easily changed without consistent effort, such as following the FEED method. Implicit memories are not readily available through insight, and insight typically doesn't change them alone. Because much of what you experience and respond to is based on implicit memories, nonconscious processes play an important role in all of your relationships.

The takeaway is that your different memory systems work together to make learning more efficient and durable. Now that you understand the difference between implicit and explicit memory, let's look at how to improve explicit memory.

Associations and Mnemonic Tricks

During the last few thousand years, a wide variety of memory improvement techniques were invented to augment learning. These techniques were built on the understanding that memory—and education more broadly—develop by association. For example, one of the interesting facets of long-term memory is that once you begin to describe an event, you may be surprised by how much you remember. As you begin to describe the event, you're reminded of other circumstances that surround the event. You unleash a whole chain of associations and rekindle a much wider spectrum of memories. This is because memory involves establishing synaptic connections among large networks of neurons. These connections represent associations with images, ideas, and feelings that you had when you coded the memories as well as every time you recall those memories.

Since memory represents associations, you can cultivate your memory skills by using mnemonic devices, which enhance memory through making associations. Mnemonic devices that grab your attention and make remembering fun are the most effective. If your mnemonic device is stale and boring, you'll forget it. Let it stand out by making it silly, funny, absurd, or even titillating.

Memory aids such as mnemonic devices provide you with ways to trick yourself into remembering. Many mnemonic devices have been used throughout history, and I recommend the following four, which are useful and easy to learn:

- Pegs
- Loci
- Story links
- Link

Pegs

Pegs do just what the name says: they peg a word to another word that is easier to remember. They are hooks that you can use to capture the word you are trying to remember. When you think of the peg word, you'll think of the word you want to remember. For instance, in "One, two, buckle my shoe; three, four, open the door," *two* is attached to *shoe* and *four* is attached to *door*.

Pegging can also associate a letter or a number with a word that you want to remember. The acronyms FEED and SEEDS are pegs. You could instead associate each letter of the alphabet with a number. You can remember a string of numbers by remembering their corresponding letters arranged as a word.

Loci

In Greek mythology, Mnemosyne, the goddess of memory, was said to know everything: the past, the present, and the future. Storytellers called bards learned how to remember long poems and epic tales by relying on Mnemosyne. They used the mnemonic technique called loci. *Loci* (LO-sigh) is the plural of *locus*, which is Latin for "place" or "location." Sometimes the loci system is referred to as the topical system. *Topo* means "location" in Greek.

When you're using loci, you're coding your memories with specific locations. If you want to be able to remember the contents of a speech you must give, you can associate each point with a specific location in the room. Then when you're giving the talk, you can look at each location and be reminded of what you want to say.

The Roman philosopher Cicero once told how the loci method was used by the poet Simonides while he chanted a lyrical poem at a large banquet in honor of the host, Scopos. When Simonides included a passage with praise for the gods Castor and Pollux, Scopos became angry and refused to pay Simonides the full fee, telling him that he could obtain the balance from the gods. During the argument Simonides was summoned by a messenger who said that two young men were waiting outside and wanted to talk to him immediately. When Simonides went outside to meet the men, they were nowhere to be seen. In the meantime, the building caught fire and collapsed, killing all the occupants inside.

As the cleanup and rescue effort got under way, no one except Simonides was able to identify the bodies of the victims. He remembered where each person had been sitting at the time he was summoned outside.

The loci system has two main steps:

1. Code into memory several locations of a place in the order that you want to remember them. The place can be your living room or a room in which you must give a presentation.
2. Associate something you want to remember with each location.

By taking these two simple steps, you can recall what you're try-ing to remember by looking at the location, walking by it, or simply picturing it in your mind.

Let's say that you want to memorize a presentation. While you are rehearsing your lines, walk around the room and make a specific association to each object in the room or each part of the room. At the lectern, remember the first part of your speech. Then go to the laptop, the projector, the first row, the back row, and so on, remem-bering a different part of your presentation at each location.

As you practice, walk around the room and time your presenta-tion to match each location with each part. Next, stand in one spot and look at each location as you go through the presentation again, matching each part with each location. Finally, leave the room phys-ically but reenter it mentally, going through your presentation and making the same matches. By the time you actually begin speaking, you'll be able to glance at areas in the room and make the presenta-tion by using each location as a cue.

Story Links

Story links have been used throughout history as people have gath-ered around storytellers, read novels, and enjoyed movies. Stories are an essential part of the fabric of culture. You can use them as a way to learn and teach by associating them with information you want to remember.

By teaching yourself a story, you can link it to information you hope to remember later. Then when you tell yourself the story again, you'll be reminded of the information you wanted to remember. Develop a story that reminds you of a list of words or a group of concepts that you have to remember. The story should weave together the items in the order that you want to remember them so that those memories connect with one another as the story unfolds.

Every time you remember that story, certain synaptic connections are strengthened and certain ones weakened, based on the details that you remember. As you discuss the events that led you to the information that you wish to present you are essentially rewiring your brain every time you review the story in your mind.

Link

One particularly powerful way to use this technique is to link an unusual visual image with something you want to remember. Advertisers use the link method when they craft ads; the positively proactive images of their products stick in your mind. For example, many companies try to link an attractive person with their product. You can use the same brain networks to link what you want to remember with a provocative visual image. Let's say that as you are about to lie down to go to sleep, you want to remember to call for a service appointment for your car in the morning because the engine light went on as you were driving home. Tell yourself that when you see the light on the coffee maker go on in the morning, you will link it with the engine light in your car.

When you don't have a lot of time and you need to develop a quick way to remember something important, it is wise to use a peg. One of the advantages of the peg over the story link is that you can pick out individual items from a list. The story link system in contrast relies on a sequence. Like the loci system, which is dependent on prememorized locations, the peg system also uses prememorized word or number links. With a peg, the information is connected to nouns or verbs (such as FEED). Whatever mnemonic system that you choose to use, make sure that it's flexible and meets the demands of what you're trying to remember. Practice using mnemonic devices so that you'll be versatile in their use.

Eduardo's Tables

Eduardo came to see me because he wanted to improve his memory at his community college classes and practice at work. He was a waiter in a high-end Nob Hill restaurant in San Francisco. He believed that his tips could be higher if he could just remember "a little something about each customer" he served. He explained,

"As it is now, I'm barely getting by remembering what table to bring the dishes to."

We explored what mnemonic system would be the most appropriate for his use in the restaurant. We settled on the loci system because he had a set arrangement of tables and chairs on which to build a system. Since Eduardo was taking a geography class, we agreed that he could assign a certain continent to each table. He entertained himself by paying attention to who sat in a particular continent and whether they ordered dishes that were from that continent. He remembered these congruities or incongruities when he served them their respective dishes. By making each evening a game, Eduardo transformed the loci mnemonic system into a great way to increase his tips and enjoy his customers. They, of course, never knew of his imaginary travels and associations.

8

The Diet Factor

Sonya came to see me because she suffered from lethargy as well as periods of anxiety, depression, insomnia, and short-term memory problems. After detailing all those complaints and thinking that they were not related, she asked that I "fix" her brain.

The first concern that I noted was that all these symptoms appeared to be related to low energy. Hearing that her primary concern was lethargy and the secondary concerns were anxiety and depression, I asked her about her diet.

She said, "I start my day with a tall skinny latte for that little boost."

"And what about breakfast?" I asked.

"An energy bar and another latte will do me until dinner," Sonya said with a shrug of her shoulders. "I sneak a few energy bars. You know, another little boost," she added, as if I would understand her special needs.

I noted that simple carbohydrates undermined her effort to boost her energy and that sugar was actually depleting her ability to generate energy, and I added that it was destructive to her brain as well.

"But I'm tired. Don't you get it?" Sonya asked in an exasperated tone.

"You're *causing* your energy problem by your diet," I informed her. "Once you start eating three or four balanced small meals per day, your energy will be on the rise."

This was not good news for Sonya. Despite everything that I explained, it all seemed counterintuitive. "Why should I cut out the things that boost my energy?" she wanted to know.

"Because you're perpetually crashing from those boosts," I explained. Then I went on to explain how mitos normally made energy and how hers were producing free radicals instead.

Sonya shook her head. "How 'bout we talk about my other problems, like memory, and give this food thing a rest?"

"Would you like to have energy for memory?" I asked.

"Of course," she said emphatically.

"Great, to get that energy you'll need to make some important changes." I suggested that she avoid drinking coffee on an empty stomach and instead eat a nutritious breakfast. Lunch, too, had to be balanced. I asked her to cut out simple carbohydrates from her diet altogether. Throughout the day she was to stay hydrated, keeping a bottle of water as her constant companion. "How 'bout I try one at a time?" she asked sheepishly.

"To make the new diet work, you'll need to do it all together."

For the next week she made all the changes that I requested. When she came back for the next session, she looked more relaxed and focused. "Okay, I feel a little better," she admitted reluctantly.

"A little?" I repeated.

"Well, more than a little, she said, not pleased to admit it. "Can we get started with my problem now?"

"You've got a good start. Without that dietary foundation, building your memory skills would be like building a house on sand."

Diet plays a major role in health and longevity. The quality of our diet has been associated with cardiovascular health and the integrity of our immune system and our epigenome. Just like Sonya discovered, a bad diet can have a major impact on your brain's ability to function properly, making you less apt to think clearly, pay attention, and cultivate neuroplasticity. The bottom line is that the food you eat is fuel for your brain that can enable you to rewire your brain or hinder you from doing so.

The field of nutritional neuroscience has shed light on how particular types of foods affect brain chemistry. Some foods enhance your brain's ability to thrive, whereas others bog it down, making it difficult to rewire your brain and adding to the risk factors for dementia.

To illustrate how your diet affects your brain, I'll start this chapter by describing how simple carbohydrates can affect the way you think. Then I'll describe how your brain chemistry develops and how you can ensure that it has what it needs to keep you from being anxious or depressed. Finally, I'll describe how to enhance the structure of your brain so that you can lower your risk for dementia and enhance your ability to rewire your brain.

Sugar Toxicity

Your brain uses glucose as fuel, but when it gets too much of it at one time, this can create a number of problems. It is no accident that many of your organs—including the pancreas, the liver, the thyroid, the adrenal glands, the pituitary gland, and the brain—are enlisted in controlling the amount of glucose in your blood. When your blood sugar drops too low, your brain (specifically, the hypothalamus) signals your pituitary gland and your thyroid gland to alert your liver to process more glucose from body fat.

If your diet consists of mostly processed foods, you are probably consuming excessive amounts of sugar. This overload may come in the form of high fructose corn syrup, which is even far more toxic for your brain. Manufacturers of fast and processed foods often use this sweetener as a way to cut costs while also making them enticing enough to make you want to keep eating these forms of sugar. These foods have become dominant in the Western diet, but not without significant costs to your health.

The foods with the highest calories per gram include beet sugar and high fructose corn syrup, accounting for 20% of the calories consumed. You're eating carbs that have already been digested for you. That may sound good, but it is quite destructive to your brain.

On average, an adult consumes about 2000 to 2500 calories per day. This quantity is equivalent to about 3 kilowatt-hours or a quarter liter of gasoline. To efficiently convert this fuel (calories to glucose) into energy, all the bodily systems must be working optimally. At any point though, your gastrointestinal, cardiovascular, and metabolic systems can break down, and your energy production can fizzle. After you consume simple carbohydrates like sugar and white flour you'll trigger a boost in stress hormones that will last for as long as 5 hours. This occurs because excess sugar makes your pancreas secrete more insulin than usual and takes too much glucose out of your system.

Many people incorrectly assume that they can burn off the extra calories they consume. Unfortunately, there is no one-to-one trade-off. Consider that one can of soda contains 140 calories. If you walk 2 miles you can burn 100 calories, which fails to burn off the 40 extra calories. Also, the soda was loaded with high fructose corn syrup, which is actually worse for you than sugar.

Carbs and Their Many Forms

There are three basic forms of carbohydrates: starches, sugars, and fiber. While starches and sugars are digested and used in a similar manner, fiber plays a critical role in your gut. Not only does fiber help digest starches and sugars, but it also feeds trillions of bacteria that make up your microbiome that I described in Chapter 2. Starches and sugars are digested as fuel to burn for energy by your mitochondria. If they are not used immediately for energy production, they are stored as glycogen or stored as fat.

The term *carbohydrate* emphasizes that it is composed of carbon and water. This is one reason complex carbohydrates are in moderation a critical part of a healthy diet to produce energy. Once the digested sugars are absorbed in your bloodstream, insulin works to get the glucose into our cells to be used by your mitos to produce energy. Blood sugar that is not burned right away is stored away as glycogen in your muscles and liver. Glycogen is a complex carbohydrate, which has a thick soupy consistency. There is a limit to how much glycogen you can store, and when you reach your limit the overflow is stored in fat cells.

High-fructose corn syrup is about 55% fructose and 45% glucose mixed with water. These simple carbs are more quickly absorbed through your intestinal wall than complex carbs. In contrast, complex carbs contain fiber and nutrients that take longer to digest, and most importantly they offer many nutritional benefits that simple carbohydrates do not.

The concept of a glycemic load (GL) is that the higher the GL of a food, the greater the expected rise in blood sugar and the greater the adverse insulin effects of the food. Long-term consumption of foods with a high GL leads to a greater risk of obesity, diabetes, and inflammation.

Since your intestines have an enormous amount of blood vessels, after a meal your blood flow to your gut doubles. If your meal was composed of simple carbs, expect a spike of blood sugar, which is almost all glucose. Complex carbohydrates, in contrast, have low glycemic index, and the fiber promotes a slow rise in blood sugar. Simple carbs promote a spike in blood sugar.

By eating a lot of food with simple carbohydrates, especially sugar, your brain cells age prematurely. They become rigid and make you less capable of rewiring your brain to learn new things. Also, instead of feeling calm in the face of stress, you will more likely feel anxiety and depression.

A diet high in sugar accelerates aging. Sugar can be destructive to protein as it toughens up the molecules by creating pigments called *advanced glycation end products* (AGEs). AGEs act like a chemical glue that attaches molecules to one another, causing *cross-linking*. For example, overcooked meat is cross-linked, which is why it is difficult to cut or chew. When your tissue has been cross-linked, many metabolic processes become impaired. AGEs alter the structure and activities of proteins and interfere with synaptic communication. When this happens to your cells, the AGEs stiffen your blood vessels, harden your lenses in your eyes, wrinkle your skin, and gunk up your brain.

Consider caramelization when sugar reacts to heat. When this happens in cooking, like with meat or bread, the browning looks, well, brown. That's all good for food that you cook, but not good for your cells. The equivalent of browning in your body is known as glycation (excess glucose), which blocks protein and thus membranes from moving freely, which slows down neural communication and causes inflammation. The destructive effects of glycation are not immediate, but over time the neurons are damaged. It is no wonder that high sugar consumption is associated with depression. In short, they accelerate your aging big time.

Refined carbohydrates (such as white flour) can increase free radical inflammatory stress on the brain. As I described in Chapter 2, a *free radical* is a molecule with a rogue electron that can rupture the structure of a cell. After a series of reactions, AGEs lead to free radicals and inflammation. Also, there is structural damage to your mitos, which causes less production of ATP to keep you alive. In short, simple carbohydrates have many ill effects on the human body, especially your brain.

Studies comparing the sugar consumption rates in countries such as Japan, Canada, and the United States find that Japan has lower consumption rates as well as lower rates of depression. Researchers have shown that when people are given the amount of sugar in two soft drinks, the free radical products of damaged fatty acids, called *isoprostanes*, rise by 34% in just 90 minutes after consumption.

Even mild isoprostane elevations have been associated with Alzheimer's disease. Another blood marker of oxidative stress (free radical damage) and damage to fatty acids is called *malondialdehyde* (MDA). Researchers have shown a relationship between increased GL and MDA.

Researchers from the Massachusetts Institute of Technology found a 25% difference between the IQ scores of children with high versus low consumption of refined carbohydrates (sugar and white flour). The differences in glucose result in significant costs to cognition and to the brain itself. Research at Britain's Swansea University found that dips in blood sugar are correlated with poor memory, poor attention, and aggressive behavior.

When researchers from Yale University gave twenty-five healthy children a drink containing the amount of glucose found in most soft drinks, the increase in blood sugar boosted their adrenaline to more than five times their normal level for up to 5 hours. Most of these children found it difficult to concentrate and were anxious and irritable.

Similarly, researchers in Finland assessed the effects of sugar consumption on 404 children ages 10 and 11. They found that withdrawal, anxiety, depression, delinquency, and aggression were twice as frequent in those who consumed 30% more sucrose in the form of soft drinks, sugary snacks, and ice cream.

The conclusions are clear: High sugar intake is bad for your brain and results in significant impairment of your ability to think clearly, maintain even moods, and behave effectively in a social situation. Keeping your blood sugar balanced and sustained is critical for your brain to operate optimally.

Go Complex and the Importance of Fiber

Most of the carbohydrates that our ancestors ate were rich in fibers. In general, fiber is composed of tough stringy molecules that give a plant structure and strength. When fiber enters your gut, it covers your intestine walls like a knit blanket that acts like a filter to slow down the absorption of sugars and other nutrients into your bloodstream. Therefore, it is not surprising that fiber plays a critical role in the microbiome in your gut, which plays multiple roles in our body (see Chapter 2).

Your microbiome digests much of the fiber you eat. It carries enzymes that your cells can't make and produces short-chain fatty acids that your cells can't absorb. Not only does it use fiber, but it also helps absorb vitamins and minerals and aids in our immune system.

The "Happy Meal" That Leaves You Sad

One of the standard American fast-food meals consists of a hamburger with fries. In fact, one fast-food chain has even branded it a "happy meal." Unfortunately, it contains bad fats, which contribute to multiple problems. For example, the *lipopolysaccharide* (LPS) molecule increases in response to a high-animal-fat diet. LPS is an endotoxin that comes with bacteria and triggers an alarming immune response. The resulting inflammation leads to a chain of events that increases the leakiness of your gut by allowing LPS to sneak between the cells in the lining of your gut and into the blood supply where it interferes with the hormone insulin and so promotes type 2 diabetes and heart disease. Regular consumption of "happy meals" with their simple carbohydrates, trans-fatty acids, and the wrong fats create insulin insensitivity, chronic inflammation, and diminished neurotransmitter levels.

Fried foods and the trans-fatty acids consumed with them are also quite destructive to your brain and result in multiple deficits that impair your ability to think clearly and control your emotions. Trans-fatty acids are found in many foods, including cookies, donuts, potato chips, candy, mayonnaise, vegetable shortening, crackers, cake, deep-fried foods, cheese puffs, and margarine.

Trans-fatty acids are destructive to the brain and can:

- Be absorbed directly by the nerve membranes
- Block the body's ability to make its own essential fatty acids that are so critical for the brain
- Alter the synthesis of neurotransmitters such as dopamine
- Negatively affect the brain's blood supply
- Increase bad (LDL) cholesterol while decreasing good (HDL) cholesterol
- Increase plaque in the blood vessels
- Increase blood clots
- Increase triglycerides, which cause the blood to be sluggish and reduce the amount of oxygen to the brain
- Cause excess body fat, which can have a destructive effect on the brain

The Amino Acid Cornucopia

The neurochemical orchestra that forms the foundation for your brain is dependent upon the food that you eat. The food that you eat provides the raw materials to build the cornucopia of neurochemicals that make your brain function efficiently. If that raw material is in short supply, or if it is composed of simple carbohydrates, trans-fatty acids, or other forms of phony food, your capacity to generate positive moods and clear thoughts deteriorates. A balanced diet contributes to balanced neurochemistry and a healthy brain. The wide spectrum of neurochemistry is dependent upon an adequate balance of nutrients, including amino acids, in the foods you consume.

As I described in Chapter 2, your genes contain the instructions to make amino acids, the ingredients of proteins. Dietary proteins are also part of a balanced diet. Though protein is a small part of your energy production, it is critical to rebuild your muscles and tissues throughout your body. Just as proteins are composed of amino acids, when consumed they are broken down to amino acids. Once digested and pulled into your bloodstream, amino acids are pulled into your cells to construct proteins. Amino acids are building blocks to the neurotransmitters that make your brain able to produce thoughts, emotions, and behaviors.

When you consume more protein than you need, it is broken down into amino acids, which travel through your bloodstream to your liver. The amino group in the amino acids is similar to ammonia, which is so named because it is an amino-like substance. It is converted to urea and sent to your kidneys to pee out in your urine. One symptom of eating too much protein is a distinctive smell in your urine.

Absorbing Amino Acids and Vitamins

The neurochemistry that serves part of the language your neurons use to communicate with one another comes from your diet. This process involves the following:

1. Food is absorbed in your gastrointestinal track.
2. Amino acids and other nutrients including vitamins and minerals are carried through your bloodstream to your brain.
3. Enzymes convert the substances such as the amino acid precursors into neurotransmitters. Or the conversion takes place indirectly by causing insulin to be released from your pancreas, which draws amino acids from your blood and tissues.
4. The neurotransmitters are stored in synaptic vesicles.
5. After the neurons fire (through an action potential) they release the neurotransmitter from the presynaptic membrane into the synapse.
6. The neurotransmitter either finds the right membrane like a "key" to fit into a "lock" on a postsynaptic membrane, making it fire, or it gets reabsorbed into the presynaptic membrane.

Balanced brain chemistry depends on obtaining specific nutrients from your diet. Specific amino acids are the crucial building blocks for proteins and neurotransmitters, which your body makes by synthesizing these amino acids from the food that you eat. For example, L-glutamine is an amino acid found in foods such as almonds and peaches; when it is digested, your body synthesizes it into the neurotransmitter GABA, which helps you stay calm. Tyrosine, which is manufactured by your body from the amino acid phenylamine, is a building block for the neurotransmitters epinephrine, norepinephrine, and dopamine, which help you stay alert. It is also an important building block of the thyroid hormone thyroxine.

Choline, found in egg yolks, serves as the raw material for the manufacture of the neurotransmitter acetylcholine. Inadequate choline causes the brain to cannibalize its own neural membrane to obtain enough to make acetylcholine. Because low levels of acetylcholine have been associated with memory problems and Alzheimer's disease, some researchers have tried to increase the body's choline level with various types of medications.

A diet low in the tryptophan, the amino acid your body uses to make serotonin, will deplete serotonin and therefore the capacity of your OFC to calm your amygdala when it gets unnecessarily overactive. Skipping breakfast alone will undermine your OFC and cause needless stress and anxiety.

Many foods contain essential amino acids. Table 8.1 shows some of the amino acid precursors, their associated neurotransmitters, and a few examples of the foods that contain them.

The foods that you eat must have a balanced spectrum of vitamins and minerals. Just like amino acids, vitamins and minerals have a direct effect on brain chemistry and the production or depletion of neurotransmitters.

Homocysteine is an amino acid in your blood made by consuming meat. Elevated homocysteine is associated with heart attacks and strokes, blood clots, and Alzheimer's disease. It can be recycled into methionine or converted into cysteine with the aid of B vitamins but elevates in the absence of consuming B vitamins. Vitamins B6 and B12 help to dispose of homocysteine.

Table 8.1   Amino Acids and Some Foods That Contain Them

Amino Acid Precursor	Neurotransmitter	Effects	Foods
L-tryptophan	Serotonin	Improves sleep, calmness, and mood	Turkey Milk Whole wheat Pumpkin seeds Cottage cheese Almonds Soybeans
L-glutamine	GABA	Decreases tension and irritability; increases calmness	Eggs Peaches Grape juice Avocado Sunflower seeds Granola Peas
Tyrosine	Dopamine	Increases feelings of pleasure	Fish Oats Wheat Dairy products Chicken Soybeans
L-phenylalanine	Norepinephrine Dopamine	Increases energy, feelings of pleasure, and memory	Peanuts Lima beans Sesame seeds Chicken Yogurt Milk Soybeans
Choline	Acetylcholine	Memory	Egg yolks Chicken Fish Wheat germ

Consider again how important energy is for your brain. Vitamin B1 (thiamine) turns glucose into fuel for the brain. Low B1 makes you tired and inattentive. B1 is particularly vulnerable to depletion by alcohol consumption. Even a glass of wine reduces the absorption of thiamine by your digestive system. Marinating meat in wine, soy sauce, or vinegar depletes 50–70% of its thiamine content. In other words, alcohol depletes your energy.

Vitamin B3 (niacin) is involved in as many as 40 different biochemical reactions in the body and the brain. One of its principal effects is to participate in the process of increasing red blood cells, which carry oxygen to the brain. It also is involved in the pathways for ATP, which, as I mentioned earlier, is your cells' principal energy substance. In moderate doses B3 lowers blood cholesterol, and in high doses it causes dilation of the blood vessels and increased blood flow to the brain. Niacin can be manufactured from L-tryptophan, which, as I have noted, is the amino acid precursor to serotonin. The amount of L-tryptophan that is converted to niacin depends on your diet, which means that niacin and L-tryptophan should be balanced in your diet.

Niacin Cheat Sheet

Good Sources of Niacin

- Chicken (white meat)
- Turkey (white meat)
- Chinook salmon
- Whole-wheat bread
- Peanuts
- Lentils

Conditions Caused by Niacin Deficiency

- Headaches
- Insomnia
- Anxiety
- Depression
- Psychosis

Vitamin B5 (pantothenic acid) is critical for your adrenal glands, which secrete epinephrine (adrenaline) to convert fat and glucose into energy. A B5 deficiency can cause feelings of malaise. B5 is required to make stress hormones and acetylcholine, which is critical for memory.

Vitamin B6 (pyridoxine) acts as a partner for more than a hundred different enzymes. It plays a role in the synthesis of serotonin, epinephrine, norepinephrine, and GABA. Estrogen and cortisone deplete B6. A word of caution: The B6 content in vegetables is reduced from 57% to 77% by freezing them. Thus, if you have primarily lived on frozen meals for much of your diet, you should shift to a significant portion of your diet from fresh foods.

Vitamin B9 (folic acid) has received a lot of attention, especially in terms of its importance for pregnancy. A B9 deficiency during pregnancy can contribute to birth defects such as spina bifida, a neural tube deficit. In general, folic acid is critical for the division and replacement of red blood cells, protein metabolism, and the utilization of glucose.

B7 (biotin) is involved in the metabolism of sugar and the formation of certain fatty acids. Although biotin deficiency is rare, the symptoms include insomnia, mild depression, anxiety, hair loss, and oversensitivity to pain. Good sources of biotin are egg yolks, liver, peanuts, mushrooms, and cauliflower.

Vitamin B12 is involved in the metabolism of every cell in your body. It affects DNA synthesis and regulation as well as fatty acid synthesis and energy production. If you are a vegan, be careful because most sources of B12 are generally animal-based foods. You can find B12 in some fortified soy products and in clams, mussels, crab, salmon, eggs, and milk.

Table 8.2 provides a sample of B vitamin deficiencies and foods that are high in B vitamins.

Table 8.2   Vitamin B Foods and Deficiencies

Low B1 Levels	Low B2 Levels	Low B6 Levels	Low B9 Levels	Low B12 Levels
↓ Alertness	Trembling	Nervousness	Memory problems	Mental slowness
Fatigue	Sluggishness	Irritability	Irritability	Confusion
Emotional instability	Tension	Depression	Mental sluggishness	Psychosis
↓ Reaction time	Depression	Muscle weakness	Depression	Stammering
Sleep disturbance	Bloodshot eyes	Headache		Weak limbs
Irritability	↑ Stress	Muscle tingling		Depression
	Fatigue	Confusion		

High B1 Foods	High B2 Foods	High B6 Foods	High B9 Foods	High B12 Foods
Oatmeal	Liver	Wheat germ	Carrots	Eggs
Peanuts	Cheese	Cantaloupe	Dark leafy vegetables	Liver
Bran	Halibut	Beans	Cantaloupe	Milk
Wheat germ	Salmon	Beef	Whole wheat	Beef
Vegetables	Milk	Liver	Apricots	Cheese
Brewer's yeast	Eggs	Whole grains	Carrots	Kidneys
Sunflower seeds	Brewer's yeast		Orange juice	Sole
	Wild rice			Crab

Vitamin C had received a great deal of attention because Linus Pauling erroneously regarded it as a cure-all. Common folklore regards it as a preventive for the common cold, but the truth is that is critical for many functions, including the manufacture of norepinephrine. Vitamin C is one of the principal antioxidants and acts as a scavenger of free radicals. Stress and bad dietary habits can, for example, produce free radicals, which steal electrons from other molecules and wreak havoc by damaging cells. As I described in Chapter 2, the cellular damage that results from free radicals can cause your energy level to wane and contribute to cognitive and emotional problems. Dietary antioxidants such as foods with vitamin C and E can minimize free radicals. But adding these supplements to eliminate free radicals has not been supported by recent research. An increase in antioxidants, as measured by blood level, is associated with enhanced memory abilities in older adults.

Dark-Skinned Fruits

Phytonutrients are antioxidants and include *flavonoids*. They are found in the pigment of many plant foods, including green tea, soy, apples, blueberries, elderberries, blackberries, and cherries. This is why blueberries and cranberries have received so much attention. Researchers have demonstrated that diets rich in blueberries are correlated with improved cognitive and motor functions. The fruits with the highest oxygen radical absorbing capacity (ORAC)—that is, the capacity to absorb free radicals—are blueberries, blackberries, strawberries, raspberries, and plums, in that order. Plums have less than half the ORAC of blueberries and blackberries.

Your dietary antioxidant defense system can help gobble up free radicals. Vitamin E works by nestling among the various fatty acids and cholesterol molecules. When free radical substances threaten or damage one of the fatty acids, vitamin E traps and neutralizes them before they trigger a chain reaction that damages the cells. Consume your vitamin E through whole foods rather than supplements.

Good Sources of Vitamin E

- Almonds
- Walnuts
- Sweet potatoes
- Sunflower seeds
- Whole wheat
- Wheat germ

Minerals and Phytonutrients

Minerals are important for the healthy functioning of your brain. Two classes of minerals are relevant to the brain: macronutrients and micronutrients. Your brain contains more macronutrients than micronutrients. The macronutrients include calcium, magnesium, sodium, potassium, and chloride. The micronutrients are also called *trace elements* because they are found in tiny amounts in the brain and the body. They include iron, manganese, copper, iodine, zinc, fluoride, selenium, chromium, aluminum, boron, and nickel. These micronutrients can cause problems when they are found in large amounts in the brain.

Calcium is the most abundant mineral in your brain and serves many functions, including the development of nerve tissue, the maintenance of a regular heartbeat, the formation of blood clots, the strength of bones and teeth, the production of iron, the maintenance of a steady metabolic rate, and the transmission of messages between your neurons. Calcium triggers the release of neurotransmitters and controls synaptic strength. After the neurotransmitters are released, calcium enhances the strength of subsequent synaptic connections.

Sources of Calcium

- Dairy products
- Kidney beans
- Salmon
- Bok choy (Chinese cabbage)
- Almonds
- Broccoli

Magnesium is involved in as many as 350 enzymatic functions in your body. It plays a role in maintaining metabolism, aiding muscle contraction, and supporting liver and kidney functions. Magnesium is important in the conversion of blood sugar into energy and is needed by cells for the creation of genetic material. Magnesium also helps with the absorption of calcium, vitamin C, phosphorous, sodium, and potassium.

Magnesium, like calcium, is involved in the conduction of nerve impulses. A magnesium deficiency contributes to irritability, nervousness, and depression. Magnesium regulates a key receptor in the hippocampus that is important in learning and memory. A proper level of magnesium is essential for maintaining the capacity for neuroplasticity. Magnesium is the gatekeeper for a crucial receptor that receives the excitatory neurotransmitter glutamate. Magnesium helps this receptor open up for input, which increases the efficacy of synaptic connections. Finally, magnesium binds to and stimulates GABA receptors in the brain, which puts the brakes on brain activity. In other words, it helps calms you down.

Good Sources of Magnesium

- Wheat and oat bran
- Brown rice
- Nuts
- Green vegetables

Iron is involved in the synthesis of serotonin, dopamine, and norepinephrine. It is a cofactor in many enzyme reactions that produce these neurotransmitters. Iron also plays an important role in the enzymes that convert dietary fatty acids into a form that is crucial for the brain.

Nancy's Wrong Fat Problem

Nancy came to see me with complaints that she was tired all the time, felt easily stressed, and had memory problems. She thought that she had "some deep buried secrets that needed airing out."

Knowing that I was trained in hypnosis, she asked me to put her in a trance and take her back to early childhood to discover "what went wrong."

When I asked her why she thought she suffered from a problem buried in the past, she answered, "Because I just feel bad, and there is nothing that should be bothering me. I should be happy. Everything is going great except how I feel."

Nancy was suffering from depression. However, what became immediately clear was that her diet was contributing to her depression. She started her day by picking up a fast-food fried breakfast burrito. During her morning break she ate a few doughnuts with coffee. For lunch she had chicken nuggets. For an afternoon snack she ate potato chips or cheese puffs. Her dinner consisted of fried chicken, French fries, fried mozzarella sticks, or some other fried foods.

Nancy had all the symptoms of essential fatty acid deficiency, including:

- Dandruff
- Dry skin
- Dry, unmanageable hair
- Brittle, easily frayed nails
- Excessive thirst
- Fatigue
- Depression

I pointed out that if she changed her diet, her energy level would probably increase and many of her depressive symptoms would evaporate.

"What are you, some kind of food fanatic?" she demanded. "I know a lot of people who eat the same things. Can you help me fix my brain or not?"

I told Nancy much of our brain is made of fats and we need the right fats for a solid foundation. Her high trans-fatty acid consumption had to be minimized because it undermined her brain's capacity to think clearly and learn anything new through neuroplasticity.

"All right," she conceded, "I'll change my diet after I feel better."

"I don't think you're going to feel better until you make those changes," I informed her. I suggested that she eliminate fried foods.

After a month without fried food, Nancy started to discover more energy and was able to think more clearly. From this foundation we were able to work together in therapy.

Digesting fats is a little more complicated than carbohydrates. Fats need helper substances to digest because they do not dissolve in water, whereas carbohydrates are partly water. Think of how washing a greasy pan needs extra soap to dissolve the grease, which is essentially fat. Your body's solution to digesting fats is a substance called bile made by your gallbladder.

Dietary imbalance in fats alters brain activity and can cause multiple problems with the blood supply to your brain, including the following:

- Poor tone in the blood vessel walls
- Blood vessel spasms
- Increasing blood viscosity, causing the blood to be sludge-like and form clots

All these factors that impede the flow of blood to the brain interfere with the delivery of oxygen and nutrients to the brain cells. This decreases your clarity of thinking, dampens your mood, and slows your behavior.

A study of 4,000 patients at Rush University Medical Center in Chicago examined the relationship among trans-fatty acids, saturated fats, copper, and cognitive decline. An increase in the level of copper in the body was found to be associated with cognitive decline, but only if the intake of trans-fatty acids and saturated fats was high. In other words, bad fats can potentiate toxicity for the brain if you consume unhealthy foods.

What Gall!

You have probably heard of the old saying, "He has the gall. . ." That metaphor for aggression has its roots in the archaic belief originating with Hippocrates that too much bile made people aggressive. Until a few centuries ago, people were treated with leeches to lower the bile level and bloodletting in hopes that they would regain the balance of body "humors" and health. Fortunately, medicine has discarded these silly beliefs. Bile acids break up the globs of fat oil into tiny emulsion droplets. As the fat is emulsified your pancreas produces an enzyme called lipases to add to the mix to break the droplets down to an even smaller size called micelles, which break apart the fats further like bubbles in a fizzy drink.

When they break apart, they release fatty acids and glycerides that are then absorbed into your intestinal walls and reformed into triglycerides, so named because they are three fatty acids attached to a glyceride molecule and the basic form of fats in your body.

When you digest fats, they are broken down into fatty acids and glycerides, which are built into fat cells in your body. Fats don't mix well with water. They tend to clump together in your blood, which is a water-based solution. This presents a problem because lumpy blood can kill you by cloggy up your blood vessels. When this happens in your brain it can cause a stroke with devastating effects on your capacity to generate a healthy mind.

To minimize this risk of neurological impairments, don't overdo your consumption of bad fats. Your body has a method to pack the triglycerides into small packets called chylomicrons minimize the fats from clumping up. They are dumped in your lymphatic system vessels, which function as a key part of your immune system. It collects 3 quarts of the plasma that leaks out of your blood vessels each day. These fat-filled chylomicrons are why a big and fatty meal can give your blood a creamy color. This material is broken down and reassembled into triglycerides and stored in fat cells.

Getting the Right Fats

Nancy's dietary fat problem is increasingly common. She didn't have to avoid consuming all fats, just the wrong kinds of fats. Nancy wasn't getting the right fats, like omega-3 essential fatty acids. Your brain is composed of 60% fat. You need the right ones to manufacture the cell membranes in your brain—and throughout the rest of your body. These fats are called *lipids,* and there is specifically a family of lipids called *fatty acids.* They serve many critical functions, and if you don't get enough your brain will not function optimally.

Linoleic acid (LA) and *alpha-linolenic acid* (ALA) are essential fatty acids, which your body cannot produce and must be incorporated into your diet. LA is an omega-6 fatty acid found in safflower, sunflower, corn, and sesame oils. ALA is found in walnuts, flaxseed, and green leafy vegetables.

The health of your synapses depends on getting the right fats. The synaptic membrane has a higher concentration of *docosahexaenoic acid* (DHA) than most tissues in your body. DHA is an omega-3 fatty acid found in salmon, mackerel, sardines, herring, anchovies, and bluefish. If you have deficiencies in DHA, the integrity of your synaptic membranes will be impaired, making learning memory difficult.

DHA is critical in keeping cell membranes soft and flexible. Saturated fats, in contrast, make cell membranes rigid. This difference has profound consequences. DHA is important for holding receptors (that receive communication from other neurons) in place. Soft and flexible membranes are capable of altering the shapes of the receptors, which is essential for the neurotransmitters to lock into place. If the receptor is made of rigid or hard fat, however, the receptor is immobilized—unable to wiggle or expand to let the neurotransmitter lock into place. Consequently, the interaction between neurons is short-circuited or interrupted. This means that your brain has trouble transmitting information between neurons.

Researchers at the National Institutes of Health have found a positive relationship between the omega-3 fatty acid DHA and the level of serotonin. The higher the DHA, the higher the serotonin. When the fat composition of cell membranes changes, this alters the actions of critical enzymes. For example, essential fatty acids are involved in the conversion of L-tryptophan to serotonin and the control of its breakdown. The body uses DHA to manufacture more synapses with more nerve endings, which in turn produces more serotonin. This makes DHA important in maintaining a stable and positive mood. DHA also plays a role in slowing cognitive decline, especially Alzheimer's disease.

Trans fats versus Good Fats

When you consume fried foods and unhealthy oils, the result-ing trans-fatty acids damage your brain. When trans-fatty acids are accompanied by a low level of omega-3, the absorption of trans-fatty acids by the brain doubles. Also, when the level of trans-fatty acids is high, omega-3 DHA is replaced.

Eicosapentaeonic acid (EPA), one of the active ingredients in omega-3 fatty acids, is associated with support for the activities of neurotransmitters such as serotonin and dopamine, and it therefore helps with mood regulation. EPA is found throughout your body, but, unlike DHA, it is not found in the brain in significant amounts. You must consume it in your diet. It is found in the same foods that are a source of DHA, but in higher amounts. It plays a role in help-ing the flow of blood in your brain, decreasing inflammation and blood clotting.

Both EPA and DHA prevent excess *arachidonic acid* (AA), an omega-6 fatty acid, from accumulating in your tissues. Although AA is found throughout your body and brain, you can get too much of it through the fat in beef, pork, chicken, and turkey. AA is a pre-cursor of many highly inflammatory conditions. For instance, high AA intake later in life increases the risk of developing dementia by more than 40%.

Prostaglandins

When triggered by viruses, bacteria, free radicals, or toxic chemicals, fatty acids are released from the cell membrane and converted into compounds called *prostaglandins*, hormone-like substances that exert a variety of functions within your brain.

(continued)

(continued)

Specific prostaglandins are formed from dietary fatty acids through a series of steps. There are three prostaglandins (PGs) of interest:

PGE1: Formed from the LA found in sunflower, corn, safflower, and sesame oils, PGE1 is important in the release of neurotransmitters. It possesses some anti-inflammatory properties, reduces fluid accumulation, and enhances the immune system.

PGE2: Formed largely by AA in animal fats, PGE2 is rarely found in plants. It is an inflammatory substance and causes swelling and increased sensitivity to pain. It can lead to increased blood viscosity (which decreases blood flow), blood platelet clumping (which increases blood clotting), and spasms in the blood vessels. It can also cause an overactive immune system, which can thereby attack your body and brain.

PGE3: Formed from the ALA found in flaxseed, walnuts, and pumpkin seeds, PGE3 is somewhat anti-inflammatory and immune enhancing. It counters many of the effects of PGE2.

Isoprostanes are prostaglandin-like compounds formed by free radical damaged fatty acids. They are found in the cerebral spinal fluid, the plasma, and the urine of people with brain-related cognitive impairment, including Alzheimer's disease. The higher level of isoprostanes in people with Alzheimer's disease implies that these substances are a possible predictor of the disease. The cerebrospinal fluid of children with traumatic brain injuries can be up to nine times higher the day after the injury than in people without a brain injury.

An omega-6 fatty acid known as gamma-linolenic acid (GLA) is used in forming brain structure, even though it is not a brain fat itself. Your body converts GLA to substances that reduce inflammation and cell growth. GLA appears to help in neurological conditions when it is converted into PGE1, which can reduce the production of inflammatory conditions caused by excessive AA. Some people with multiple sclerosis who have been treated with GLA derived from primrose oil have been reported to have fewer symptoms.

Omega-3 fatty acids can lower the cellular damage that results from free radicals. It can also help minimize the inflammation associated with neurological and psychological disorders. While both inflammation and oxidative stress interfere with BDNF production, omega-3 promotes the critical neural chemical BDNF, which as you learned in Chapter 1 plays an essential role in neuroplasticity and neurogenesis. This fertilizer for brain cells is critical for memory and new learning. Low levels of BDNF have been associated with neurological and psychological disorders.

Essential fatty acids balance the influences of the immune system in your brain indicated by cytokine activity. Cytokines can have either pro- or anti-inflammatory effects. When essential fatty acids are not balanced, proinflammatory cytokines are activated, leading to chronic inflammation and as a result to depression, anxiety, and cognitive problems.

As I described in the first chapter, your brain contains neurons and *glial cells*, which are more numerous than neurons. One type of glial cells (oligodendroglia cells) coat the nerve fibers. Called *myelin*, this coating is like the plastic that coats electrical wire that makes your neurons fire more efficiently. Myelin is made up of various fats, fatty acids, phospholipids, and cholesterol. As much as 75% of myelin is fat.

Cholesterol: Good versus Bad

Since cholesterol makes up part of myelin, it is essential for its development. Contrary to the oversimplified bad rap that cholesterol has received, high-density lipoprotein (HDL) is considered good cholesterol. It is low-density lipoprotein (LDL) that

(continued)

(continued)

is considered the bad cholesterol. To minimize the LDL cholesterol, cut foods from your diet that add to it (such as fatty meat
and fried foods). LDL cholesterol tends to burrow into the walls
of arteries, especially when your blood pressure is high. This
damage to arteries invites inflammation that generates plaque.

The body needs high amounts of good cholesterol. HDL
is associated with exercise, which helps scavenge and return
LDL cholesterol back to your liver. A diet built on a foundation
of vegetables and fruits, complex carbohydrates, and proteins
such as fish and other nonsaturated fats minimizes LDL and
increases HDL.

When myelin is inadequate or damaged, nerve impulses do not
send messages efficiently. Damaged myelin is a major factor in
multiple sclerosis. This devastating neurological disease results in
multiple impairments, including an inability to walk, memory problems, cognitive and emotional regulation, and depression.

Phospholipids

Phospholipids are another family of brain fats. They are actually
both fat and mineral: *phospho* refers to the mineral phosphorus, and
lipid refers to fat molecules. Phospholipids are important in forming
nerve membranes and protecting them from toxic injury and free
radical attack.

The phospholipid *phosphatidylserine* (PS) is one of the structural
molecules of the nerve cell membranes. PS is formed when the
phospholipid complex combines with the amino acid serine. PS
influences the fluidity of the nerve cell membranes and fosters the
incorporation of membrane proteins that bind neurotransmitters in
the brain. A good source of PS is soy, meat, and fish.

Another phospholipid, *phosphatidylcholine* (PC), is an important part of the nerve cell membrane, because it manufactures
acetylcholine. The common name for PC is lecithin. Lecithin is
found in eggs and soy. It can also be bought in granulated form

and sprinkled on your food, and some vegans use it as a substitute for eggs in recipes.

Lecithin has been reported to keep the level of the amino acid homocysteine in check. A high level of homocysteine has been associated with neurodegenerative diseases. It contributes to the clotting of the blood vessel linings and the development of plaque in the arteries. It can also block the synthesis of neurotransmitters and trigger metabolic changes that injure the neurons.

When neurotransmitters are released by the cell membrane, they float across the gap between the neurons (the synapse) and link with a receptor site like a key in a lock. The receptors are held in place by phospholipids and fatty acids. If the structures of the phospholipids and the fatty acids are damaged or are poorly formed, the receptor can't receive the neurotransmitter. It's partly for this reason that fatty acid supplements have been shown to improve the action of antidepressant medications.

Fats and Depression

During the past century, the amount of omega 3 essential fatty acids consumed in the typical American diet has declined by more than 80%. Moreover, the types of fats have changed for the worse, with an increase in animal fats, vegetable oils, and processed foods. The balance of fats has also changed dramatically: although there was once a balance between omega-6 and omega-3, that ratio has been skewed to 30:1. The vast reduction in omega-3 fatty acid consumption has occurred for the following reasons:

- The reduction of cereal germ (which contains essential fatty acids) by current milling practices
- Decreased fish consumption
- A 2500% increase in trans-fatty acid consumption (which interferes with essential fatty acid synthesis)
- A 250% increase in sugar intake (which interferes with the enzymes of essential fatty acid synthesis)
- An increase in the consumption of LA oils
- The hydrogenation of oils in commercial processing

Studies throughout the world have shown that there is a link between the levels of fatty acids and depression. For example, a study of 3884 patients in Rotterdam, the Netherlands, found that the higher the ratio of omega-6 to omega-3, the higher the rate of depression. The researchers concluded that an adequate level of omega-3 is associated with positive moods.

In Melbourne, Australia, a similar correspondence was found between the ratio of omega-6 to omega-3 and the incidence of depression. As the omega-6 level was elevated over the omega-3 level, there was a corresponding increase in the symptoms of depression. Similar results were found in a study in Belgium: people with depression had a higher ratio of omega-6 to omega-3. Supplementing one's diet with omega-3 has been a consistent recommendation in all these studies.

Brain fats must be nourished and protected. Since brain fats can be damaged by oxidative stress (free radical damage), they rely on a network of antioxidants for protection. Antioxidant nutrients and enzymes keep stray electrons from damaging the delicate unsaturated fatty acids of the cell membranes.

A diet the emphasizes fatty fish tends to promote mental health. In Finland, approximately 1800 people were assessed for depression. Those who consumed fish twice a week or more significantly reduced their depressive symptoms and suicidal thoughts. In a study in Japan, 256,118 people who consumed fish daily were found to have a lower suicide rate than people who consumed less fish. Among those who had attempted suicide, low levels of EPA were strongly correlated with impulsivity, guilt, and future suicide risk.

Fasting and calorie restriction break down fatty acids and increase mitochondrial protein acetylation, but without the ill effects. This is because of the increased activity of the anti-aging SIRT enzymes, which remove acetyl groups from various acetylated proteins. In fact, SIRT enzymes are known as de-acetylases. SIRT enzymes work when our energy levels drop in the cell and mitochondria. Our body needs to use up energy before we can generate more energy. However, overeating and lack of exercise will not spur the production of more energy.

Hype versus a Balanced Diet

A balanced diet is just what it says: "balanced." Along with oxygen, the raw fuel for your metabolism includes the principal macronutrients of carbohydrates, fats, and proteins. It turns out that despite all the anti-carb hype, moderate amounts of complex carbohydrates are an essential part of a healthy diet. Your concern should be on what type of carbohydrates because they are not all the same. Simple carbohydrates are destructive to your body.

One of the unfounded beliefs is that our ancestors supposedly ate considerable amounts of meat. The truth is that our ancestors consumed complex carbohydrates as the basis of their diets in the form of fibrous carbohydrates as the main source of fuel. For a few million years our ancestors dug up roots with digging sticks and gathered fruits as their main source of food. Meat was consumed, but not every day.

The emphasis on meat and fats is based on Inuit and Eskimo diets. Historically, they were only marginal populations that occupied their environments since the advent of agriculture in other parts of the world. In other words, they have occupied their environments for a fraction of our evolutionary history.

Spices and Tea

The Indian spice turmeric has garnered a lot of attention during the last few decades for its health benefits. It has been found to inhibit the action of proteins that transfer acetyl groups onto histones.

Green tea inhibits the action of proteins that transfer methyl groups onto DNA. In fact, the field of neuroepigenetics has been exploring the activity of various nutritional and metabolic factors and our genome. Even broccoli sprouts have been shown to increase histone acetylation of specific white blood cells as quickly as 3–6 hours after consumption.

A consistent body of research has demonstrated that the Mediterranean and Okinawan diets are the best for longevity and brain health and that those who eat foods aligned with these diets live to be 100 years old. These diets emphasize fruits and vegetables with complex carbohydrates as the foundation; protein in forms of fish and meat is not a daily ingredient. Most recently the MIND diet is a brain-healthy diet that stands for Mediterranean-DASH Intervention for Neurodegenerative Delay. It's a hybrid of the DASH diet (Dietary Approaches to Stop Hypertension) and the Mediterranean diet. While not cutting out dairy and meat, the MIND diet emphasizes fish, nuts, legumes, and beans.

While the general Western diet with its processed foods and simple carbohydrates has been shown to be detrimental, the Mediterranean and most recent MIND diet have been shown to support overall health.

In summary, a healthy diet promotes a healthy brain. Healthy brain functioning depends on keeping brain chemistry at healthy levels and eating a balanced diet. A balanced diet can be the optimal foundation for your thoughts and emotions. Notice that I said *can be*, not *is*. That's because a healthy diet only lays the foundation. You can rewire your brain and build on this foundation by changing your behavior and your thoughts upon the foundation of a brain healthy diet.

9

The Sleep Factor

Sleep accounts for roughly one-third of your life. Most people think that sleep provides only "rest" so that you can face the next day with more energy. This is true, but sleep does so much more for your brain. The most dramatic evidence to anyone who had a bad night sleep is that you are compromised at the very least during the activities the next day.

By nature, the quality of your sleep plays a significant part in your health and so the health of your brain. Healthy sleep performs multiple functions that include metabolism, gene expression, and memory consolidation. So it makes sense to understand what healthy sleep looks like and to dispel the myths about it.

Melody had suffered from sleep problems for years. She had trouble going to sleep and staying asleep. She said that she tried everything to deal with her problems, including over-the-counter and prescription sleep aids and marijuana. She was surprised to learn that though all these methods produce sedation, they actually promote garbage sleep. They essentially contribute to the breakdown in the healthy sleep architecture. What's more, they contribute to tolerance and withdrawal. This means you need more of the substance to get the same effect, and when you abruptly cut it off the insomnia is worse than ever. They are like quicksand. The more you use them, the more you use them, and the more you "feel like" you need them, and your sleep becomes impaired. In this chapter, I describe all the factors involved in healthy, clean sleep, including what it provides for you and how you can repair this critical function for your brain.

Your Circadian Rhythm

Your sleep should conform to a cycle that is significantly affected by daylight and darkness. This cycle is called the *circadian rhythm*. Light comes in through your eyes, to your retina, which sends the information that it is daytime to your pineal gland, which is positioned in the middle of your brain. It responds to light by suppressing the production of melatonin, your circadian rhythm neurohormone, convincing the brain that it is daytime and not the time to become sedated. When it's dark, your retina sends that information to your pineal gland that it should produce melatonin to induce sedation.

Your circadian rhythm should be in sync with the rotation of the earth. With night and day you optimally maintain an internal clock, linking your body temperature and the external signal, involving light. Not only is it optimal for your sleep when it is dark and your body temperature is cool, but during the day our exposure to full spectrum light also synchronizes your circadian rhythm.

The Circadian Rhythm Clock

Your biological clock sits at the middle of your brain. Its technical name is the suprachiasmatic nucleus, so named because the *supra* means "above" and *chiasm* means "crossing point" near your optic nerve coming from your eyes. This biological clock samples light before the signals are sent to the back of your brain (occipital lobes) for visual processing.

Since the amount of light you are exposed to during the day affects your sleep, you should maximize your exposure to full spectrum light in the daytime to set your circadian rhythm to match the natural day–night cycle of the world. If you suffer from insomnia, don't use a computer in the late evening because you're essentially looking at light. The light of a computer screen at night will trick your brain into adjusting to a daytime pattern. Since your circadian rhythm can shift away from the actual day–night cycle, you need soft light a few hours before going to bed.

Your circadian rhythm is tied not only to the exposure to light but also to your body temperature. Ideally, when you go to sleep at night, your body temperature should be in the process of dropping. Just before you get out of bed in the morning, your body temperature is on the rise. As you get out of bed and expose yourself to light and move around, you promote a further rise in your body temperature.

Body Temperature—Stay Cool

Just as light and darkness play major roles in your circadian rhythm, so does the temperature. When the sun goes down, it gets cooler. To be in sync with the Earth's rotation over evolutionary time, our ancestors slept when it was cool as well as dark. Our circadian rhythm therefore is not only aligned with the light and dark of day and night but also the cool of the night (Figure 9.1).

If you wake up in the middle of the night and can't get back to sleep, you may have difficulty regulating your body temperature. Your body temperature may actually increase at night when it should be going down. This can occur if you don't exercise. By exercising during the day, you can promote a dip in your body temperature at night.

Melatonin and Adenosine

The two main neurohormones that regulate your sleep–wake cycle's circadian rhythm are adenosine and melatonin. While darkness promotes melatonin, sleep pressure is influenced by the concentration

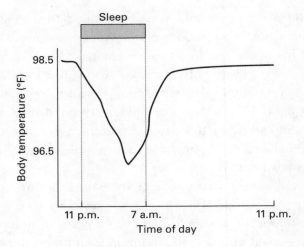

Figure 9.1   Body temperature through the sleep cycle

of adenosine. This means that darkness and high levels of adenosine promote sleep, whereas full spectrum light plus low levels of adenosine promote alertness. Melatonin is sometimes called the darkness hormone. It signals the rest of your brain that it is dark and time to get ready for sleep. As the darkness hormone it plays a crucial part of your circadian rhythm, in sync with the day and night cycle of the earth. In this sense it provides your brain with the switch for "lights out." Once asleep is under way, the concentration of melatonin in your brain decreases, and your pineal gland shuts off its release.

Adenosine plays a principal role in your sleep–wake cycle. Higher levels of adenosine promote sleep, while lower levels lead to wakefulness. As the level of adenosine builds up in your brain, you begin to feel sleep pressure. The longer you are awake the greater the sleep pressure and the higher level of adenosine in your brain. We can observe the role of adenosine for sleep when we drink a cup of coffee before bedtime. Obviously, people who drink coffee at night have trouble falling and staying asleep. The reason coffee—and caffeine in general—keeps you awake is that it blocks the receptors for adenosine in your brain. In other words, caffeine tricks your brain into feeling alert despite the levels of adenosine building up in your brain. In fact, the caffeine withdrawal, sometimes simply called a crash, is partly because of the build-up of adenosine. Once the receptors are not blocked, the accumulated adenosine floods the available receptors.

Those of us who enjoy a rich cup of coffee but also require good-quality sleep must ask ourselves: How late in the day can we drink without suffering from caffeine-induced insomnia? More specifically, how long does it take for caffeine to clear out of our system and get away from our adenosine receptors? To answer these questions, we must consider the pharmacology of a drug, referred to as half-life, which represents the length of time that it takes for your body to remove 50% of a drug's concentration. Caffeine has on average a half-life of 5–7 hours. This means if you drink a cup of coffee at 7 p.m., by midnight to 2 a.m. 50% of the caffeine with still be working against your ability to enjoy a healthy level of sleep. Notice that I specified "healthy level": some people may get to sleep, but it is unhealthy sleep. To makes matters worse, as you age, the enzyme produced by your liver to clear caffeine becomes less effective. This means that the older you are the longer it takes for your body to remove caffeine. We simply become more sensitive to the effects of caffeine as we age.

To promote this combination of sleep-inducing neurochemicals, expose yourself to full spectrum light early in the day and low levels in the evening and avoid anything that blocks adenosine after noon, such as consuming caffeine.

Sleep and Brain Health

Sleep is critical for brain health. If you do not get an adequate amount of good-quality sleep on a regular basis, you can impair your brain. Sleep has been shown to be crucial for certain genetic processes, protein synthesis, and myelin formation. Myelin is like the plastic on electric wires that keeps them insulated and protected from shorting out. Sleep is critical for the synthesis and transport of cholesterol, which forms a significant portion of myelin. Without myelin, the neurons do not fire efficiently.

Thousands of genes in your brain depend upon a stable amount of sleep. Disruption in sleep can adversely affect your DNA. The caps on the ends of your chromosomes, called telomeres, will shrink without quality sleep, exposing genes to potential mutations. If you deprive yourself of good sleep, the healthy activity of your genes will drop and you may become more vulnerable to a wide range of illnesses such as metabolic syndrome, chronic inflammation, and cellular stress. Your good cholesterol (HDL) will drop, and your bad cholesterol (LDL) will rise.

Quality sleep is also critical for your immune system. Have you ever wondered why when you become ill you become sleepy? This is for good reason: to boost your immune system. And when you lose sleep, you undermine your immune system. This is one of the reasons you may tend to catch the latest virus going around after a poor night's sleep. In fact, studies have shown that people who get a good night's sleep after a vaccination generate a greater number of antibodies than people who slept poorly. Getting as little as 4 hours of sleep can knock out 70% of your natural killer cells circulating in your body, relative to having enjoyed 8 hours of sleep.

Poor sleep can destabilize your mood and clarity of thought. This is a vicious cycle of dysregulating the levels of stress hormones such as cortisol, which will make you feel easily stressed. If that is not enough to concern you, high levels of cortisol also impair your hippocampus and your prefrontal cortex. This means that your memory and decision-making capacities will falter.

Even just 1 week of sleep deprivation can lead to weight gain because of an increase in the production of the hormone ghrelin, which promotes appetite. Simultaneously, there is a decline in the production of the hormone leptin, which curbs appetite. This increase in appetite does not seem to be for fruits, vegetables, or high-protein foods. It is for starchy, high-carbohydrate foods, sweets, and other high-calorie foods. If you are sleep deprived, you may consume 33–45% more of these foods than people who get enough sleep.

Sleep deprivation promotes obesity and is associated with heart disease, type 2 diabetes, depression, dementia, and even cancer. Snoring and sleep apnea are associated with all those risks. Sleep deprivation can compromise your attention, new learning, and memory. The longer you endure sleep deprivation, the more compromised these essential functions become. One of the most revolutionary findings in neuroscience was the discovery that new neurons can grow in a certain area of the hippocampus. Studies have shown that sleep deprivation impairs the ability of these stem cells to grow and become new neurons. In other words, losing sleep blocks neurogenesis.

Synaptic consolidation (strengthening of synaptic connections) is critical for the formation of memories. During sleep, unstable memory traces are reconfigured into more permanent ones for long-term storage. Thus, during sleep the experiences of the day are reactivated and consolidated.

Stages of Your Sleep

Sleep is not one simple state. Your sleep pattern goes through a variety of stages, each with different brain wave patterns and metabolic rates, as illustrated in Figure 9.2. This sleep architecture needs to be preserved. Think of it as a cycle that you must transition through each night for brain maintenance.

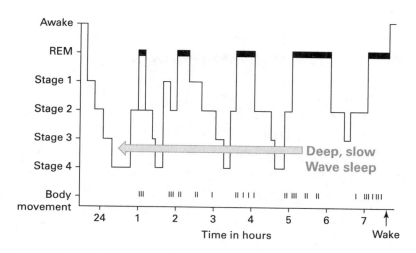

Figure 9.2   The sleep cycle

An electroencephalograph (EEG) shows that the first stage of sleep is a transition state. Here the brain waves are fast. If you wake up from this stage of sleep, you'll probably report that you were not really asleep. Think of this stage as dozing off. The second stage of sleep is light—what scientists call theta brain waves. Many people suffering from insomnia complain that they do not sleep when in fact they are experiencing this stage of sleep. You spend half the night in light sleep. During periods of stress, this stage increases relative to the next stage. As we age, we spend more time in this stage of sleep and less time in deeper levels of sleep.

Stages 3 and 4 are considered deep sleep. In this phase you produce slow brain waves, called delta waves. Deep sleep gives your immune system a boost while allowing your bodily functions and overall metabolism to slow down. If you are deprived of deep sleep, your immune system tends to be suppressed, which can lead to body aches. Since stress increases the release of norepinephrine, epinephrine, and cortisol, you will probably suffer a decrease in the amount of slow wave sleep you get during the night. Your cortisol level should be at its lowest during your slow wave sleep. If you are sleep deprived, the first stage of sleep to rebound is deep sleep, indicating its importance to your overall health.

Slow Wave Sleep

Before and during non-rapid eye movement sleep (NREM sleep) your brain produces a burst of brain waves called sleep spindles. They act to protect your sleep by shielding you from external noises. Adding meaning to deep sleep, the protection of sleep spindles tails off when your deep sleep fades.

During deep sleep your brain waves move from your prefrontal cortex (PFC) and travel to the back of your brain. This deep sleep is also called slow wave sleep where your brain experiences a sort of neural synchrony. The hum of tens of thousands of brain waves can occur at a slower frequency, in contrast to waking states, which are at a higher frequency. These slower frequency synchronous waves sweep across your brain in a way not evident with waking consciousness. This is one of the reasons slow wave sleep is critical for memory consolidation. It serves to take recent information stored in the short-term location to long-term consolidation.

The stage of sleep called rapid eye movement (REM) sleep is so named because your eyes move back and forth as if you are watching something. In fact, this is the stage at which people who are awakened report vivid dreams. Like slow wave sleep, REM sleep decreases as you age. In REM, most of your body functions are at an almost wakeful level of activation, except your limbs. Unlike slow wave sleep, your metabolism energizing neurotransmitters rise during REM sleep. For this reason, REM sleep is called *paradoxical sleep*. You may dream that you're running, and most of your organs will function as if you are doing exactly that. In fact, some areas of your brain are 30% more active during REM sleep than waking. This is because your brain wave activity looks like you are awake, but you are not.

You generally go through a REM period every 90 minutes, and most of your REM sleep occurs later in your sleep cycle. It constitutes 25% of sleep time in healthy adults.

Throughout the day you store memories in your hippocampus, which acts like a librarian for newly acquired books in the library. During early NREM sleep your hippocampus sorts out the important parts of your memories and stores them in your in cortex, just like a librarian does for the library. Instead of storing the color of the car that almost hit you on the morning commute, you store the fact that you were almost hit and where it happened. Think of your waking state as receptive to experiences. Your NREM sleep stores memories gained from those experiences and REM sleep as the integration.

Brain Cleaning

Early in your sleep cycle, your metabolism slows along with your body temperature. Slow wave sleep, which is non-REM (NREM), performs a critical janitorial service. Because your brain is a high-energy consumer, it produces a multitude of waste products called metabolites that build up over the day. They are flushed out in your cerebral spinal fluid in slow wave sleep. If all those metabolites, such as beta amyloid, are not flushed out, you run the risk of developing dementia.

This brain cleaning happens when your glial cells shrink up to 20% during slow wave sleep to allow enough space between your neurons to flush out these destructive metabolites. Deep sleep provides the time for this critical janitorial service when we are not conscious. During this flushing-out process, enzymes come in to repair any damaged cells and rejuvenate receptors for neurotransmitters.

The suggestion "Why don't you sleep on it?" actually describes an important function that your brain provides. Not only do you arise with a new vitality in the morning, but your enlarged and fresh perspective is also based on having consolidated important memories from the previous day. It's from this extension of the neuroplastic process—begun during the day and extended through sleep—that you can arrive at new insights. In fact, throughout history there have been anecdotal stories of great insights being gained after a good night's sleep.

For example, this is how the Russian chemist Dmitry Mendeleyev conceived the idea of organizing the elements by atomic weight into the periodic table. German pharmacologist Otto Loewi, winner of the 1936 Nobel Prize in Physiology and Medicine, reported that he woke during the middle of the night with the insight of how neurons communicate through the chemical messengers we now call neurotransmitters.

The take home point is that your brain is constantly rewiring even when you are asleep. And while you are asleep, some important house cleaning is happening. NREM and REM sleep both cycle through the night to perform essential brain functions. Early in your sleep cycle NREM sleep weeds out and removes unnecessary neural connections. REM sleep plays a role in strengthening important connections. So first you sweep away superfluous memories with NREM, then with REM sleep your brain wires up those memories that are important to make them more durable and useful.

Nighttime Imagery—Dreaming

You probably noticed that the plotlines of your dreams shift abruptly. One moment you are dreaming about cooking dinner, and the next moment you're dreaming about hiking up a mountain. This is because the area of your brain responsible for making decisions and regulating your emotions (your prefrontal cortex, the CEO of your brain) is deactivated. In contrast to NREM sleep, during REM a variety of areas of your brain became activated. For example, while you are imagining seeing things in your dreams, your occipital lobes are processing visual information. Also, the areas of your brain associated with emotions are more activated than when you are awake.

During REM sleep, the two neurotransmitters serotonin and norepinephrine tend to not be active. However, during a nightmare there tends to be a surge of norepinephrine. High levels of norepinephrine are associated with anxiety. The fact that norepinephrine is absent in REM sleep suggests that your dreams could provide an opportunity to reprocess unsettling experiences so that they may be remembered differently. More importantly, memories can be rewired without the association to anxiety. As a result, the memories can become safe to bring up again for reconsolidation. This overnight rewiring of your brain allows you to bring up what is salient emotionally and weed out the emotionally painful parts. To illustrate how this works, Matthew Walker and his colleagues at the University of California–Berkeley showed that REM periods reduced the reactivity of the amygdala in people who had been given emotionally disturbing stimuli before sleeping. Prior to sleeping, their amygdala activity was high and their prefrontal cortex (PFC) was low. After sleep, their PFC was reengaged, which allowed them to better manage their emotions.

REM sleep has been shown to be important for the cultivation of emotional intelligence. Instead of the tuning up of emotion intelligence provided by REM sleep, its deprivation tends to ramp up your fear reactivity. Not only are you less likely to sense the emotional feelings of others, but you are also more likely to misjudge even neutral feelings as threatening or ill-willed.

The REM cycle is different for people who suffer from trauma experiences. One of the symptoms of posttraumatic stress disorder (PTSD) is called reexperiencing, during which someone is overwhelmed with feelings they had during the trauma. This occurs during the day and also at night with nightmares. The critical ingredient to REM sleep that fuels nightmares is the neurotransmitter norepinephrine, which as noted earlier is normally turned off. Unfortunately, instead of benefiting from the therapeutic rewiring of the brain during REM sleep, the person rewires more traumatic memories with repetitive nightmares.

To deal with this rewiring-gone-bad problem, people suffering from PTSD sometimes take a medication for high blood pressure before sleep, which lowers norepinephrine. This allows the REM cycle to perform its therapeutic rewiring to help the person recover.

Waking Up Inside a Dream

During REM sleep, your PFC activates during the rare occurrence that you realize that you are dreaming during the dream. This is called lucid dreaming because it involves your volitional control over what you are dreaming. Instead of describing the plotline of the dream as jumping around you say, "and the next thing I knew I was . . ." With lucid dreaming you decide what you will do next. And it is no wonder that unlike normal dreaming, your PFC is activated so that there is a director to this movie that is your dream.

Unraveling Sleep Loss

Brad came in for help for insomnia. He complained that he typically woke up about 3 hours after going to bed and then had trouble falling back asleep for the next 2 hours. He added that during that time he felt a raw sense of anxiety. This pattern is called mid-sleep cycle insomnia, when he went to sleep at his normal time but woke up and could not go back to sleep. One of the most common causes of mid-sleep cycle insomnia is alcohol consumed in the evening. So, right away, I asked Brad if he drank any alcohol in the evening.

He responded, "Of course! We live in Napa Valley, don't we?"

I explained that in addition to minimizing deep sleep, alcohol often contributes to waking up about 3 hours into the sleep cycle. This is because it dampens the activating neurotransmitter glutamate (the gas pedal), which wears off in about 3 hours. Meanwhile, the alcohol hits the GABA receptors (the breaks) but wears off in about 3 hours. So, what had been a foot on the breaks reverses and becomes a foot off the breaks and a stomp on the gas pedal.

Brad was slightly amused by the analogy but quickly responded by saying, "But Doc it's good wine! It is not one of those $15 bottles. I pay big bucks to keep my wine cellar stocked with the best wine." I acknowledged that while there was a difference in quality of wines, alcohol is alcohol and the negative effects on your brain cannot be eliminated by the cost.

Sleep loss is associated with weight gain, type 2 diabetes, and metabolic syndrome. As I have described in previous chapters, these problems add to the risk of depression, cognitive problems, and brain shrinkage. Two areas of the brain include the hippocampus and PFC, making you less able to the remember things, control your emotions, and make decisions.

Disruption in sleep also disrupts your cardiovascular system. Even moderate sleep loss for 1 week can disrupt blood sugar levels so dramatically that a snapshot blood test would raise the alarm for prediabetes. Your blood vessels also become impaired, and your coronary arteries can become blocked. These impairments lead to the risk of cardiovascular diseases, strokes, and heart disease.

Sleep loss dismantles your body's ability to control blood sugar. Your cells become less responsive to the presence of insulin and set you up on an express path for type 2 diabetes. Now you have high levels of glucose floating around your body with no way of using or disposing of it. As a result, many systems such as vision and brain function dysfunction and can cause brain shrinkage, Alzheimer's disease, and type 3 diabetes.

The Sleep Loss and "Comfort Food" Spiral

The combination of sleep loss, junk food, and weight gain hijacks the reward circuit of your brain. As a result, you can become addicted to "comfort food," which only provides momentary "comfort" and leads to body systems breaking down, ironically causing major discomfort. The downward spiral does not stop there. The hijacking of the reward circuit may lead to addiction to comfort food or other substances or other bad habits. Also, the reward circuit in your brain involves motivation, so addiction hijacks your motivational drive.

Ghrelin is a neurohormone that promotes hunger. Leptin is a neurohormone that tells your brain that you are full. Short sleeps promote a rise in ghrelin and a drop in leptin, making you hungrier the next day and not know when to stop eating. To make matters worse, you crave high-calorie nutrient poor foods. Combined with feeling tired because of the loss of sleep, you burn fewer calories with less regular exercise. It is no wonder that chronic sleep loss is associated with weight gain.

Sleep deprivation has been shown to impact our DNA. For example, the lack of sleep dampens the expression of genes in the hippocampus, which impairs memory and so learning. These adverse epigenetic effects lead to an increase in inflammation as well as shortened telomeres. Sleep has been shown to be crucial for gene transcription involving synaptic consolation, protein synthesis, and myelin formation. Sleep is critical for the synthesis and transportation of cholesterol, and cholesterol forms a portion of myelin.

Cancer and Sleep Loss

A study of over 25,000 people in Europe found that sleeping 6 or fewer hours was associated with a 40% increased risk of developing cancer. This dramatic increase in vulnerability occurs for a variety of reasons. Sleep loss is associated with a drop in natural killer cells that would normally attack malignant tumors. There is also increased activation of stress involving the overreaction of your sympathetic nervous system triggering your fight–flight reaction. All this triggers inflammatory activity, and malignant tumors are known to lure inflammatory factors into their mass to help initiate growth of blood vessels to feed them with nutrients and oxygen. These inflammatory factors also help metastasize some of the tumor cells, allowing the cancer to spread to other areas of your body.

Periodic sleep loss is common. Virtually everyone has had insomnia at least once in their lives, and for many it's an ongoing problem. Approximately half the population reports trouble sleeping once a week, and 15% have trouble sleeping two or more nights a week. If it is an ongoing problem, following the recommendations at the end of this chapter will help.

Sleep problems are especially common among people who are experiencing anxiety or depression. If you're tense and preoccupied, it's difficult to unwind enough to fall asleep. Stress raises the levels of the activating neurotransmitters norepinephrine, epinephrine, and cortisol, which should subside at night. They increase not only stress but also your metabolic rate and core body temperature. If you don't lower these neurochemicals, even if you are able to sleep, the quality of your sleep is extremely poor. If you experience

Insomnia Symptoms

The American Sleep Disorders Association lists the following symptoms of primary insomnia:

- A problem initiating and maintaining sleep
- Daytime fatigue associated with the sleep disturbance
- Significant distress in or impairment of one's social life or occupation
- Duration of more than 1 month
- Frequency of three or more nights a week
- A sleep latency, or time awake after sleep onset, longer than 30 minutes
- Waking more than 30 minutes before the desired time
- A total sleep time of 6.5 or fewer hours
- A sleep efficiency lower than 85%

stress, anxiety, or depression, you may keep yourself charged up and tense by thinking about what is waiting for you the next day. In the evening, the alertness-promoting neurochemicals that need to be moderated are adrenalin, norepinephrine, and cortisol. Those neurochemicals can be lowered with relaxation.

Many factors contribute to insomnia, including stress, ill health, alcohol, and drugs. And to make matters worse, as you age, the quality of your sleep can deteriorate. Though you can't stop aging you can do something about the other factors.

These indicators of primary insomnia are also associated with general anxiety and depression. Indeed, a significant number of people who are depressed or anxious seek treatment for insomnia. Ironically, excessive worry about the lack of sleep contributes to anxiety-related insomnia.

As I described at the beginning of this chapter, caffeine causes insomnia because it blocks the adenosine receptors in the brain. Adenosine is a sleep promoter, especially for slow wave (deep) sleep. Even if you are able to sleep after consuming caffeine it will probably be shallow sleep and you will be prone to wake up during the night.

Lifestyle and environmental factors that contribute to insomnia include:

- Poor air quality in the bedroom
- High body temperature
- Caffeine afternoon
- Nicotine
- Alcohol in the evening
- Sugar
- Heavy meals before bedtime
- Hunger
- Exercise just before bedtime
- No exercise at all
- Daytime naps
- Computer use in the late evening
- Arguing with your partner before bed
- Warm bedroom
- Sporadic and novel noise
- Light

It has been estimated that 10% of all sleep problems are caused by alcohol. Yet there is a common myth that alcohol helps you get to and stay asleep. The truth is that if you drink alcohol in the evening, you will suffer a reduction in deep sleep and REM sleep. Alcohol is one of the most powerful suppressors of REM. When your body metabolizes alcohol, it produces aldehydes and ketones. Aldehydes, in particular, block your brain's capacity to generate REM sleep. Part of REM sleep pressure erupts during your waking hours, causing a wide variety of cognitive and emotional problems. If you suffer from insomnia and you drink, you should stop drinking several hours before bedtime or consider not drinking at all.

Medical Conditions Associated with Insomnia

- Fibromyalgia
- Huntington's disease
- Kidney disease
- Hyperthyroidism
- Parkinson's disease
- Epilepsy
- Cancer
- Asthma
- Hypertension
- Heart disease
- Bronchitis
- Arthritis

You could have insomnia related to a disruption of your circadian rhythm. If you typically wake up too early in the morning and can't get back to sleep, you should expose yourself to full spectrum light in the early morning. This will ensure that your pineal gland will not produce melatonin throughout the day and that your body temperature will be at its lowest when you sleep. If you wake up in the middle of the night and can't get back to sleep, you should expose yourself to full spectrum light in the late morning. This will encourage a lower body temperature in the middle of the sleep cycle and promote staying asleep.

There are no medications that will minimize insomnia without adverse consequences. Over-the-counter sleep aids tend to suppress the important stages of sleep. They can also lead to tolerance buildup (that is, more of the drug will be needed to achieve the same effect) and withdrawal. Yet millions of people treat their insomnia with either over-the-counter sleep drugs or physician-prescribed sleeping pills. Over-the-counter aids contain the allergy medicine diphenhydramine (Benadryl) and therefore produce some sedation. Upon awakening the next morning, you may experience grogginess and have more difficulty concentrating.

Two major surveys of hundreds of studies on the effectiveness of treatment for insomnia have shown that sleep medications are relatively ineffective over the long term. Prescription sleep medications (benzodiazepines) are half as effective as behavioral approaches. Benzodiazepines are simply not as effective as long-term treatments for insomnia. There is tolerance and withdrawal. If you take them on a regular basis, you'll experience daytime grogginess, shallow sleep, and withdrawal (making it even harder to sleep).

The World Health Organization put out a report indicating that over-the-counter drugs like Benadryl and prescribed drugs like benzodiazepines contribute to dementia. This is because they impair the glymphatic system and as a result build up toxins such as tau proteins and beta amyloid. These sleep medications not only give you poor sleep but also impair your glymphatic system.

Some medications cause insomnia. Unfortunately, many physicians do not take the time to warn their patients that insomnia is a side effect of the medications they prescribe. If you're taking a sleep medication, you should not stop abruptly but should gradually taper off. And don't do it alone. Withdrawal from benzodiazepines should be supervised by a physician.

Some of the Medications That Contribute to Insomnia

• Decongestants	• Parkinson's medications
• Corticosteroids	• Asthma medications
• Diuretics	• Appetite suppressants
• Heart medications	• Kidney medications

Sleep Hygiene

I always liked the term *sleep hygiene* because it suggests clean sleep. In other words, you can benefit best from sleep when not complicated by unnatural chemicals, either prescribed or over the counter. There are several natural methods for improving sleep, including exercise, proper diet, light exposure during the day, and a cool bedroom.

Researchers at Stanford University studied the effect of exercise on sleep in adults ages 55 to 75 years and found that those who exercised for 20–30 minutes in the afternoon reduced the time that it took to go to sleep by one-half. Two meta-analyses have shown that exercise can increase overall sleep quality. These studies showed that exercise promotes not only an increase in sleep time but also an increase in slow wave, deep sleep.

Exercising 3–6 hours before bedtime enhances sleep because it elevates your heart rate and your body temperature but also allows your body time to return to baseline before bedtime. Aerobic exercise will provide you with a calming and antidepressant effect that also promotes sleep.

If you experience a particularly stressful period of time, your cortisol and epinephrine (adrenalin) levels will tend to be high, even throughout the night when you should be resting peacefully at sleep. Exercise—as long as it's not right before you sleep—will gradually lower basal cortisol and epinephrine (adrenalin) levels and body temperature and help sync your circadian clock. This helps you access your parasympathetic nervous system (part of your autonomic nervous system), which is also called the "rest and mend system." As we discussed earlier, the other part of the autonomic nervous system is called the sympathetic nervous system, which provides the flight-or-flight response.

While a cool bedroom promotes the deepest sleep, warm bedrooms, in contrast, promote light sleep. Paradoxically, a hot bath can be helpful as a winding-down activity as long as you don't go right to bed after the bath. The body temperature is raised in the tub, but it drops sharply by bedtime.

To successfully enter slow wave sleep, your body temperature must drop. This decrease is body temperature is detected by a group of thermosensitive cells that live right next to your 24-hour clock, the suprachiasmatic nucleus. Once your core body temperature dips below a threshold in the evening, the message goes to your nearby suprachiasmatic nucleus. Together with the fading light your gland can release melatonin. One way to hasten the drop in body temperature is to allow your hands and feet out of the covers. Taking a hot bath or shower dilates blood vessels on the surface of your body, which can help your body core temperature to drop. Generally, getting your bedroom temperature down to or below 65 degrees is ideal for sleep.

Your diet also has a major effect on the quality your sleep. Food rich in L-tryptophan (an amino acid that converts to serotonin and melatonin) contributes to sedation, whereas protein-rich foods (such as fish) may make you less sleepy. Protein increases the plasma-rich, large, neutral amino acids. Simple carbohydrates (such as white bread) are not helpful for those who have sleep problems. Simple carbohydrates result in increased blood glucose and may awaken you during the sleep cycle. Complex carbohydrates, in contrast, trigger serotonin conversion long term and create a slow and sustained rise in glucose.

Make sure that your bed is for two purposes only: sleep and sex. If you toss and turn for more than an hour, you should get up and go to another room. Getting out of bed allows your body temperature to drop.

Almost all sleep departments in medical centers strongly advise against having a television in your bedroom. Since your brain is geared to pay attention to novelty, try to minimize nonrepetitive sounds. A television will periodically grab your attention and wake you up. White noise, in contrast (such as the noise of a fan), is monotonous and makes a good screen for other noises, such as a barking dog or road noise outside. Some people keep a fan on all night long just to provide white noise. Good-quality earplugs can also filter out noises.

Try to minimize your exposure to bright and blue light (from screens) 2–3 hours prior to bedtime because the light suppresses the release of melatonin by 20–50%. If you read on a device prior to bed, you can count on feeling less rested and will suffer from shallow sleep.

Sleep scheduling is another way to reestablish a normal sleep pattern. This involves adjusting the time you go to bed. For example, by staying up later than usual, you'll build up pressure to go to sleep and stay asleep through the night. This is because a sleep-deprived person will fall asleep earlier the next night to catch up on lost sleep. If insomnia has become a habit and you assign considerable importance to the problem, it's usually a good practice to establish a schedule commensurate with reconditioning your sleep cycle. Sleeping late in the morning, which might seem sensible, is only likely to make it more difficult for you to fall asleep the next night. Sleep scheduling, in contrast, requires that you get up in the morning at the usual time no matter how much sleep you had the previous night.

Calculate how many hours you actually sleep on average, and then add an hour to the total. Use this formula to schedule how much sleep time you should allow yourself. For example, if you averaged 5 hours of sleep a night for the past month despite staying in bed for 8 hours, you can allow yourself 6 hours of potential sleep time. If your normal wake-up time has been 6 a.m., you should be in bed at midnight. You should use this schedule for at least 4 weeks. Your goal should be to fill up most of your time in bed with sleep. Eventually your body temperature will adjust, and the sleep pressure will build up so that you can add another hour.

This approach is useful if you have chronic insomnia, not if you have experienced a night or two of poor sleep. If you're a chronic insomniac, the task is to repair your sleep cycle. If your sleep cycle is out of sync, sleep scheduling helps you to move it back into sync and reestablish sleep efficiency.

Don't try too hard to go to sleep. Your brain activity increases when you worry about not getting enough sleep. Research has shown that *trying* to fall asleep promotes increased muscle tension, heart rate, blood pressure, and stress-hormones. One study offered a cash prize to the participant who could get to sleep first. The participants took twice as long as they usually did to fall asleep, because they were trying so hard.

Negative sleep thoughts (NSTs) push temporary insomnia into long-term insomnia. NSTs are essentially inaccurate ideas about sleep that create a self-fulfilling prophecy. If you believe these NSTs, then you'll have more difficulty falling asleep again because of the buildup of stress. NSTs result in negative emotions such as anger and in all the biochemical changes that are associated with anger, all of which are activating rather than sedating. NSTs set off a chain of events that result in insomnia.

Identify your NSTs and replace them with accurate information about sleep. For example, if you wake up in the middle of the night, try to interpret your wakefulness in one of the following ways:

- I might get back to sleep or I might not. Either way, it isn't the end of the world.
- This isn't great, but at least I've got my core sleep.
- If I don't get a good night's sleep tonight, I will tomorrow night.

Adopting these thoughts will, paradoxically, help you to get back to sleep. This is because by adopting reasonable thoughts about sleep, you'll take the pressure off yourself and relax enough to get to sleep. In addition, while you're lying in bed, use the opportunity to relax. Relaxation methods, such as deep, diaphragmatic breathing, quiet your mind. Relaxation during the daytime will help you to sleep at night. They work best if practiced twice daily, once during the day and once before bed.

In summary, several techniques can help you to achieve a healthy sleep pattern. Follow these guidelines:

- Don't do anything in bed other than sleep and have sex. Don't watch television, balance the checkbook, discuss finances with your spouse, or argue. Associate your bed with sleep.
- Reading in bed is fine and often relaxing.
- If you can't sleep, get up and go to another room.
- Don't try too hard to go to sleep as the antidote to NSTs. It will increase your stress and lead to a paradoxical effect. Try telling yourself one of the three statements listed earlier. The change in expectation will free you up to be able to relax and get to sleep. The harder you try to go to sleep, the harder it will be to induce sleep.
- Avoid drinking large quantities of liquid at night, which lowers the sleep threshold and causes you to wake up to urinate.
- Avoid bright light at least a few hours before going to sleep. Don't work on the computer or iPad late in the evening.
- Do all planning for the next day before you get into bed. If you think of something you need to remember, get up and write it down. This will help to postpone thinking or worrying about anything until the next day.
- Avoid long daytime naps. Think of these naps as stealing sleep from the nighttime.
- Exercise 3–6 hours before going to bed.
- If noise bothers you, use earplugs or a source of white noise such as a fan.
- Avoid alcohol for 5 hours before bedtime.
- If you're troubled by chronic insomnia, try sleep scheduling.

- Use relaxation exercises. These will help you go to sleep or go back to sleep if you awaken during the night.
- Keep your body temperature cool. Don't cover yourself too heavily. Crack your window open in cool weather, use air conditioning in the summer, and make sure that your bedroom is not overheated in the winter.
- Cut your caffeine intake, don't drink caffeine on an empty stomach, and don't drink any in the afternoon.
- Eat three meals a day.
- Avoid sugar and other simple carbs.

Part 3

Your Mind-Brain

10

Resiliency
to Wisdom

Maria came to see me after a series of losses. First her father died. That loss was hard, and as she emerged slowly from her grief 6 months later, her cat died. She had been very attached to him and had spent many years holding him on her lap in the evenings. It took 2 months for her to move beyond the sadness of his loss. Then, when all seemed to be going well again, she was transferred to a new unit at work. She had grown very close to her coworkers, and the prospect of having to get to know an entire new group of people was daunting. Finally, she found that this new group was as easy to get along with as her old group had been. A few months later she twisted her ankle and had to walk with crutches. This occurred just as she had begun to take a walk every evening with a neighbor.

Maria complained, "I'm just not as durable as most people. Why is it that it takes me so long to bounce back after something bad happens?"

No one in her past had ever served as a resilient role model. In fact, many members of her family were the opposite of resilient. Her father complained woefully about everything, even when things were going well. He always found a flaw in whatever was going on: whether his favorite restaurant was closed, or his favorite television show was being preempted by a special newscast, he sulked for hours after these minor disappointments.

Maria's mother spent much of her time trying to make sure that everything went easily for Maria's father, but she silently loathed the role. Like her father, her older brother was quite passive-aggressive, always manipulating his wife, who babied him. In fact, all of Maria's role models were anything but resilient or vibrant people. This, coupled with the fact that she married an alcoholic right after high school, meant that she entered adulthood with few durable supports and role models. Now, 30 years old and with an 11-year-old daughter, she was ill-prepared for the general stresses of life. Even when her daughter caught a cold, it took her quite a while to emotionally adjust to taking care of her while also managing the household and going to work.

Maria told me that she was both a pessimist and a perfectionist. I wondered out loud if those attitudes set her up to react to whatever occurs in her life by making the situation worse rather than better. Her pessimism meant that she could foresee no good options and no light at the end of the tunnel. This was a prescription for despair and anxiety to return. Her neural circuitry ramped up a worry loop by ruminating about the possible causes of that threat. She also overactivated her right prefrontal cortex (PFC) and underactivated her left. She didn't know that her pattern of neglect and withdrawal in response to stress made her feel worse.

My plan to help her rewire her brain entailed inoculations of manageable periods of stress. Simultaneously, she needed to activate her left PFC, which involved taking action to kindle all the positive emotions associated with it being engaging in the world around her. Initially, she was resistant, but after I explained how neuroplasticity works she indicated that she was willing to give it a try. Since she thought that she was doomed to a series of bad experiences over which she had no control, she needed to learn to put herself in the driver's seat by making decisions about whatever occurred in her life. As she slowly began to gain a reasonable sense of control, Maria was better able to build self-esteem. Rewiring her brain required that she decide to make changes rather than to react to her life as she were a victim. I introduced her to the FEED acronym as a mnemonic device for remembering the steps required to rewire the brain.

Since Maria needed a place to practice, I suggested that she take initiative at work by volunteering to be on a committee with the new team. Her reaction was, "I finally got comfortable with them."

"It's time to expand your comfort zone," I said. "Think of this as a sort of initiation. You're building up your stress tolerance." After some gentle encouragement followed by enthusiastic support, she reluctantly agreed. I noted that she could be playing the passive victim by dragging herself into the exercise. She employed the first steps of the FEED plan, which she acknowledged was against her "nature."

Maria volunteered the next day. When she returned to see me a week later, she reported that the members of the committee were pleased by her initiative and thanked her for volunteering. After the committee assignment was completed, she asked if I thought it would be wise to "resign now because I have done my bit."

"On the contrary," I continued, "You're just getting started. Keep expanding your comfort zone. Remember, the second E in FEED highlights the importance of making a continued *effort* until you find it effortless."

Maria swallowed hard but did agree to stay on the committee. In fact, she proposed an expansion of the last project. I praised her on her initiative and suggested that she volunteer to chair the subcommittee. She said, "Are you kidding?"

"What do you think?" I retorted.

She smiled coyly then nodded yes, noting that she got it.

Maria adopted the strategy to generate a moderate degree of manageable stress to promote the optimum level of neuroplastic changes. Later, obstacles and unfortunate situations would naturally arise on their own, but she was prepared for them because she was inoculated by a moderate degree of stress while volunteering for projects.

A more than moderate challenge came soon enough. One of her subcommittee members disagreed with one of her proposals. Although there was no way of determining whether his motivation for the criticism was constructive or personal, initially, Maria reacted as if he were being critical of her personally. I suggested that she stick to the facts and use his critique as an opportunity to examine her idea. By shifting to the content of his critique rather than wondering about its motives, she leaned into constructive action with her left PFC. This allowed her to come up with a logical strategy to modify her idea while still moderating stress. Had she remained defensive and felt overwhelmed by a presumed personal attack, she would have pushed her panic button and activated her amygdala to detect a threat.

The experience with her committee member and several subsequent experiences provided her with opportunities to rewire her brain. Maria became increasingly more resilient. She found herself craving new experiences instead of shrinking from them.

Attitude and Resiliency

Resilient people turn frustrating situations into opportunities to learn something new. They adapt to bad circumstances by focusing on hidden opportunities. For example, you may run into financial problems and have to change your job to one that pays more. You were pretty comfortable in the old position, so switching means that you have to expand yourself in areas that you had never explored. After pushing yourself out of your comfort zone, you may actually find the new one more rewarding than the old one.

Changing circumstances and conditions are part of life. Adapting to those changes is part of resiliency. Since things generally don't occur in the way that you eagerly anticipate, you can either roll with whatever does occur or bemoan the fact that what you had expected didn't happen. In each situation, you script yourself in or out of enjoying the present moment.

It's much easier to deal with disappointment if the failed expectation was simple and within normal human experience, but how about when terrible things happen? There are people who have experienced great trauma, yet with resiliency they have made new lives for themselves. As I write this second edition of this book, I am in daily contact with my friends in Ukraine I met while lecturing there before the war. They are working long hours providing therapy for those traumatized by the war. I also think of my own Armenian ancestors, who survived the genocide perpetrated by the Ottoman Turks. They made new, flourishing lives for themselves in the United States and France. Although they never forgot what they had endured, they didn't sit around passively waiting for good things to happen. Instead, they made things happen. They became successful in their adopted countries by crafting careers and building new families. I continue to be inspired by their resiliency.

During the last few decades there has been a considerable amount of research on the role of positive attitudes on mental health. The characteristics of these attitudes the following:

- Gratitude
- Compassion
- Acceptance
- Optimism
- Forgiveness

Resiliency consists of maintaining hope in the face of adversity that things will eventually get better while doing what it takes to make those things happen. This type of optimism forms part of what is called emotional intelligence. In fact, optimism is good for both your mental and physical health. In one study, people who were assessed to be either pessimistic or optimistic were assessed again 30 years later for their health. Pessimism was found to be a poor risk factor for physical and mental health as well as interfering with longevity. Pessimists essentially paint themselves into a depressing corner. Their negative thinking allows them no opportunity to feel good about anything that happens in their lives.

Pessimism can have a negative effect on your health for the following reasons:

- You believe that nothing you do makes a difference.
- You unknowingly promote negative life events by reacting to neutral events negatively and creating more negative events because of your wasted and misdirected efforts.
- It depresses the immune system.

If you focus on what something isn't, you block your perception of what it is. In such cases, you're hung up on a negative frame of reference. Let's say that you expect things to turn out a specific way and they don't. Instead of appreciating how things did turn out, you're stuck on the fact that they didn't turn out the way you hoped. This dilemma is similar to what psychologists call *cognitive dissonance,* which means that once you develop an opinion about something, it's difficult to hold an opinion contrary to it.

The Neuroscience of Optimism

The following findings from neuroscience show that optimism promotes positive changes in your brain:

- Increased left prefrontal activation, associated with approach behaviors and positive emotions
- Increased orbitofrontal cortex activation, associated with increased resiliency
- Enhanced emotional regulation results in decreased anxiety and decreased amygdala activation

Optimism is more than just seeing the glass as half full. Cultivating an optimistic attitude might seem like a broad jump if you are experiencing a high degree of stress, because you might think that there is nothing to feel optimistic about. However, a sense of optimism will emerge if you look past your current situation to focus on possibilities and potentialities, thus unlocking yourself from a self-limiting attitude. A stressful situation can present an opportunity to explore new ways of managing stress as well as growing from the experience. By focusing on possibilities, you can see more than a potential light at the end of the tunnel. The light doesn't have to be at the end of the tunnel; it can illuminate an opportunity wherever you are.

Gratitude is another key ingredient to a brain-healthy attitude. Maintaining a sense of gratitude for what you do have instead of what you do not have promotes mental health. Gratitude has many benefits. For example, highly grateful people compared to their counterparts tend to experience greater life satisfaction and hope. And for those who embrace a sense of spirituality, they tend to believe that all things are connected. Research has shown that the combination of expressing compassion for others and intentionally expressing gratitude enhances positive emotional states.

Gratitude and Your Brain

Gratitude and positive emotional states correlate with the following:

- Causes synchronized activation in multiple brain regions
- Activates parts of the brain's reward pathways and the hypothalamus

The emotions cultivated with a healthy attitude feed off one another so that your overall life satisfaction gets a boost. Gratitude promotes a wide variety of mental health benefits. Stress associated with depression and anxiety fades away, and a sense of joy and enthusiasm as well as optimism can permeate your attitude and emotional well-being.

The combination of optimism and gratitude revamped Taylor's life. He came to see me complaining that this life was too "routine and boring." The only emotion that he was able to vaguely identify was a dull and nagging feeling of stress. He was a dutiful father, husband, and employee. Yet, he felt little joy and found himself bracing for the "next demand." None of the demands were particularly stressful but they stood out because of his lack of attention to the positive aspects of his life. He took everything for granted, which made it all blur together in a stale dullness.

As he began to use the FEED formula to focus and cultivate a greater degree of depth on what he did have, his pessimism began to fade. He began to act with compassion toward family members and friends who he had previously related to out of a "sense of duty." Slowly he found himself looking forward to upcoming events with a sense of optimism and gratitude.

Prior to cultivating gratitude and compassion, Taylor had described himself as fundamentally a pessimist. He eventually discovered that his cliché old motto "No good deed goes unpunished" boxed him into an odd form of self-punishment. He learned that whereas pessimism is a retreat, optimism is a lean-forward attitude.

As he expressed compassion toward his family and friends, he began to feel self-compassion, which also provided successful, self-referential integration to project him into the future with an optimistic bias. He mobilized his attention and working memory to support a positive stream of thought. When he reflected on his past, he accessed a library of memories to plan for a meaningful future which he then moderated with his newly developed optimistic feelings.

Benefits of Self-Compassion

The benefits of self-compassion include:

- Psychological: such as lower rates of depression, anxiety, recovery from PTSD, and eating disorders.
- Physical: such as alleviating chronic pain, improved lower back pain, and reduced inflammatory response.

Shifting Your Emotional Tone

A few decades ago, Richard Davidson of the University of Wisconsin pioneered research on cerebral asymmetry and mood. He showed that people who overactivate one hemisphere relative to the other tend to have a particular emotional tone, he referred to as *affective style*. For example, people whose left PFC is dominant tend to be more positive, take a more active role in their lives, and embrace a more "can do" attitude than people whose right PFC is dominant. People who overactivate the right PFC tend to have a more negative affective style. They tend toward anxiety, sadness, worry, passivity, and withdrawal.

You might ask, "What happened to all the press about the right hemisphere being so creative, receptive socially, and more aware of the big picture?" That is all generally true, and I am not saying that the right hemisphere is not important. It most certainly is! What I am saying is that balance between the hemispheres is important, and engagement in the world is critical for your mental health, as it is associated with activation of the left hemisphere.

These asymmetrical emotional tendencies have been shown to occur early in life. Even infants who are crying or sad show greater right hemisphere activity, whereas infants who display emotions such as happiness show more left hemisphere activity. Another study found that female undergraduates who rated themselves as quite shy showed right hemisphere overactivation, whereas their more socially oriented counterparts displayed left hemisphere dominance.

One of the key features of a positive (left PFC) affective style is the capacity to neutralize negative emotions. The connections between the PFC and the amygdala play a significant role in this type of affect regulation. In other words, your stress tolerance is based on your ability to inhibit negative emotions, including threat detected by the amygdala. Resilience is the ability to maintain positive emotions in the face of adversity.

The capacity to recover from negative emotional states is an important aspect of resiliency. People who *practice* positive moods and well-being—for example, through mindfulness meditation—become more resilient. After a stressful event they easily bounce back to the usual positive attitude and mood. In one study, Davidson put a very experienced Tibetan meditator through a thorough electrophysiological assessment and found that the activity in his left PFC was associated with positive moods. He was actually six standard deviations higher than the average Western subject in the measure. These studies indicate that the tendency toward resilience is a left rather than a right hemispheric function.

The idea of an emotional tone is consistent with this research on hemispheric asymmetry and resiliency. A tone is a sort of emotional gravitational force. Although you might experience a great tragedy, such as the loss of a loved one, or a great fortune, such as winning the lottery, you will eventually move back to your tone after a period of adjustment.

If your emotional tone is not as positive and calm as you want it to be, you'll have to feed your brain by inducing increased activation of positive left PFC states long enough to induce a new trait. The difference between states and traits represents two critical steps in inducing neuroplasticity. A *state* can be a mood, such as happiness or sadness. As I explained in Chapter 1, people fluctuate between different states throughout the day, depending on what is going on in the moment. A *trait*, however, is an enduring tendency. For example, most people experience an anxious or depressed state from time to time, but not all people experience anxiety or depression as an enduring trait. Your traits and emotional tone are not hardwired.

If your emotional tone tends to be anxious or depressing, you can rewire a new trait by using the FEED technique (see Chapters 3 and 4) to activate the fundamental neuroplastic connections between states of mind and traits. The more frequently you induce balance among your states of mind, such as calmness or hope, the greater is the chance that those states will FEED a new trait. The more often you activate the neurons that represent that state, the easier it will be to induce that state again, and the more likely it will be that the feeling of calmness or hope will become a stable trait of your emotional tone.

Psychological Hardiness

Your attitude has a significant effect on your stress level and whether you can shift your emotional tone. Your attitude is your way of approaching your life. And you can learn to approach your life with greater resiliency and hardiness. To explore the range of differences in attitude, Salvatore Maddi and Suzanne Kobasa, two research psychologists, identified attitudinal characteristics that help a person deal with stress. They studied busy and successful executives and identified three characteristics they had in common:

- **Commitment:** People feel invested in what they are doing. They have energy for and are interested in their duties.
- **Control:** People have the realistic sense that what they are doing is in their realm of control; that is, they consider themselves to be active participants in their work instead of feeling hopeless and victimized by the work conditions. This is in contrast to developing learned helplessness.
- **Challenge:** People view change as an opportunity to act differently rather than as a crisis from which to defend themselves.

These three Cs are the attitudes that can help you to stay healthy despite having to deal with high levels of stress. They are essential in developing what is called a stress-hardy person. By developing stress hardiness, you will be able to deal with stress that many people find unbearable.

As you cultivate stress hardiness, keep in mind that you still need the social factor in the form of the support of friends and family members. Stress-hardy people tap into social support, which helps them to blunt the impact of stressful events. The social support must be directed toward caring and encouragement rather than fostering self-pity and dependence, however. It should help you to explore your options and to challenge yourself.

Consistent with the principle that a moderate degree of stress will help you to rewire your brain and inoculate you from greater stress, challenge focuses your energy on goals that require extra effort. This moderate stress activation can also keep you from becoming bored. Mihaly Csikszentmihalyi described how people can avoid being overwhelmed with anxiety from stimulation while also avoiding boredom. By investing your energy in finding a healthy balance between the two, you can experience flow, and enjoyment.

If you recall from Chapter 1, I described the inverse U that is optimum for learning and neuroplasticity. A moderate degree of stress is a good thing! The concept of flow and the insight from the inverse "U" are consistent with the development of resiliency. Engage in the world and make an effort to challenge yourself.

Your attitude affects not only how you feel about your life and how you approach stress, but also whether you believe that you have options. Do you invest your energy in becoming greater than you have been in the past? This investment can have a major bearing on your capacity to rewire your brain and respond with resiliency to stress.

Ambition and curiosity play a dynamic role in how well your brain thrives. Cultivating these two characteristics enables you to approach the future with vitality and a hunger for life. They open the door to your future and say yes to new experiences. By cultivating an insatiable curiosity, you make whatever environment you encounter an enriched environment. Enriched environments stimulate neuroplasticity, whereas impoverished environments damage your brain.

Stir up the motivation to turn possibilities into actualities. By cultivating ambition, you'll reach for a bright future with vast possibilities. Healthy ambition is *not* competitive or aggressive. It does <u>not</u> involve stepping on or over other people to attain one's goals. Healthy ambition involves curiosity and a goal-driven sense of purpose to expand beyond your current understanding.

My Father and Beethoven

My father admired and listened to Beethoven's symphonies until the last days of his life. When I spoke at his memorial service,

I described how his life was similar in theme to that of his favorite composer. My father's life and Beethoven's life carried the same themes of resilience and transcendence over adversity.

For Beethoven, resiliency emerged from struggles with his family. After Beethoven studied briefly with Haydn in Vienna, his mother died, so he returned to Bonn to care for his two younger brothers. His father should have managed the responsibility of raising his sons, but his alcoholism and abusiveness destroyed any capability for or interest in doing so. Beethoven drove his father out of town and raised his brothers by himself. After completing the role of father figure for his brothers, he returned to Vienna to launch a self-made career as the first composer who was not on the payroll of the nobility. He transformed Western music. Then tragedy hit. By the time of his *Third Symphony*, he knew he was becoming deaf with no hope of recovery. How could a composer with such great promise lose his hearing?

Surpassing this incredible limitation, Beethoven went on to write revolutionary symphonies, piano sonatas, and piano concertos. Each piece of music surpassed the last. The only constant was that each piece of music was transcendent. The culmination of all his work, the *Ninth Symphony*, was itself about transcendence and unity. Just days before my father died, he exclaimed, "How could he write something so magnificent?"

My father, too, transcended many potentially limiting obstacles. He and his two brothers were born soon after his father and his mother fled to the United States as refugees. His parents were deeply traumatized by having barely escaped genocide. Many of their close relatives were slaughtered by the Turks—some right in front of them. My father began his life in a household with parents who spoke little English and who had experienced horrific trauma, but this did not hold him back.

After growing up during the Depression and serving in the US Marine Corps in the Pacific during World War II, he became a prosecuting attorney who took three cases to the Supreme Court and convicted three people of murder even though the victims' bodies were never found. After serving as a judge, he retired and became a graduate student in art. Throughout his life he earned enough college credits for three Ph.Ds. He earned the title by which he was described in the front-page headline of the newspaper: "Superstar Judge Dies at 81."

Beethoven and my father defied limitations; they both made major efforts to transcend potentially limiting factors and pushed forward until the very end. Biographers of Beethoven have described him as the most generous famous person in history. And I have described my father as the most generous person I have ever met. Both transcended adversity and both thrived in their fields while always being generous to others.

These characteristics of a resilient attitude will expand your life and possibilities. Limitations that hold you back need not hold you back. A resilient attitude allows you to maintain a strong effort to attain your goals, to keep yourself from giving up, and to be open to the world around you along the way.

A Wise Sense of Humor

Wisdom involves humility and the ability to laugh at yourself. As you strive to improve yourself with realistic expectations, you should not take yourself too seriously. Lighten the load by acknowledging your humanity. Humor, especially if it's self-directed, is a liberating way to transcend your fixation on the petty details that bind you to unrealistic expectations.

Developing a sense of humor about yourself is incredibly liberating. It ensures that you don't take your current situation and yourself too seriously. Laughing at yourself allows you to see yourself as part of a greater whole. By not taking yourself too seriously, you can let things slide off you and not "sweat the small stuff." By developing a sense of humor, you'll cultivate positive thoughts and feelings.

Cultivating a sense of humor and practicing laughter are good for your brain and mind. There are several physiological changes that occur, particularly in the cardiovascular system, immune system, and brain.

Benefits of Laughter and Humor

- Improves cognitive function
- Exercises and relaxes the muscles
- Momentarily increases the heart rate and the blood pressure
- Decreases the cortisol level
- Increases natural killer cell activity
- Alters gene expression
- Stimulates dopamine
- Increases longevity
- Lowers anxiety, stress, and depression
- Raises self-esteem, energy, and sense of empowerment

It's critical that the type of humor you cultivate is positive. Negative humor, the kind of humor that belittles another person, is not wise; it's petty, mean, and not actually humor. Humor is light irony, metaphorical, incongruent, unbelievable believability, and elevates rather than degrades. Cultivating humor enhances mental health.

Psychological Benefits of Humor

↓ Anxiety
↓ Stress
↓ Depression
↑ Self-esteem
↑ Energy and hope
↑ Sense of empowerment

Humor boosts your biochemistry and helps lower the levels of the stress hormone cortisol while increasing immunoglobulin, natural killer (NK) cells, and plasma cytokine gamma interferon levels. Immunoglobulin consists of the antibodies that help the immune system to fight infections; it serves as one of the body's primary defense mechanisms. NK cells seek out and destroy abnormal cells; they are a key mechanism for *immunosurveillance*. Plasma cytokine gamma interferon orchestrates or regulates anticellular activities and turns on specific parts of the immune system.

Humor boosts the vitality of your thoughts and your emotions and enhances your self-esteem and your ability to deal with stress, anxiety, and depression. Given all the health benefits that it provides, humor can be understood as emotional wisdom. So, lighten up and cultivate humor for wisdom! Have a good laugh. It's good for your brain.

Maximize the time you spend in the emotional state you want to be in so that it comes naturally to you and serves as your baseline emotional tone. Do everything that you can do to promote the thoughts, perspective, and behaviors that kindle emotional wisdom.

References

Chapter 1

Allman, J., Hakeem, A., & Watson, K. (2002). Two phylogenetic specializations in the human brain. *Neuroscientist, 8,* 335–346.

Doidge, N. (2007). *The brain that changes itself.* New York: Viking Press.

Elbert, T., Pantev, C., Weinbruch, C., Rockstrob, B., & Taub, E. (1995). Increased cortical representation of the fingers of the left hand in string players. *Science, 270,* 305–307.

Frings, L., Wagner, K., Unterrainer, J., Spreer, J., Halsband, V., & Schulze-Bonhange, A. (2006). Gender-related differences in lateralization of hippocampal activation and cognitive strategy. *Brain Imaging, 17,* 417–421.

McEwen, B., & Morrison, J. (2013). Brain on stress: Vulnerability and plasticity of the prefrontal cortex over the course. *Neuron, 79,* 16–29.

MacPherson, S. E., Philips, L. H., & Della Salla, S. (2002). Ages, executive function, and social decision making: A dorsolateral prefrontal theory of cognitive aging. *Psychology and Aging, 17,* 598–609.

Oomen, C. A., Behinschtein, P., Kent, B. A., Saksida, L. M., & Bussey, T. J. (2014). Adult hippocampal neurogenesis and its role in cognitive. *Wiley Interdiscip. Rev. Cognitive Science,* 5(5), 573–587.

Pascual-Leone, A., Amedi, A., Fregi, F., & Merabet, L. B. (2005). The plastic human brain cortex. *Annual Reviews of Neuroscience,* 28, 380.

Pascual-Leone, A., Hamilton, R., Tormos, J. M., Keenan, J. P., & Catala, M. D. (1999). Neuroplasticity in the adjustment to blindness. In J. Grafman & Y. Christen (Eds.), *Neural plasticity: Building a bridge from the laboratory to the clinic* (pp. 94–108). New York: Springer-Verlag.

Postle, B. R. (2020). *Essentials of cognitive neuroscience,* 2nd ed. Hoboken, NJ: Wiley.

Rosenzweig, E. S., Barnes, C. A., & McNaughton, B. L. (2002). Making room for new memories. *Nature Neuroscience,* 5(1), 6–8.

Witelson, S. F., Beresh, H., & Kigar, D. L. (2006). Intelligence and brain size in 100 postmortem brains: Sex, lateralization and age factors. *Brain,* 129, 386–398.

Chapter 2

Benros, M. E., Waltoft, B. L., Nordentoft, M., Ostergaard, S. D., Eaton, W. W., Krogh, J., & Mortensen, P. B. (2013). Autoimmune disease and severe infections as risk factors for mood disorders: A nationwide study. *JAMA Psychiatry,* 70(8), 812–20.

Bested, A. C., Logan, A. C., & Selhub, E. M. (2013). Intestinal microbiota, probiotics, and mental health: From Metchnikoff to modern advances: Part II—Contemporary contextual research. *Gut Pathology,* 5(1), 3.

Cao, Y., Zhang, X., Shang, W., Xu, J., Wang, X., Hu, X., Ao, Y., & Cheng, H. (2013). Proinflammatory cytokines stimulate mitochondria superoxide flashes in articular chondrocytes vitro and in situ. *PLoS ONE,* 8(6), e66444.

Cerf, M. E. (2013). Beta cell dysfunction and insulin resistance. *Frontiers in Endocrinology,* 4, 37–45.

Clark, W. (2008). *In defense of self: How the immune system really works*. New York: Oxford University Press.

Cryan, J. E., & Dinan, T. G. (2012). Mind-altering microorganisms: The impact of the gut microbiota on the brain and behavior. *Nature Reviews Neuroscience, 13*, 701–712.

De La Monte, S. M. (2008). Alzheimer's disease in type 3 diabetes— Evidence reviewed. *Journal of Diabetes Science and Technology, 22*(6), 1101–1113.

De Meyer, T. (2011). Telemere length integrates psychological factors in successful aging story, but what about biology? *Psychosomatic Medicine, 73*(7), 524–527.

Denham, J., et al. (2016). Increased expression of telomere-regulating genes in endurance athletes with long leukocyte telomere. *Journal of Applied Physiology, 120*(2), 148–158.

Eisenberger, N. I., Berkman, E. T., Inagaki, T. K., Rameson, L. T., Mashal, N. M., & Irwin, M. R. (2010). Inflammation-induced anhedonia: Endotoxin reduces ventral striatum responses to reward. *Biol. Psychiatry, 68*(8), 748–754.

Esparza, J., Fox, C., Harper, I. T., Bennett, P. H., Schultz, L. O., Valencia, M. E., & Rasussin, E. (2000). Daily energy expenditure in Mexican and US Pima Indians: Low physical activity as a possible cause of obesity. *International Journal of Obesity and Related Metabolic Disorders, 24*, 55–59.

Francis, D. D., & Meany, M. J. (1999). Maternal care and the development of stress responses. *Current Opinion. Neurobiology, 9*(1), 128–134.

Frayn, K., & Evans, R. (2019). *Human metabolism: A regulatory perspective*, 4th ed. Hoboken, NJ: Wiley.

Gustafson, D., Lissner, L., Bengtsson, C., Björkelund, C., & Skoog, I. (2004). A 24-year follow-up of body mass index and cerebral atrophy. *Neurology, 23;63*(10):1876–81. doi: 10.1212/01.wnl .0000141850.47773.5f. PMID: 15557505.

Janelidzes, S., Matte, D., Westrin, A., Traskman,-Bendz, L., & Brundin, L. (2011). Cytokine levels in the blood may distinguish suicide attempters from depressed patients. *Brain, Behavior, and Immunity, 25*, 335–339.

Kendler, K. S. (2005). "A gene for . . ." The nature of gene action in psychiatric disorders. *American Journal of Psychiatry, 162,* 1243–1252.

Esteves, A. R., Gozes, I., & Cardoso, S. M. (2014). The rescue of microtubule-dependent traffic recovers mitochondrial function in Parkinson's disease. *Biochimica et Biophysica Acta: Molecular Basis of Disease, 1842*(1), 7–21.

Lane, N., & Martin, W. (2010). The energetics of genome complexity. *Nature, 467*(3318), 929–934.

Ledderose, C., Bao, Y., Lidicky, M., Zipperle, J., Li, L., Strasser, K., Shapiro, N. I., & Junger, W. G. (2014). Mitochondria are gate-keepers of T cell function by purinergic signaling. *Journal of Biological Chemistry, 289*(37), 25936–25945.

Liang, Q., & Kobayashi, S. (2016). Mitochondrial quality control in the diabetic heart. *Journal of Molecular and Cellular Cardiology, 95,* 57–69.

Lupski, J. R. (2013). Genetics: genome mosaicism—One human, multiple genomes. *Science, 341,* 358–386.

Lin, J., Epel, E. S., & Blackburn, E. H. (2009). Telomere, maintenance, and the aging of cells and organisms. In G. G. Berntson & J. T. Cacioppo (Eds.), *Handbook of neuroscience for the behavioral sciences* (vol. 2, pp. 1280–1296). Hoboken, NJ: Wiley.

Lin, A., & Marsland, A. (2014). Peripheral pro-inflammatory cytokines and cognitive aging: The role of metabolic risk. In A. W. Kusnecov & H. Anisman (Eds.), *Psychoneuroimmunology* (pp. 330–346). New York: Wiley.

Maes, M., Kubera, M., & Leunis, J. C. (2008). The gut–brain barrier in major depression: Intestinal mucosal dysfunction with an increased translocation of LPS from gram-negative enterobacteria (leaky gut) plays a role in inflammatory pathophysiology of depression. *Neuro. Edcrinol. Lett., 29*(1), 117–124.

Maier, S. F., & Watkins, L. R. (2009). Neuroimmunology. In G. G. Berntson & J. T. Cacioppo (Eds.), *Handbook of neuroscience for the behavioral sciences* (vol. 1, pp. 119–135). Hoboken, NJ: Wiley.

Mayer, E. (2016). *The mind–gut connection: How the hidden conversation within our bodies impact our mood, our choices, and overall health*. New York: HarperWave.

McGowan, P. O., Sasaki, A., D'Alessio, A. C., Dymov, S., Lobonte, B., Szyf, M., Turecki, G., & Meany, M. (2009). Epigenetic regulation of the glucocortion receptor in human brain associates with child abuse. *Nature Neuroscience, 12*(3), 342–348.

Morgan, N., Irwin, M. R., Chung, M., & Wang, C. (2014). The effects of mind-body therapies on the immune system: Meta-analysis. *PLoS ONE, 9*(7), e100903.

Moynihan, J. A., Heffner, K. L., Caserta, M. T., & O'Connor, T. G. (2014). Stress and immune function in humans: A life-course perspective. In A. W. Kusnecov & H. Anisman (Eds.), *The Wiley Blackwell handbook of psychoneuroimmunology* (pp. 251–265). New York: Wiley.

Murgatroyd, C., Patchev, A. V., Wu, Y., Micale, V., Bockmühl, Y., Fischer, D., Holsboer, F., Wotjak, C. T., Almeida, O. F. X., & Spengler, D. (2009). Dynamic methylation programs persistent adverse effects of early-life stress. *Nature Neuroscience, 12,* 1559–1565.

Nezu, A. M., Raggio, G., Evans, A. N., & Nezu, C. H. (2013). Diabetes mellitus. In A. M. Nezu, C. H. Nezu, & P. A. Geller (Eds.), *Handbook of psychology: Health psychology* (vol. 9, pp. 200–217). Hoboken, NJ: Wiley.

Nivison, M., Guillozet-Bongaarts, A. L., & Montine, T. J. (2010). Inflammation, fatty acid oxidation, and neurodegeneration. In K. Kendall-Tacket (Ed.), *The psychoneuroimmunology of chronic disease* (pp. 23–53). Washington, DC: American Psychological Association.

Naik, E., & Dixit, V. M. (2011). Mitochondrial reactive oxygen species drive proinflammatory cytokine production. *Journal of Experimental Medicine, 208*(3), 417–420.

Nurse, D. (2020). *What is life?* New York: Norton.

Parrington, J. (2015). *The deeper genome: Why there is more to the human genome than meets the eye*. New York: Oxford University Press.

Pontzer, H. (2021). *Burn: The misunderstood science of metabolism*. New York: Penguin Books.

Procaccini, C., Pucino, V., Mantzoros, C. S., & Matarese, G. (2015). Leptin in autoimmune disease. *Metabolism: Clinical and Experimental, 64*(1), 92–104.

Reul, L. M. H., Collins, A., & Gutierrez-Mecinas, M. (2011). Stress effects on the brain: Intracellular signaling cascades, epigenetic mechanisms, implications in behavior. In C. D. Conrad (Ed.), *Handbook of stress: Neuropsychological effects on the brain*. Hoboken, NJ: Wiley-Blackwell.

Sompayrac, L. (2016). *How the immune system works*, 6th ed. Hoboken, NJ: Wiley.

Tammen, S. A., Friso, S., & Choi, S. W. (2013). Epigenetics: The link between nature and nurture. *Molecular Aspects of Medicine, 34,* 753–764.

Thoudam, T., Jeon, J. H., Ha, C. M., & Lee, I. K. (2016). Role of mitochondria-associated endoplasmic reticulum membrane in inflammation-mediated metabolic diseases. *Mediators of Inflammation,* 1–18.

Uher, R. (2014). Gene–environment interactions in severe mental illness. *Frontiers of Psychiatry, 5,* 48.

Vieira-Potter, V. J. (2014). Inflammation and macrophage modulation in adipose tissues. *Cellular Microbiology, 16*(10), 1484–1492.

Wahlsten, D. (2019). *Genes, brain function, and behavior*. Cambridge, MA: Academic Press.

Zhang, T. Y., & Meany, M. J. (2010). Epigenetics and the environmental regulation of the genome and its function. *Annual Review of Psychology, 61,* 439–466.

Chapter 3

Arden, J. (2015). *Brain2Brain*. Hoboken, NJ: Wiley.

Arden, J. (2019). *Mind–brain–gene: Toward psychotherapy integration*. New York: Norton.

Arden, J. B. (2014). *The brain-based anxiety workbook*. PESI Press.

Arden, J. B., & DalCorso, D. (2014). *The brain-based OCD workbook*. PESI Press.

Hartley, C. A., & Phelps, E. A. (2012). Anxiety and decision making. *Biological Psychiatry, 72,* 113–118.

Hill, R., & Dahliz, M. (2022). *The practitioner's guide to the science of psychotherapy.* New York: Norton.

Knapska, E., Macias, M., Mikosza, M., Nowaka, A., Owczarekb, D., Wawrzyniakb, M., Pieprzyk, M., et al. (2012). Functional anatomy of neural circuits regulating fear and extinction. *Proceedings of the National Academy of Sciences, 109,* 17093–17098.

LeDoux, J. (2016). *Anxious: Using the brain to understand and treat fear and anxiety.* New York: Penguin.

Lebow, M.A., & Chen, A. (2016). Overshadowed by the amygdala: the bed nucleus of the stria terminalis emerges as key to psychiatric disorders. *Mol Psychiatry. 21*(4): 450–463. doi: 10.1038/mp.2016.1.

O'Doherty, J., Kringelback, M. L., Rolls, E. T., Hornak, J., & Andrews, C. (2001). Abstract reward and punishment representation in the human orbital frontal cortex. *Nature Neuroscience, 4,* 95–102.

Chapter 4

Arden, J. (2015). *Brain2Brain,* Hoboken, NJ: Wiley.

Arden, J. (2019). *Mind–brain–gene: Toward psychotherapy integration.* New York: Norton.

Bansal, Y., & Kuhad, A. (2016). Mitochondrial dysfunction of depression. *Current Neuropharmacology, 14*(6), 610–618.

Davidson, R. J., Jackson, L., & Kalin, N. H. (2000). Emotion, plasticity, context, and regulation. *Psychological Bulletin, 126,* 890–909.

Goldapple, K., Segal, Z., Garson, C., Lau, M., Bieling, P., Kennedy, S., & Mayberg, H. (2004). Modulation of cortical-limbic pathways in major depression: Treatment-specific effects of cognitive behavioral therapy. *Archives of General Psychiatry, 61,* 34–41.

Kirsch, I. (2002). Are drug and placebo effects in depression addictive? *Biological Psychiatry, 47,* 733–735.

Lambert, K. (2008). *Lifting depression: A neuroscience hands-on approach to activating your brain's healing power.* New York: Basic Books.

Leuchter, A., Cook, I. A., Witte, E. A., Morgan, M., & Abrams, M. (2002). Changes in brain function of depressed subjects during treatment with placebo. *American Journal of Psychiatry, 159,* 122–129.

Lockwood, L. E., Su, S., & Youssef, N. A. (2015). The role of epigenetics in depression and suicide: A platform for gene-environment interactions *Psychiatry Res., 228,* 235–242.

Maletic, V., & Raison, C. (2017). *The new mind–body science of depression.* New York: Norton.

Montgomery, M. K., & Turner, N. (2015). Mitochondrial dysfunction and insulin resistance: An update. *Endocrine Connections, 4*(1), R1–R15.

Moore, D. S. (2015). *The developing genome: An introduction to behavioral epigenetics.* New York: Oxford University Press.

Morris, G., et al. (2015). Central pathways causing fatigue in neuroinflammatory and autoimmune illness. *BMC Medicine, 13*(1), 28.

Morrison, S. F., Madden, C. J., & Tupone, D. (2014). Central neural regulation of brown adipose tissue thermogenesis and energy expenditure. *Cell Metabolism, 19,* 741–756.

Moussavi, S., Chatterji, S., Verdes, E., Tandon, A., Patel, V., & Ustun, B. (2007). Depression, chronic diseases, and decrements, in health: Results from the World Health Surveys. *Lancet, 370*(9590), 85–88.

Muoio, D. M., & Newgard, C. B. (2008). Mechanisms of disease: Molecular and metabolic mechanisms of insulin resistance and β-cell failure in type 2 diabetes. *Nature Review: Molecular Cell Biology, 9*(3), 193–205.

Marsden, W. N. (2013). Synaptic plasticity in depression: Molecular, cellular and functional correlates. *Progress in Neuro-Psychopharmacology and Biological Psychiatry, 43,* 168–184.

Mayberg, H., Silva, J. A., Brannan, S. K., Tekell, J. L., Mahurin, R. K., McGunnis, S., & Jarebek, P. A. (2002). The functional neuroanatomy of the placebo effect. *American Journal of Psychiatry, 159,* 728–737.

Murgatroyd, C., Patchev, A. V., Wu, Y., Micale, V., Bockmuhl, Y., Fischer, D., Holsboer, F., et al. (2009). Dynamic DNA methylation programs persistent adverse effects of early-life stress. *Nature Neuroscience, 12,* 1559–1566.

Nanni, V., Uher, R., & Danese, A. (2011). Childhood maltreatment predicts unfavorable course of illness and treatment outcome in depression: A meta-analysis. *American Journal of Psychiatry, 169*(2), 141–151.

Niemi, M. J. (2009). Cure in the mind. *Scientific American Mind, 20,* 42–50.

Nixon, N. L., Liddle, P. F., Nixon, E., Worwood, G., Liotti, M., & Palaniyappan, L. (2014). Biological vulnerability to depression: Linked structural and functional brain network findings. *British Journal of Psychiatry, 204,* 283–289.

O'Doherty, J., Kringelback, M. L., Rolls, E. T., Hornak, J., & Andrews, C. (2001). Abstract reward and punishment representation in the human orbital frontal cortex. *Nature Neuroscience, 4,* 95–102.

Posner, J., Hellerstein, D. J., Gat, I., Mechling, A., Klahr, K., Wang, Z., McGrath, P. J., et al. (2013). Antidepressants normalize the default mode network in patients with dysthymia. *JAMA Psychiatry, 70*(4), 373–382.

Stieglitz, J., Trumble, B. C., Thompson, M. E., Blackwell, A. D., Kaplan, H., & Gurven, M. (2015). Depression as sickness behavior? A test of the host defense hypothesis in a high pathogen population. *Brain, Behavior, and Immunity, 49,* 130–139.

Verhoeven, J. E., Révész, D., Epel, E. S., Lin, J., Wolkowitz, O. M., & Penninx, B. W. (2014). Major depressive disorder and accelerated cellular aging: Results from a large psychiatric cohort study. *Molecular Psychiatry, 19*(8), 895–901.

Chapter 5

Ainsworth, M. D. S., Blehar, M. C., Waters, E., & Wall, S. (1978). *Patterns of attachment: A psychological study of the strange situation.* Hillsdale, NJ: Erlbaum.

Arbib, M. A. (2002). Language evolution: The mirror system hypothesis. In M. Aribib (Ed.), *The handbook of brain theory and neural networks* (2nd ed., pp. 606–611). Cambridge, MA: MIT Press.

Allman, J., Tetreault, N. A., Hakeem, A. Y., & Park, S. (2011). The von Economo neurons in apes and humans. *American Journal of Human Biology, 23,* 5–21.

Berns, G. S., McClure, S. M., Pagnoni, G., & Montague, P. R. (2001). Predictability modulates human brain response to reward. *Journal of Neuroscience, 21,* 2793–2798.

Barnett, L. (2017). *How emotions are made.* New York: Houghton Mifflin Harcourt.

Bartels, A., & Zekis, S. (2000). The neural basis of romantic love. *Neuro Report, 11,* 3829–3834.

Bassuk, S. S., Glass, T. A., & Berekman, L. F. (1998). Social disengagement and incident cognitive decline in community-dwelling elderly persons. *Annals of Internal Medicine, 131,* 165–173.

Baylin, J., & Hughes, D. (2016). *The neurobiology of attachment-focused therapy: Enhancing connection and trust in the treatment of children and adolescents.* New York: Norton.

Chungani, H. (2001). Local brain functional activity following early deprivation: A study of postinstitutional Romanian orphans. *Neuro Image, 14,* 184–188.

Cohen, S. (2004). Social relationships and health. *American Psychologist, 59,* 676–684.

Cohen, S., Doyle, W. J., Turnes, R., Alper, C. M., & Skoner, D. F. (2003). Sociability and susceptibility to the common cold. *Psychological Science, 14*(5), 389–395.

Cozolino, L. (2014). *The neuroscience of human relationships: Attachment and the developing social brain,* 2nd ed., Norton Series on Interpersonal Neurobiology. New York: Norton.

Damasio, A. (2003). *Looking for Spinoza's joy, sorrow, and the feeling brain.* New York: Harcourt.

Field, T. (2001). *Touch.* Cambridge, MA: MIT Press.

Field, T. (2002). Violence and touch deprivation in adolescents. *Adolescence, 37,* 735–749.

Field, T. M., Healy, B., Goldstein, S., & Bendell, D. (1988). Infants of depressed mothers show "depressed" behavior even with non-depressed adults. *Child Development, 59,* 1569–1579.

Fiori, L. M., & Turecki, G. (2012). Broadening, our horizons: Gene expression profiling to help better understand the neurobiology of suicide and depression. *Neurobiology Disorders, 45*, 14–22.

Fischer, L., Ames, E. W., Chisholm, K., & Savoie, L. (1997). Problems reported by parents of Romanian orphans adopted in British Columbia. *International Journal of Behavioral Development, 20*, 67–87.

Francis, D. D., Diorio, J., Liu, D., & Meany, M. J. (1999). Variations in maternal care form the basis for a non-genomic mechanism of intergenerational transmission of individual differences in behavioral and endocrine responses to stress. *Science, 286*(5442), 1155–1158.

Fries, A. B., Ziegler, T. E., Kurian, J. R., Jacoris, S., & Pollak, S. D. (2005). Early experience in humans is associated with changes in neuropeptides critical for regulating social behavior. *Proceedings of the National Academy of Sciences, 102*, 17237–17240.

Frith, C. D., & Frith, U. (1999). Interacting minds: A biological basis. *Science, 286*, 1692–1695.

Gallese, V. (2001). The shared manifold hypothesis: From mirror neurons to empathy. *Journal of Consciousness Studies, 8*(5–7), 33–50.

Gallese, V., Fadiga, L., Fogassi, L., & Rizzolatti, G. (1996). Action recognition in the premotor cortex. *Brain, 119*, 593–609.

Goleman, D. (2006). *Social intelligence: The new science of human relationships*. New York: Bantam Books.

Goodfellow, L. M. (2003). The effects of therapeutic back massage on psychophysiologic variables and immune function in spouses of patients with cancer. *Nursing Research, 52*, 318–328.

Grossman, K. E., Grossman, K. F., & Warter, V. (1981). German children's behavior toward their mothers at 12 months and their father at 18 months in Ainsworth's Strange Situation. *International Journal of Behavioral Development, 4*, 157–181.

Gunmar, M. (2001). Effects of early deprivation: Findings from orphanage-reared infants and children. In C. Nelson & M. Luciana (Eds.), *Handbook of developmental cognitive neuroscience* (pp. 617–629). Cambridge, MA: MIT Press.

Hawkley, L. C., & Cacioppo, J. T. (2010). Loneliness matters: A theoretical and empirical review of consequences and mechanisms. *Annals of Behavioral Medicine, 40*, 218–227.

Iacoboni, M. (2008). *Mirroring people*. New York: Farrar, Straus & Giroux.

Ijzendoorn, M. H. van, & Bakerman-Kranenburg, M. J. (1997). Intergenerational transmission of attachment: A move to the contextual level. In L. Atkinson & K. Zucker (Eds.), *Attachment and psychopathology* (pp. 135–170). New York: Guilford Press.

Kiecolt-Glaser, J. K., Rickers, D., George, J., Messick, G., Speicher, C. E., Garner, W., & Glaser, R. (1984). Urinary cortisol levels, cellular immunocompetency, and loneliness in psychiatric inpatients. *Psychosomatic Medicine, 46*(1), 15–23.

Kosfeld, M., Heinrichs, M., Zak, P. J., Fischbacher, V., & Fehr, E. (2005). Oxytocin increases trust in humans. *Nature, 435*(7042), 673–676.

Koski, L., Iacoboni, M., Dubeau, M. C., Woods, R. P., & Mazziotta, J. C. (2003). Modulation of cortical activity during different imitative behaviors. *Journal of Neurophysiology, 89*, 460–471.

Kuhn, C. M., & Shanberg, S. M. (1998). Responses to maternal separation: Mechanisms and mediators. *International Journal of Developmental Neuroscience, 16*, 261–270.

Kumsta, R., & Heinrichs, M. (2013). Oxytocin, stress, and social behavior: Neurogenetics of the human oxytocin system. *Current Opinion in Neurobiology, 2*, 11–16.

Lepore, S. J., Allen, K. A. M., & Evans, G. W. (1993). Social support lowers cardiovascular reactivity to an acute stress. *Psychosomatic Medicine, 55*, 518–524.

Lieberman, M. D. (2013). *Social: Why our brains are wired to connect*. New York: Crown.

Main, M., & Goldwyn, R. (1994). *Adult attachment scoring and classification system*. Unpublished manuscript, University of California, Berkeley.

McClelland, D., McClelland, D. C., & Kirchnit, C. (1988). The effect of motivational arousal through films on salivary immunoglobulin. *Psychology and Health, 2*, 31–52.

Meany, M. J., Aitken, D. H, Viau, V., Sharma, S., & Sarrieau, A. (1989). Neonatal handling alters adrenocortical negative feedback sensitivity in hippocampal type II glucocorticoid receptor binding in the rat. *Neuroendocrinology, 50,* 597–604.

Mesulam, M. M. (1998). From sensation to cognition. *Brain, 121,* 1013–1052.

Mikulincer, M., Saber, P. R., Gillath, O., & Nitzberg, R. A. (2005). Attachment, caregiving and altruism: Boosting attachment security increases compassion and helping. *Journal of Personality and Social Psychology, 89,* 817–839.

Mikulincer, M., & Shaver, R. (2001, July). Attachment theory and intergroup bias: Evidence that priming the secure base schema attenuates negative reactions to outgroups. *Journal of Personality and Social Psychology, 81,* 97–115.

Miller, G. (2005). New neurons strive to fit in. *Science, 311,* 938–940.

Miyake, K., Chen, S., & Campos, J. (1985). Infant temperament, mother's mode of interaction, and attachment in Japan. In I. Bretheron & E. Waters (Eds.), *Growing points in attachment theory and research* (pp. 276–297). Ann Arbor, MI: Society for Research in Child Development.

Panksepp, J. (1998). *Affective neuroscience: The foundations of human and animal emotions.* New York: Oxford University Press.

Phillips, M. L., Young, A. W., Senior, C., Brammer, M., Andrew, C., Calder, A. J., Bullmer, E. T., et al. (1997). A specific substrate for perceiving facial expression of disgust. *Nature, 389,* 495–498.

Remington, R. (2002). Calming music and hand massage with agitated elderly. *Nursing Research, 54,* 317–323.

Rizzolatti, G., & Arbib, M. A. (1998). Language within our grasp. *Trends in Neurosciences, 21*(5), 188–194.

Rolls, E. T., O'Doherty, J., Kringelbach, M. L., Francis, S., Bowtell, R., & McGlone, F. (2003). Representations of pleasant and painful touch in the human orbital frontal and cingulated cortices. *Cerebral Cortex, 13,* 308–317.

Russell, D. W., & Cutrona, C. E. (1991). Social support, stress, and depression symptoms among the elderly: Test of a process model. *Psychology and Aging, 6,* 190–201.

Rutter, M., Kreppner, J., & O'Connor, T. (2001). Specificity and heterogeneity in children's responses to profound institutional deprivation. *British Journal of Psychiatry, 179*, 97–103.

Saarni, C., Mumme, D. L., & Campos, J. J. (2000). Emotional development: Action, communication, and understanding. In W. Damon & N. Eisenberg (Eds.), *Handbook of child psychology: Vol. 3. Social, emotional, and personality development* (5th ed., pp. 237–309). Hoboken, NJ: Wiley.

Sabbagh, M. A. (2004). Understanding orbital frontal contributions to the theory-of-mind reasoning: Implications for autism. *Brain and Cognition, 55*, 209–219.

Sapolsky, R. M. (1990). Stress in the wild. *Scientific American, 262*, 116–123.

Siegal, D., & Varley, R. (2002). Neural systems involved in the "theory of mind." *Nature Reviews Neuroscience, 3*, 267–276.

Spitzer, S. B., Llabre, M. M., Ironson, G. H., Gellman, M. D., & Schneiderman, N. (1992). The influence of social situations on ambulatory blood pressure. *Psychosomatic Medicine, 54*, 79–86.

Thomas, P. D., Goodwin, J. M., & Goodwin, J. S. (1985). Effect of social support on stress related changes in cholesterol level, uric acid level, and immune function in an elderly sample. *American Journal of Psychiatry, 142*, 732–737.

Wallin, D. (2007). *Attachment in psychotherapy*. New York: Guilford Press.

Weaver, I. C. G., Cervoni, N., Champagne, F. A., D'Alessio, A. C., Sharma, S., Seckl, J. R., Dymov, S., et al. (2004). Epigenetic programming by maternal behavior. *Nature Neuroscience, 7*, 847–854.

Weller, A., & Feldman, R. (2003). Emotion regulation and touch in infants: The role of cholecystokinin and opioids. *Peptides, 24*, 779–788.

Wexler, B. (2006). *Brain and culture: Neurobiology, ideology, and social change*. Boston: MIT Press.

Chapter 6

Adlard, P. A., Perreau, V. M., & Cotman, C. W. (2005). The exercise-induced expression of BDNF within the hippocampus varies across life-span. *Neurology of Aging, 26*, 511–520.

Arden, J. (2014). *The brain bible*. New York: McGraw Hill.

Carro, E., Trejo, J. L., Busiguina, S., & Torres-Aleman, I. (2001). Circulating insulin-like growth factor 1 mediates the protective effects of physical exercise against brain insults of different etiology and anatomy. *Journal of Neuroscience, 21*, 5678–5684.

Chekroud, S. R., Gueorguieva, R., Zheutlin, A. B., Paulus, M., Krumholz, H. M., Krystal, J. H., & Chekroud, A. M. (2018). Association between physical exercise and mental health in 1.2 million individuals in the USA between 2011 and 2015: A cross-sectional study. *Lancet Psychiatry, 5*, 739–747.

Chilton, W. L, Marques, F. Z., West, J., Kannourakis, G., Berzins, S. P., O'Brien, B. J., & Charchar, F. J. (2014). Acute exercise leads to regulation of telomere-associated genes and microRNA expression in genes. *PLOS One, 9*(4), e92088.

Cotman, C. W., & Berchtold, N. C. (2002). Exercise: A behavioral intervention to enhance brain health and plasticity. *Trends in Neuroscience, 25*, 295–301.

Dietrich, A., & McDaniel, W. W. (2004). Endocannabinoids and exercise. *British Journal of Sports Science in Sports and Exercise, 38*, 536–578.

Fabel, K., Fabel, K., Tam, B., Kaufer, D., Baiker, A., Simmons, N., Kuo, C. J., et al. (2003). VEGF is necessary for exercise-induced adult hippocampus neurogenesis. *European Journal of Neurogenesis, 18*, 2803–2812.

Farmer, J., Zhao, X., Praag, H. van, Wodtke, K., Gage, F. H., & Christie, B. R. (2004). Effects of voluntary exercise on synaptic plasticity and gene expression in the two dentate gyrus of adult male Sprague-Dawley rats in vivo. *Neuroscience, 124*, 71–79.

Ford, E. S. (2002). Does exercise reduce inflammation? Physical activity and C-reactive protein among U.S. adults. *Epidemiology, 13*, 561–568.

Frank, M. G., Issa, N. P., & Stryker, M. P. (2001). Sleep enhances plasticity in the developing visual cortex. *Neuron, 30*, 275–287.

Geffken, D. F., Cushman, M., Burke, G. L., Polak, J. F., Sakkinen, P. A., & Tracy, R. P. (2001). Association between physical activity and markers of inflammation in a healthy elderly population. *American Journal of Epidemiology, 153*, 242–260.

Kohut, M. L., McCann, D. A., Konopka, D. W. R., Cunnick, J. E., Franke, W. D., Castillo, M. C., & Vanderah, R. E. (2006). Aerobic exercise, but not flexibility/resistance exercise, reduces serum IL-18, CRP, and IL-6 independent of β-blockers, BMI, and psychosocial factors in older adults. *Brain, Behavior, and Immunity, 20*, 20–209.

Larson, E. B., Wang, L., Bowen, J. D., McCormick, W. C., Teri, L., Crane, P., & Kukull, W. (2006). Exercise is associated with reduced risk for the incidence of dementia among persons 65 years of age and older. *Ann Intern, 144*, 73–81.

Lieberman, D. E. (2020). *Exercised: Why something we never evolved to do is healthy and rewarding.* New York: Pantheon

Manger, T. A., & Motta, R. W. (2005). The impact of an exercise program on post traumatic stress disorder, anxiety and depression. *International Journal of Emergency Mental Health, 7*, 49–57.

McFadden, K. L., Cornier, M. A., Melanson, E. L., Bechtell, J. L., & Tregellas, J. R. (2013). Effects of exercise on resting-state default mode and salience network activity in overweight/obese adults. *Neuroreport, 24*(15), 866–871.

Neeper, S. A., Gomez-Pinilla, F., Choi, J., & Cotman, C. W. (1996). Physical activity increases mRNA from brain-derived neurotrophic factor and nerve growth factor in the rat brain. *Brain Research, 726*, 49–56.

O'Connor, P. J., & Youngstedt, M. A. (1995). Influence of exercise on human sleep. *Exercise and Sport Science Reviews, 23*, 105–134.

Pascual-Leone, A., Dang, N., Cohen, L. G., Brasil-Neto, J. P., Cammarota, A., & Hallet, M. (1995). Modulation of muscle responses evoked by transcranial magnetic stimulation during the acquisition of new fine motor skills. *Journal of Neurophysiology, 74*(3), 1037–1045.

Ratey, J. (2008). *Spark: The revolutionary new science of exercise and the brain.* New York: Little, Brown.

Ristow, M., Zarse, K., Oberbach, A., Klöting, N., Birringer, M., Kiehntopf, M., Stumvoll, M., Kahn, C. R., & Blüher, M. (2009).

Antioxidants prevent health-promoting effects of physical exercise in humans. *Proceedings of the National Academy of Sciences of the United States of America, 106*(21), 8665–8670.

Strohle, A., Feller, C., Onken, M., Godemann, F., Heinz, A., & Dimeo, F. (2005). The acute anti-panic activity of aerobic exercise. *American Journal of Psychiatry, 162*, 2376–2378.

Swain, R. A., Harris, A. B., Wiener, E. C., Dutka, M. V., Morris, H. D., Theien, B. E., Konda, S., et al. (2003). Prolonged exercise induces angiogenesis and increases cerebral blood volume in primary cortex of the rat. *Neuroscience, 117*, 1037–1046.

Van Praag, H., Shubert, T., Zhao, C., & Gage, F. H. (2005). Exercise enhances learning and hipppocampal neurogenesis in aged mice. *Journal of Neuroscience, 25*(38), 8680–8685.

Yan, Z., Lira, V. A., & Greene, N. P. (2012). Exercise training-induced regulation of mitochondrial quality. *Exercise and Sport Sciences Reviews, 40*(3), 159–164.

Chapter 7

Arden, J. (2014). *The brain bible*. New York: McGraw Hill.

Buchanan, T. W., & Adolphs, R. (2004). The neuroanatomy of emotional memory in humans. In D. Reisberg & P. Hertel (Eds.), *Memory and emotion* (pp. 42–75). New York: Oxford University Press.

Cohen, N. J., & Squire, L. R. (1980). Preserved learning and retention of pattern-analyzing skill in amnesia: Dissociation of knowing how and knowing that. *Science, 210*, 207–209.

Cozolino, L. (2013). *The social neuroscience of education: Optimizing attachment and learning in the classroom* (The Norton Series on the Social Neuroscience of Education). New York: Norton.

Golomb, J., deLeon, M. J., Kluger, A., George, A. E., Tarshish, C., & Ferris, S. H. (1993). Hippocampal atrophy in normal aging: An association with recent memory impairment. *Archives of Neurology, 50*(9), 967–973.

Kapur, N., Scholey, K., Moore, E., Barker, S., Brice, J., Thompson, S., Shiel, A., et al. (1996). Long-term retention deficits in two cases of disproportionate retrograde amnesia. *Journal of Cognitive Neuroscience, 8*, 416–434.

LeDoux, J. E., Romanski, L. M., & Xagorasis, A. E. (1989). Indelibility of subcortical emotional memories. *Journal of Cognitive Neuroscience, 1,* 238–243.

Milner, B. (1965). Memory disturbances after bilateral hippocampal lesions in man. In P. M. Milner & S. E. Glickman (Eds.), *Cognitive processes and brain.* Princeton, NJ: Van Nostrand.

Nader, K., & Einarsson, E. O. (2010). Memory reconsolidation: An update, *Annals of the New York Academy of Sciences, 1191,* 27–41.

Ochs, E., & Capps, L. (1996). Narrating the self. *Annual Review of Anthropology, 25,* 19–43.

Reisberg, D., & Heuer, F. (2004). Memory for emotional events. In D. Reisberg & P. Hertel (Eds.), *Memory and emotion* (pp. 3–41). New York: Oxford University Press.

Rudy, J. W., & Morledge, P. (1994). Ontogeny of contextual fear conditioning in rats: Implications for consolidation, infantile amnesia, and hippocampal system function. *Behavioral Neuroscience, 108,* 227–234.

Schacter, D. L. (1996). *Searching for memory: The brain, the mind, and the past.* New York: Basic Books.

Smith, P. J., Blumenthal, J. A., Hoffman, B. M., Cooper, H., Strauman, T. A., Browndyke, J. N., & Sherwood, A. (2010). In P. J. Smith, J. A. Blumenthal, et al. (Eds.), Aerobic exercise and neurocognitive performance: A meta-analytic review of randomized controlled trials, *Psychosomatic Medicine, 72,* 239–252.

Sherry, D. F., & Schacter, D. L. (1987). The evolution of multiple memory systems. *Psychological Review, 94,* 439–454.

Chapter 8

Adams, P., Lawson, S., Sanigorski, A., & Sinclair, A. J. (1996). Arachidonic acid to eicosapentaenoic acid ratio in blood correlates positively with clinical symptoms of depression. *Lipids* (Suppl.), *31,* S157–S161.

Amaducci, L., Crook, T. H., & Lippi, A. (1980). Phospholipid methylation and biological signatransmission. *Science, 64,* 245–249.

Arden, J. (2014). *The brain bible.* New York: McGraw Hill.

Bayir, H., Kagan, V. E., Tyurina, Y. Y., Tyurin, V., Ruppel, R., Adelson, P., Graham, S. H., et al. (2002). Assessment of antioxidant reserves and oxidative stress in the cerebrospinal fluid after severe traumatic brain injury and children. *Pediatric Research, 51*, 571–578.

Benton, D. (2001). The impact of the supply of glucose to the brain on mood and memory. *Nutritional Review, 59*(1), S20–21.

Bested, A. C., Logan, A. C., & Selhub, E. M. (2013). Intestinal microbiota, probiotics, and mental health: From Metchnikoff to modern advances: Part II – contemporary contextual research. *Gut Pathology, 5*(1), 3.

Cai, N., et al. (2015). Molecular signatures of major depression. *Current Biology, 25*(9), 1146–1156.

Cain, S. W., Filtness, A. J., Phillips, C. L., & Anderson, C. (2015). Enhanced preference for high-fat foods following a simulated night shift. *Scandinavian J Work Environ Health, 41*(3), 288–293.

Dittman, J. S., & Regher, W. G. (1997). Mechanisms and kinetics of hetrosynaptic depression at a cerebella synapse. *Journal of Neuroscience, 17*(23), 9048–9059.

Epstein, F. G. (1996). Mechanisms of disease. *New England Journal of Medicine, 334*(6), 374–381.

Esposito, K., Maiorino, M. I., Bellastella, G., Chiodini, P., Panagiotakos, D., & Giugliano, D. A. (2015). A journey into a Mediterranean diet and type 2 diabetes: A systematic review with meta-analyses. *BMJ Open, 5*(8), e008222.

Fahn, S. (1989). The endogenous toxin hypothesis of the etiology of Parkinson's disease and a pilot trail of high-dose antioxidants in an attempt to slow the progression of the illness. *Annals of the New York Academy of Sciences, 570*, 186–196.

Farquharoson, J., Jamieson, E. C., Abbasi, K. A., Patrick, W.J.A., Logan, R. W., & Cockburn, F. (1995). Effect of diet on fatty acid composition of the major phospholipids of the infant cerebral cortex. *Archives of Disease in Childhood, 72*, 198–203.

Glen, A. I. M. (1994). A red cell membrane abnormality in a subgroup of schizophrenic patients: Evidence for two diseases. *Schizophrenic Research, 12*, 53–61.

Glueck, C. J., Tieger, M., Kunkel, R., Tracy, T., Speirs, J., Streicher, P., & Illig, E. (1993). Improvements in symptoms of depression and in an index of life stressor accompany treatment of severe hypertriglyceridemia. *Biological Psychiatry, 34*(4), 240–252.

Gustafson, D., Lissner, L., Bengtsson, C., Björkelund, C., & Skoog, I. (2004). A 24-year follow-up of body mass index and cerebral atrophy. *Neurology, 63,* 1876–1881.

Haapalahti, M., Mykkänen, H., Tikkanen, S., & Kokkonen, J. (2004). Food habits in 10- to 11-year-old children with functional gastrointestinal disorders. *European Journal of Clinical Nutrition, 58*(7), 1016–1021.

Haatainen, K., Honkalampi, K., & Viinamaki, H. (2001). *Fish consumption, depression, and suicidality in a general population.* Paper presented at the Fourth Congress of the International Society for the Study of Lipids and Fatty Acids, Tsukuba, Japan.

Hibbelin, J. R. (1998). Fish consumption and major depression. *Lancet, 351,* 1213.

Hu, Y., Block, G., Norkus, E., Morrow, J. D., Dietrich, M., & Hudes, M. (2006). Relations of glycemic load with plasma oxidative stress marker. *American Journal of Clinical Nutrition, 84*(1), 70–76.

Jeong, S. K., Nam, H. S., Son, E. J., & Cho, K. H. (2005). Interactive effect of obesity indexes on cognition. *Dementia, Geriatric Cognitive Disorders, 19*(2–3), 91–96.

Johnson, H., Russell, J. K., & Torres, B. A. (1998). Structural basis for arachiadonic acid and second messenger signal in gamma-interon induction. *Annual New York Academy of Sciences, 524,* 208–217.

Jones, T., Borg, W., Boulware, S. D., McCarthy, G., Sherwin, R. S., & Tamborlane, W. V. (1995). Enhanced adrenomedullary response and increased susceptibility to neuroglycapenia: Mechanisms underlying the adverse effects of sugar ingestion in healthy children. *Journal of Pediatrics, 126*(2), 1717.

Joseph, J. A., Shukitt-Hale, B., Denisova, N. A., Bielinski, D., Martin, A., McEwen, J. J., & Bickford, P. C. (1999). Reversals of age-related declines in neuronal signal transduction, cognitive, and motor behavior deficits with blueberry, spinach or strawberries dietary supplementation. *Journal of Neuroscience, 19*, 8114–8121.

Kikuchi, S., Shinpo, K., Takeuchi, M., Yamagishi, S., Makita, Z., Sasaki, N., & Tashiro, K. (2003, March). Glycation—a sweet tempter for neuronal death. *Brain Research Review, 41*, 306–323.

Laganiere, S., & Fernandez, G. (1987). High peroxidizability of subcellular membrane induce by high fish oil diet is reversed by vitamin E. *Clinical Research, 35*(3), 565A.

Lee, J. Y., Jun, N. R., Yoon, D., Shin, C., & Baik, I. (2015). Association between dietary patterns in the remote past and telomere length, *European Journal of Clinical Nutrition, 69*(9), 1048–1052.

Leung, C. W., Laraia, B. A., Needham, B. L., Rehkopf, D. H., Adler, N. E., Lin, J., Blackburn, E. H., & Epel, E. S. (2014). Soda and cell aging: Association between sugar-sweetened beverage consumption and leukocyte telomere length in healthy adults from the National Health and Nutrition Examination Surveys. *American Journal of Public Health, 104*(12), 2425–2431.

Logan, A. C. (2007). *The brain diet*. Nashville, TN: Cumberland House.

Maes, M. (1996). Fatty acid composition in major depression: Decreased n-3 fractions in cholesteryl esters and increased C20: 4n-6/c20: 5n-3 ratio in cholesteryl esters and phospholipids. *Journal of Affective Disorders, 38*, 35–46.

Martin, A., Cherubini, A., Andres-Lacueva, C., Paniagua, M., & Joseph, J. (2002). Effects of fruits and vegetables on levels of vitamins E and C in the brain and their association with cognitive performance. *Journal of Nutrition, Health, and Aging, 6*(6), 392–404.

Morris, M. (2006, November). Docosahexaenoic acid and Alzheimer's disease. *Archives of Neurology, 63*, 1527–1528.

Murphey, J. M., Pagano, M. E., Nachmani, J., Sperling, P., Kane, S., & Kleinman, R. E. (1998). The relationship of school breakfast and psychosocial and academic functioning. *Archives of Pediatric Adolescent Medicine, 152*, 899–907.

National Institute of Alcohol Abuse and Alcoholism. (1985). *Alcohol health and research world.* (U.S. Department of Health and Human Services Pub. No. ADM 85–151.) Washington, DC: U.S. Government Printing Office.

Petersen, J., & Opstvedt, J. (1992). Trans fatty acids: Fatty acid consumption of lipids of the brain and other organs in suckling piglets. *Lipids,* 27(10), 761–769.

Practico, D., Clark, C., Liun, F., Lee, V., & Trojanowski, I. (2002). Increase of brain oxidative stress in mild cognitive impairment: A possible predictor of Alzheimer's disease. *Archives of Neurology,* 59, 972–976.

Reichenberg, A., Yirmiya, R., Schuld, A., Kraus, T., Haack, M., Morag, A., & Pollmächer, T. (2001, May). Cytokine-associated emotional and cognitive disturbance in humans. *Archives of General Psychiatry,* 58, 445–452.

Rudin, D. O. (1985). Omega-3 essential fatty acids in medicine. In J. S. Bland (Ed.), *1984–85 yearbook in nutritional medicine* (p. 41). New Canaan, CT: Keats.

Rudin, D. O. (1987). Modernization disease syndrome as a substitute pellagra-beriberi. *Journal of Orthomolecular Medicine,* 2(1), 3–14.

Sampson, M. J., Nitin Gopaul, N., Isabel, R, Davies, I. R., Hughes, D. A., & Carrier, M. J. (2002). Plasma F2 isoprostanes: Direct evidence of increased free radical damage during acute hypoglycemia in type 2 diabetes. *Diabetes Care,* 25(3), 537–541.

Sanchez-Villegas, A., Delgado-Rodríguez, M., Alonso, A., Schlatter, J., Lahortiga, F., Serra Majem, L., & Martínez-González, M. A. (2009). Association of the Mediterranean dietary pattern with the incidence of depression: The Seguimiento Universidad de Navarra/University of Navarra Follow-up (SUN) Cohort. *Archives of General Psychiatry,* 66(10), 1090–198.

Sano, M. (1997). Vitamin E supplementation appears to slow progression of Alzheimer's disease. *New England Journal of Medicine,* 336, 1216–1222.

Schauss, A. (1984). Nutrition and behavior: Complex interdisciplinary research. *Nutritional Health,* 3(1–2), 9–37.

Schmidt, M. A. (2007). *Brain-building nutrition: How dietary fat and oils affect mental, physical, and emotional intelligence* (3rd ed.). Berkeley, CA: Frog Books.

Sehub, J., Jacques, P. F., Bostom, A. G., D'Agostino, R. B., Wilson, P. W. F., Belanger, A. J. B., O'Leary, D. H., Wolf, P. A., Schaefer, E. J., & Rosenberg, I. H. (1995). Association between plasma homocystine concentrations and extracranial carotid stenosis. *New England Journal of Medicine, 332*(5), 286–291.

Simopoulos, A. P. (1996). Omega-3 fatty acids. In G. A. Spiller (Ed.), *Handbook of lipids in human nutrition* (pp. 51–73). Boca Raton, FL: CRC Press.

Slutsky, I., Sadeghpour, S., Li, B., & Lui, G. (2004). Enhancement of synaptic plasticity through chronically reduced Ca2+ flax during uncorrelated activity. *Neuron, 44*(5), 835–849.

Smith, D. (2002). Stress, breakfast, cereal consumption and cortisol. *Nutritional Neuroscience, 5*, 141–144.

Smith, D. (2006). Prevention of dementia: A role for B vitamin? *Nutrition Health, 18*(3), 225–226.

Sublette, M. E., Hibbeln, J. R., Galfalvy, H., Oquendo, M. A., & Mann, J. J. (2006). Omega-3 polyunsaturated essential fatty acids status as a predictor of future suicidal risk. *American Journal of Psychiatry, 163*(6), 1100–1102.

Shivappa, N., Steck, S. E., Hurley, T. G., Hussey, J. R., & Hébert, J. R. (2014). Designing and developing a literature-derived, population-based dietary inflammatory index. *Public Health Nutrition, 17*(8), 1689–1696.

Steck, S., EShivappa, N., & Tabung, F. K. (2014). The Dietary Inflammatory Index: A new tool for assessing diet quality based on inflammatory potential. *The Digest, 49*(3), pp. 1-9.

Subramanian, N. (1980). Mini review on the brain: Ascorbic acid and its importance in metabolism of biogenic amines. *Life Sciences, 20*, 1479–1484.

Tanskanen, A., Hibbeln, J. R., Hintikka, J., Haatainen, K., Honkalampi, H., & Vjinamaki, H. (2001). Fish consumption, depression, and suicidality in a general population. *Archives of General Psychiatry, 58*(5), 512–513.

Tiemeir, H., Tuijl, R. van, Hoffman, A., Kilaan, A. J., & Breteler, M.M.B. (2003). Plasma fatty acid composition and depression are associated in the elderly: The Rotterdam Study. *American Journal of Clinical Nutrition, 78*(1), 40–46.

Warnberg, J., Nova, E., Moreno, L. A., Romeo J., Mesana, M. I., Ruiz J. R., Ortega, F. B., & Sjöström, M. (2006). Inflammatory proteins are related to total and abdominal adiposity in a healthy adolescent population: The AVENA Study. *American Journal of Clinical Nutrition, 84*(3), 503–512.

Wesnes, K. A., Pincock, C., Richardson, D., Helm, G., & Hails, S. (2003). Breakfast reduces declines in attention and memory over the morning in schoolchildren. *Appetite, 41*, 329–331.

Winter, A., & Winter, R. (2007). *Smart food: Diet and nutrition for maximum brain power.* New York: ASJA Press.

Wurtman, R. J., & Zeisel, S. H. (1982). Brain choline: Its sources and effects on the synthesis and release of acetylcholine. *Aging, 19*, 303–313.

Young, C. D., & Anderson, S. M. (2008). Sugar and fat—that's where it's at: Metabolic changes in tumors. *Breast Cancer Research, 10*(1), 202.

Youqing Hu, Y., Block, G., Norkus, E. P., Morrow, J. D., Dietrich, M., & Hudes, M. (2006). Relations of glycemic index and glycemic load with plasma oxidative stress markers1,2,3. *American Journal of Clinical Nutrition, 84*(1), 70–76.

Chapter 9

American Sleep Disorders Association. (1997). *International classification of sleep disorders: Diagnostic and coding manual.* Rochester, MN: Author.

Andreasen, N. C. (2001). *Brave new brain: Conquering mental illness in the era of the genome.* New York: Oxford University Press.

Arden, J. (2009). *Heal your anxiety workbook.* Boston: Fair Winds Press.

Cirelli, C. (2005). A molecular window on sleep: Changes in gene expression between sleep and wakefulness. *Neuroscientist, 11*, 63–74.

De Havas, J. A., Parimal, S., Soon C. S., & Chee, M. W. (2012). Sleep deprivation reduces default mode network connectivity and anti-correlation during rest and task performance. *Neuroimage, 16*(2), 1745–1751.

Guzman-Marin, R., Suntsova, N., Methippara, M., Greiffenstein, R., Szymusiak, R., & McGinty, D. (2005). Sleep deprivation suppresses neurogenesis in adult hippocampus of rats. *European Journal of Neuroscience, 22*(8), 2111–2116.

Fang, Z., Spaeth, A. M., Ma, N., Zhu, S., Hu, S., Goel, N., Detre, J. A., Dinges, D. F., & Rao, H. (2015). Altered salience network connectivity predicts macronutrient intake after sleep deprivation. *Scientific Reports, 5,* 8215.

Hauri, P. J., & Fischer, J. (1986). Persistent psychophysiologic (learned) insomnia. *Sleep, 9,* 38–53.

Jeannerod, M., & Decety, J. (1995). Mental motor imagery: A window into the representation stages of action. *Current Opinion in Neurobiology, 5,* 727–732.

Kubitz, K. K., Landers, D. M., Petruzzello, S. J., & Han, M. W. (1996). The effects of acute and chronic exercise on sleep. *Sports Medicine, 21*(4), 277–291.

Macquet, P. (2001). The role of sleep in learning and memory. *Science, 294,* 1048–1052.

Magee, L., & Hale, L. (2012). Longitudinal associations between sleep duration and subsequent weight gain: A systemic review. *Sleep Med Rev., 16*(3), 231–241.

Samann, P. G., Wehrle, R., Hoehn, D., Spoormaker, V. I., Peters, H., Tully, C., Holsboer, F., & Czisch, M. (2011). Development of the brain's default mode network from wakefulness to slow wave sleep. *Cerebral Cortex, 21,* 2082–2093.

Singh, A., Meshram, H., & Srikanth, M. (2019). American Academy of Sleep Medicine guidelines 2018. *International Journal of Head and Neck Surgery, 10*(4), 102–103.

Spiegel, K., Tasali, E., Penev, P., & Van Cauter, E. (2004). Sleep curtailment in healthy young men is associated with decreased leptin levels, elevated ghrelin levels and increased hunger and appetite. *Annals of Internal Medicine, 141,* 846–850.

Strickgold, R. (2015). Sleep on it! Your nightly turns out to affect your mind and health more than anyone suspected. *Scientific American,* October, 32–57.

Venkatraman, V., Chuah, Y. M., Huettel, S. A., & Chee, M. W. (2007). Sleep deprivation elevates expectation of gains and attenuates response to losses following risky decisions. *Sleep, 30*(5), 603–609.

Xie, L., Kang, H., Xu, Q., Chen, M. J., Liao, Y., Thiyagarajan, M., O'Donnell, J., Christensen, D. J., Nicholson, C., Iliff, J. J., et al. (2013). Sleep initiated fluid flux drives metabolite clearance from the adult brain. *Science,* October 18.

Chapter 10

Bartzokis, G., Cummings, J. L., Sultzer, D., Henderson, V. M., Nuechtherlein, K. H., & Mintz, J. (2004). White matter structural integrity in healthy aging adults and patients with Alzheimer's disease. *Archives of Neurology, 60,* 393–398.

Bellert, J. L. (1989). Humor: A therapeutic approach in oncology nursing. *Cancer Nursing, 12*(2), 65–70.

Berk, L. S., Tan, S. A., Nehlsen-Cannrella, S., Napier, B. J., Lee, J. W., Lewis, J. E., & Hubbard, R. W. (1988). Humor-associated laughter decreases cortisol and increases spontaneous lymphocyte blastogenesis. *Clinical Research, 36,* 435A.

Bigler, E. D., Anderson, C. V., & Blatter, D. D. (2002). Temporal lobe morphology in normal aging and traumatic brain injury. *American Journal of Neuroradiology, 23,* 255–266.

Cabeza, R. (2002). Hemispheric asymmetry reduction in older adults. The HAROLD model. *Psychology and Aging, 17*(1), 85–100.

Cabeza, R., Anderson, N. D., Locantore, J. K., & McInosh, A. (2002). Aging gracefully: Compensatory brain activity in high performing older adults. *NeuroImage, 17,* 1394–1402.

Cozolino, L. (2008). *The healing aging brain.* New York: Norton.

Davidson, R. J., Jackson, L., & Kalin, N. H. (2000). Emotion, plasticity, context, and regulation. *Psychological Bulletin, 126,* 316–321.

De Maritino, B., Kumaran, D., Seymour, B., & Dola, R. J. (2006). Frames, biases, and rational decision-making in the human brain. *Science, 313,* 684–687.

Deaner, S. L., & McConatha, J. T. (1993). The relationship of humor to depression and personality. *Psychological Reports, 72,* 755–763.

Fry, W. F. Jr. (1992). The physiological effects of humor, mirth, and laughter. *Journal of the American Medical Association, 267* (4), 1874–1878.

Gunning-Dixon, F. M., Head, D., McQuain, J., Acker, J. D., & Raz, D. (1998). Differential aging of the human striatum: A prospective MR imaging study. *American Journal of Neuroimaging, 19,* 1501–1507.

Gustafson, D., Lissner, L., Bengtsson, C., Björkelund, C., & Skoog, I. (2004). A 24-year follow-up of body mass index and cerebral atrophy. *Neurology, 63,* 1876–1881.

Hayashi, T., Urayama, O., Kawai, K., Hayashi, K., Iwanaga, S., Ohta, M., Saito, T., & Murakami, K. (2006). Laughter regulates gene expression in patients with type 2 diabetes. *Psychotherapy and Psychosomatics, 75,* 62–65.

Kuhn, C. C. (1994). The stages of laughter. *Journal of Nursing Jocularity, 4*(2), 34–35.

Lawrence, B., Myerson, J., & Hale, S. (1998). Differential decline on verbal and visual spatial processing speed across the adult life span. *Aging, Neuropsychology, and Cognition, 5*(2), 129–146.

Levine, B. (2004). Autobiographical memory and the self in time: Brain lesion effects, functional neuroanatomy, and lifespan development. *Brain and Cognition, 55,* 54–68.

Maddi, S. R., & Kobasa, S. C. (1984). *The hardy executive.* Homewood, IL: Dow Jones-Irwin.

McCullough, M. E., Emmons, R. A., & Tsang, J. (2002). The grateful disposition: A conceptual and empirical topography. *Journal of Personality and Social Psychology, 82,* 112–127.

Martin, R. A., Kuiper, N. A., Olinger, L. J., & Dance, D. A. (1993). Humor, coping with stress, self-concept, and psychological well-being. *Humor: International Journal of Humor Research, 6*(1), 89–104.

Maruta, I., Colligan, R. C., Malinchoc, M., & Offord, K. P. (2002). Optimism–pessimism assessed in the 1960s and self-reported health status 30 years later. *Mayo Clinic Proceedings, 77*, 748–753.

McEwen, B., & Wingfield, J. C. (2003). The concept of allostasis in biology and biomedicine. *Hormones and Behavior, 43*, 2–15.

McEwen, B. S. (1998). Stress, adaptation, and disease: Allostasis and allostatic load. *Annals of the New York Academy of Science, 8*, 840–844.

McEwen, B. S., & Stellar, E. (1993). Stress and individual-mechanisms leading to disease. *Archives of Internal Medicine, 153*, 2093–2101.

McGraty, R., & Atkinson, M. (2004). The grateful heart: The psychophysiology of appreciation. In R. A. Emmons & M. E. McCullough (Eds.), *The psychophysiology of gratitude* (pp. 230–255). New York: Oxford University Press.

Mobbs, D., Greicius, M. D., Abdel-Azim, E., Menon, V., & Reiss, A. L. (2003). Humor modulates the mesolimbic reward centers. *Neuron, 40*, 1041–1048.

Morrison, J. H., & Hoff, P. R. (2003). Changes in cortical circuits during aging. *Clinical Neuroscience Research, 2*, 294–304.

Pearce, J. M. S. (2004). Some neurological aspects of laughter. *European Neurology, 52*, 169–171.

Raz, N., Gunning, F. M., Head, D., Dupuis, J. H., McQuain, J., Briggs, S. D., Loken, W. J., Thornton, A. E., & Acker, J. D. (1997). Selective aging of the human cerebral cortex observed in vivo: Differential vulnerability of the prefrontal gray matter. *Cerebral Cortex, 7*, 268–282.

Raz, N., Gunning, F. M., Head, D., Williamson, A., & Acker, J. D. (2001). Age and sex differences in the cerebellum and the ventral pons: A prospective MR study of healthy adults. *American Journal of Neuroradiology, 22*, 1161–1167.

Reuter-Lorenz, P. A., Stanczak, K. L., & Miller, A. C. (1999). Neural recruitment and cognitive aging: Two hemispheres are better than one, especially as you age. *Psychological Science, 10*, 494–500.

Richards, M., & Deary, I. J. (2005). A life course approach to cognitive reserve: A model for cognitive aging and development? *Annals of Neurology, 58,* 617–622.

Salat, D. H., Buckner, R. L., Synder, A. Z., Greve, D. N., Desikan, R. S. R., Busa, E., Morris, J. C., Dale, A. M., & Fischl, B. (2004). Thinning of the cerebral cortex in aging. *Cerebral Cortex, 14,* 721–730.

Salat, D. H., Kaye, J. A., & Janowsky, J. S. (2001). Selective preservation and degeneration within the prefrontal cortex in aging and Alzheimer's disease. *Archives of Neurology, 58,* 1403–1408.

Schmidt, L. A. (1999). Frontal brain electrical activity in shyness and sociability. *Psychological Sciences, 10,* 316–321.

Seeman, T. E., Lusignolo, T. M., Albert, M., & Berkman, L. (2001). Social relationships, social support, and patterns of cognitive aging in healthy, high-functioning older adults. *Health Psychology, 4,* 243–255.

Seligman, M. (2001). Optimism, pessimism and mortality. *Mayo Clinic Proceedings, 75*(2), 133–134.

Shiota, M. N., Campos, B., Oveis, C., Hertenstein, M. J., Simon-Thomas, E., & Keltner, D. (2017). Beyond happiness: Building a science of discrete positive emotions. *American Psychologist, 72*(7), 617–643.

Singer, B., & Ryff, C. D. (1999). Hierarchies of life histories and associated health risks. *Annals of the New York Academy of Sciences, 896,* 96–116.

Singer, T., Seymore, B., O'Doherty, J., Kaube, H., Dolan, R. J., & Firth, C. D. (2014). Empathy for pain involves the affective but not the sensory components of pain. *Science, 303,* 1157–1161.

Snowden, D. (1997). *Aging with grace: What the Nun Study teaches us about leading longer, healthier, and more meaningful lives.* New York: Bantam Books.

Sowell, E. R., Peterson, P. M., Thompson, P. M., Welcome, S. E., Henkenius, A. L., & Toga, A. W. (2003). Mapping cortical change across the human life span. *Nature Neuroscience, 2,* 850–861.

Sterling, P., & Eyer, J. (1988). Allostasis: A new paradigm to explain arousal pathology. In S. Fischer & J. Reason (Eds.), *Handbook of stress, cognition, and health* (pp. 269–249). Hoboken, NJ: Wiley.

Sullivan, E. V., Marsh, L., Mathalon, D. H., Lim, K. O., & Pfefferbaum, A. (1995). Age-related decline in MRI volumes in temporal lobe gray matter but not hippocampus. *Neurobiology of Aging, 16*, 591–606.

Sullivan, R. M., & Gratton, A. (2002). Prefrontal cortical regulation of hypothalamic-pituitary-adrenal function in the rat and implications for psychopathology: Side matters. *Psychoneuroendochrinology, 27*, 99–114.

Takahashi, K., Iwase, M., Yamashita, K., Tatsumoto, Y., Ve, H., Kurasune, H., Shimizu, A., & Takeda, M. (2001). The elevation of natural killer cell activity induced by laughter in a crossover designed study. *International Journal of Molecular Medicine, 8*, 645–650.

Tang, Y., Nyengaard, J. R., Pakkenberg, B., & Gundersen, H. J. (1997). Age-induced white matter changes in the human brain: A stereological investigation. *Neurobiology of Aging, 18*, 609–615.

Taylor, S. E., Kemeny, M. E., Reed, G. M., Bower, J. E., & Gruenewald, T. L. (2000). Psychological resources, positive illusions, and health. *American Psychologist, 5*, 99–109.

Terry, R. D., DeTeresa, R., & Hansen, L. A. (1987). Neocortical cell counts in normal human adult aging. *Annals of Neurology, 21*, 530–539.

Tessitore, A., Hariri, A. R., Fera, F., Smith, W. G., Das, S., Weinberger, D. R., & Mattay, V. S. (2005). Functional changes in the activity of brain regions underlying emotion processes in the elderly. *Psychiatry Research: Neuroimaging, 139*, 9–18.

Vaillant, G. E. (2002). *Aging well: Surprising guide points to a happier life from the landmark Harvard study of adult development.* Boston: Little, Brown.

Van Patten, C., Plante, E., Davidson, P. S. R., Kuo, T. Y., Bjuscak, L., & Glisky, E. L. (2004). Memory and executive function in older adults: Relationships with temporal and prefrontal volumes and white matter hyperintensities. *Neuropsychologia, 42*, 1313–1335.

Whalley, L. J. (2001). *The aging brain*. New York: Columbia University Press.

Whalley, L. J., Deary, I. J., Appleton, C. L., & Starr, J. M. (2004). Cognitive reserve and the neurobiology of cognitive aging. *Aging Research Reviews, 3*, 369–382.

Willis, M. W., Ketter, T. A., Kimbell, T. A., George, M. S., Herscovitch, P., Danielson, A. L., et al. (2002). Age, sex, and laterality effects on cerebral glucose metabolism in healthy adults. *Psychiatry Research Neuroimaging, 114*, 23–37.

Wilson, R. S., Beckett, L. A., Barnes, L. L., Schneider, J. A., Bach, J., Evan, D. A., et al. (2002). Individual differences in rates of change in cognitive abilities of older persons. *Psychology and Aging, 17*, 179–193.

Wooten, P. (1996). Humor: An antidote for stress. *Holistic Nursing Practice, 10*(2), 49–55.

Wueve, J., Kang, J. H., Manson, J. E., Breteler, M. M. B., Ware, J. H., & Grodstein, F. (2004). Physical activity, including walking, and cognitive function in older women. *Journal of the American Medical Association, 292*, 1452–1461.

Yoder, M. A., & Haude, R. H. (1995). Sense of humor and longevity. Older adults' self-ratings for deceased siblings. *Psychological Reports, 76*, 945–946.

Yovetich, N. A., Dale, J. A., & Hudak, M. A. (1990). Benefits of humor in the reduction of threat-induced anxiety. *Psychological Reports, 66*, 51–58.

About the Author

John Arden, Ph.D., has written 15 books (translated into over 20 languages), including *Mind-Brain-Gene: Toward the Integration of Psychotherapy, Brain2Brain, The Brain Bible, Rewire Your Brain* (1st edition), *Improving Your Memory for Dummies,* and *Brain-Based Therapy with Adults.* He worked previously for Kaiser Permanente, where he served as the Northern California regional director of training and developed one of the largest mental health training programs in the United States. In this capacity he oversaw more than 150 interns and postdoctoral psychology residents in 24 medical centers. Arden's study of neuropsychology has inspired him to integrate neuroscience and psychotherapy, synthesizing the biological and psychological. He has presented seminars in all U.S. states and 30 countries.

Acknowledgments

I would like to thank as well as praise the editorial team at Wiley. Ashante Thomas, Mary Beth Rosswurm, Pete Gaughan, Kristi Bennett, and Kim Wimpsett have been exceptional in many ways. They are not only highly professional and talented but are also always helpful and gracious. It was a pleasure to work with them. And finally, I want to thank Dr. Olivia Lesslar, a star in Functional and Integrative Medicine, for her thoughtful contributions and expertise, and Dr. Jean Annan for her insightful contributions regarding the field of Positive Psychology.

Index

Runner's high, 139
Rutter, Michael, 115, 120

SAD. *See* Seasonal affective disorder
Sadness, cultivated, 82–83
Safety behaviors, 70–71
Said, Edward, 122
Saturated fats, 184
Scheduling worrying time, 75
Scopos, 160
Seasonal affective disorder (SAD), 87
Secure attachment, 120
SEEDS factors, 13, 27, 89
    education and, 146
    as peg, 159
    telomeres and, 39–40
Selective serotonin reuptake inhibitors
        (SSRIs), 142
Self-care, 25
Self-compassion, 228
Self-esteem, 120–121, 223
Semantic memory, 151
Septal region, 126–127
Serotonin, 87, 90, 97, 141–
        142, 175–178
    REM sleep and, 205
    spindle cells and, 112
SgACC. *See* Subgenual anterior
        cingulate cortex
Short-term memory, 150
Shoulds and should nots, 92
Sickness behavior, 43–44, 88–89
Simonides, 160
SIRT enzymes, 192
Sitting, 131
Skin, receptors in, 113–114
Sleep, 195
    alcohol and, 207, 211
    anxiety and, 209–210
    body temperature and, 197–198,
        214–215, 218
    brain cleaning in, 204
    brain health and, 199–201
    circadian rhythm and, 196–197
    cortisol and, 140, 200
    depression and, 209–210

    diet and, 214
    DNA and, 200, 208
    exercise and, 213–214
    hippocampus and, 201, 203, 207
    immune system and, 200
    light and, 215, 217
    mood and, 200
    PFC and, 202, 207
    relaxation and, 217–218
    stages of, 201–205
    stress and, 202, 209
    type 2 diabetes and, 208
Sleep aids, 212
Sleep hygiene, 213–218
Sleep loss, 207–213
Sleep scheduling, 215–217
Slow wave sleep, 202, 204, 214
Smoking, 130
Smokodiabesity, 130
Snap judgment, 111
Social boosting, 93–94
Social brain, systems of, 113
Social connectedness, 109
Social contact, 106
Social media, 146
Social nourishment, 109
Socialization
    anxiety and, 107
    health benefits, 110
Sodium, 181
Solomon, George, 52
Spices, 193
Spindle cells, 111–112
SSRIs. *See* Selective serotonin reuptake
        inhibitors
Starches, 168
States, 230
Stem cells, 139
Story links, 161
Stress
    building tolerance to, 223
    depression and, 88
    excitotoxic, 132
    exercise benefits and, 132–
        136, 139–142
    false alarms and, 59–65
    focus and, 61–62